ST. KILDA REVISITED

ii

ST. KILDA REVISITED

by DAVID A. QUINE, FLS

Drawings and photographs by the author except where acknowledged

For the St. Kildans
and the St. Kilda Club

ISBN 0 9508135 0 8

CONTENTS

COLOUR PHOTOGRAPHS

MAPS OF ST. KILDA

MONOCHROME PHOTOGRAPHS

Acknowledgements

Many groups of people and individuals have co-operated and assisted me in the production of this book. The National Trust for Scotland has given me the opportunity to visit St. Kilda on several occasions and has given me permission to reproduce a number of photographs taken by A. M. Cockburn which are now in the Trust's photographic Library. Many personnel of the Royal Artillery Detachment have enabled visits to be made to Dun and the use of their amenities has improved the quality of life, they have also provided two excellent photographs. The Nature Conservancy has kindly supplied the basic information and figures of the population of Soay sheep on Hirta, and the Trustees of the National Library of Scotland have given permission for me to include part of Nicolas de Nicolay's chart of 1583.

I am also greatly indebted to all the authors mentioned in the bibliography. In particular I would like to thank the following individuals, Lachlan Mac-Donald, who was born on Hirta, for his first hand description of life on St. Kilda; Alick MacLeod for his help over many of the Gaelic names; Dr. R. R. Harding for his advice and guidance on the Geology; Dr. Christine Howson for her help with the Marine Biology. Malcolm Bangor-Jones for pursuing a number of queries in the National Library and to Mary Harman for the use of her illustration of the 'crosses' and Dr. M. B. Cottam for the use of his plans of some of the archaeological sites. The book would have been the poorer if Mrs. Askham, the daughter of George Murray, had not graciously given her permission to quote from her father's diary of his stay as school-master, 1886-87; her sister Mrs. J. R. Naish kindly provided the photograph. Mrs. Charlotte Lyon of Inverness found the photograph of some of the inhabitants, taken in 1884, which was being used as backing for a picture she had bought in Aberdeen, and kindly allowed me to reproduce it. Mrs. Gladstone, widow of John Gladstone, permitted me to read and quote from her husband's diaries. I have also greatly appreciated the leaders of the parties visiting St. Kilda, Richard Castro, George Thomson and George Perry. I am also most grateful to Joe Keppie and Alex Warwick for their helpful and constructive criticisms. Lastly, but by no means least, to my own family, my wife Mary, Christopher and Timothy, for their considerable patience, severely tested at times, for their encouragement and assistance in countless ways, also to Brian Thomas and his staff at the Dowland Press, for all their care over the text and the illustrations.

Foreword

Although a tremendous amount has been written about St. Kilda many of the earlier writings are not easily accessible and some of the fascinating diaries are privately owned. During the last five years I have enjoyed delving into the earlier material and talking to several of the St. Kildans. I have found many delightful descriptions and comments; in order to give the true flavour I have quoted these at length. In writing the book I have endeavoured to collect together this material with recent findings and studies in as many fields as possible.

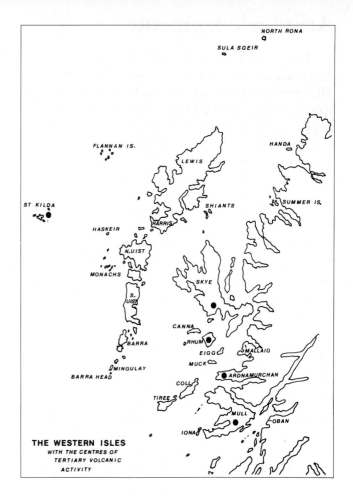

THE WESTERN ISLES
WITH THE CENTRES OF
TERTIARY VOLCANIC
ACTIVITY

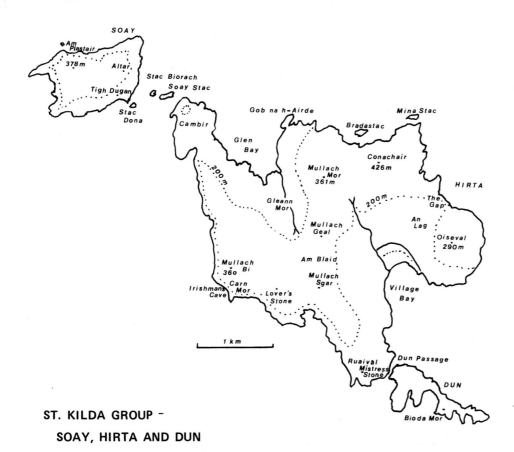

SOAY

Am Plastair

378m

Altar

Tigh Dugan

Stac Dona

Stac Biorach
Soay Stac

Cambir

Gob na h-Airde

Glen Bay

Mullach Mor
361m

Conachair
426m

Bradastac

Mina Stac

HIRTA

Gleann Mor

200 m

Mullach Geal

200m

The Gap

An Lag

Oiseval
290m

Mullach Bi
360

Am Blaid

Mullach Sgar

Carn Mor

Irishmans Cave

Lover's Stone

Village Bay

1 km

Ruaival
Mistress Stone

Dun Passage

DUN

Bioda Mor

ST. KILDA GROUP -
SOAY, HIRTA AND DUN

THE ST· KILDA GROUP

Stac an Armin

4 km

Stac Lee

Boreray

Soay

Hirta

Dun

Levenish

ST. KILDA —
THE VISITORS' BOOK

Sunrise over Boreray and the Stacs from Conachair.
Photo: J. Keppie.

STONE AGE TO NUCLEAR AGE

Visitors came to St. Kilda well before the Stone Age – sea-birds breeding in the summer by their thousands and seals haunting the caves in the winter storms. Nearly 4,000 years ago man arrived and made his home on the main island and left behind him a few stone monuments – the 'boat-shaped settings' and cairns on An Lag. Through the centuries man has visited or inhabited these islands, just managing to eke out an existence, until he finally capitulated at the evacuation in 1930. Since then few have stayed for any length of time apart from a Royal Air Force unit which began to construct the Radar Tracking Station, and those Army personnel who maintain and man it. National Trust Working Parties stay for a couple of weeks at a time to repair and restore the buildings. Visitors – geographers, archaeologists, historians and naturalists – usually come for short spells to investigate the tremendous wealth of the islands in their own particular field.

Lachlan MacLean visited St. Kilda in July 1838 on the Vulcan, one of the first steamships for tourists; on setting foot on the main island he wrote in his Journal, "I am at length, thank God, arrived on terra firma in St. Kilda, the place which, of all other places within the British dominions, I longed most to see; and I had not certainly been led to form a false or exaggerated conception of it; nay, the half had not been told me."

THE NAME

There are many mysteries about St. Kilda and one of the most puzzling is the derivation of the name itself.

1

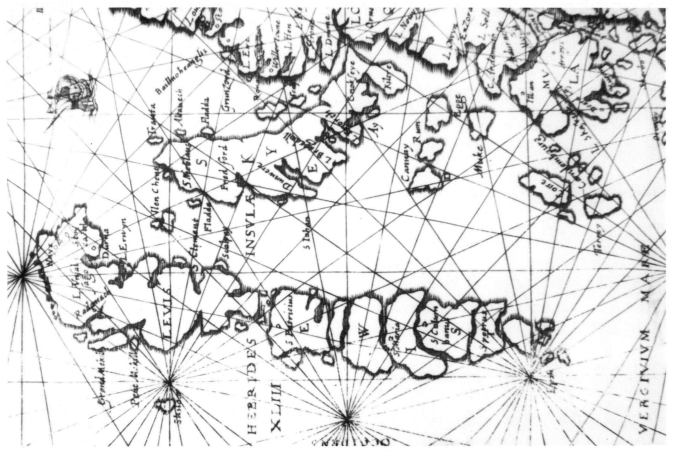

Map by Nicolas de Nicolay, Chart of Scotland, 1583.

The most likely answer is that it evolved from a copyist error. Three theories have been put forward. Martin Martin, who visited the islands in 1697 believed that the present name was derived from a man named 'Kilder' who lived on the island and after whom the well was named. Another suggestion, now under suspicion, is that it may have come from 'Kelda', the Old Norse for a 'well'; Kilda appeared on some of the first maps and the early settlement was centred on the Tobar Childa. Having studied all the old maps of the vicinity the late A. B. Taylor (1969) was quite convinced that the name had developed from a copyist's mistake. 'Skildir' is the Old Norse for 'shields' which could describe the islands when seen from a distance as they appear to rest flat on the surface of the water. 'Skilder' was marked on many contemporary Dutch and French maps, designed to assist fishermen to navigate in these waters and 'Skildar' on that produced by Nicholas de Nicolay, published in Paris in 1583. On this map the 'r' was almost invisible due to a line on the page. It is thought that when Lucas J. Waghenaer copied it he also separated the 'S' and the 'K', putting a full stop in between them so that 'S.Kilda' appeared in his book of Charts published in 1592. An extraordinary story indeed – certainly no 'Saint' of that name has ever been recorded or known.

St. Kilda has a grandeur and magic of its own with some of the highest and most spectacular cliffs and sea-stacks in Europe; a huge sea-bird breeding population and some creatures found nowhere else in the world. It provides the setting for the fascinating story of a human community in its struggle to survive on this lonely and exposed archipelago.

THE EARLIEST DESCRIPTION

The earliest description of St. Kilda is that of Sir Donald Monro, High Dean of the Isles, who travelled through many of the Western Isles in 1549 although his book was not published until 1774. "Hirta. To the west north west of this ile (Haysker) foresaid, out in the mayne ocean seas, be three-score of myle by sea, layes an ile callit Hirta, ane maine laiche ile, as far as is manurit of it, abundant in corne and gressing, namelie for sheipe, for ther are fairer and graiter sheip ther, and larger tailed, than ther is in any uther ile about. The inhabitants thereof ar simple poor people, scarce learnit in aney religion, but M'Cloyd of Herrey, his stewart, or he quhom he deputs in sic office, sailes anes in the sear ther at midsummer, with some chaplaine to baptise bairnes ther, and if they want a chaplaine, they baptise ther bairnes themselfes. The said stewart, as he himself tauld me, uses to take ane maske of malt ther with a masking fatt, and makes his malt, and ere the fatt be ready, the commons of the town, baith men, weemin, and bairns, puts their hands in the fatt, and findis it sweeit, and eets the greyns after the sweeitness thereof, quhilk they leave nather wirt or draffe unsuppit out ther, quharwith baith men, women and bairns, were deid drunken, sua that they could not stand upon their feet. The said stewart receives thir dewties in miell and reistit (salted) mutton, wyld foullis reistit, and selchis (seals). This ile is maire nor ane mile lange, and narrest als meikle in braid quhilk is not seine of aney shore, bot at the shoresyde of it lyes three grate hills, quhilk are ane pairt of Hirta, quhilk are seen affar off from the fore landis. In this ile is fair sheipe, falcon nests and wyld fouls biggand, but the streams of the sea are starke, and are verey eivil entring in aney of the saids iles. This ile of Hirta perteins of auld to M'Cloyd of Herray."

THE FIRST MAP

The first detailed map appeared together with a much fuller description of St. Kilda in 1698, published by Martin Martin. He was born on Skye and after obtaining his degree at Edinburgh University he was appointed governor or tutor to the younger MacLeod of Dunvegan on Skye. He was a great traveller and conversed with members of the Royal Society. He wrote two books – "A Late Voyage to St. Kilda" (1698) and "A Description of the Western Isles of Scotland" (1703). The late James Fisher (1952) described them as "naturalists' classics, accurate and full of facts; without them the history of the animals of the Western Isles would be very meagre." The books and map were the fruit of a voyage with the Rev. John Campbell, minister of Harris, in 1697. In his preface he tells us that he was "prompted by a generous curiosity to undertake a voyage through several isles to St. Kilda . . . and that in an open boat, to the almost manifest hazard of his life, since the seas and tides in those rocky islands are more inconstant and raging than in most other places."

So great is the captivating spell cast by St. Kilda that many have been compelled to write after simply gazing at the islands from the sea, others after setting foot for only a few hours. The real wealth of literature down the years comes from those who have stayed for longer periods, either as true inhabitants or ministers, schoolmasters, nurses, journalists or scientists who have recorded their observations and experiences in their fascinating books, diaries and journals.

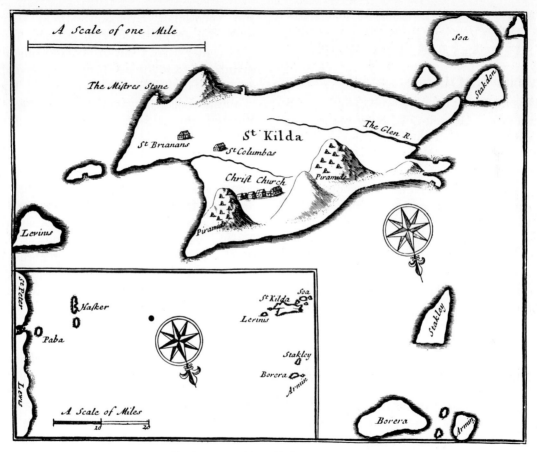

The First Map of St. Kilda by Martin, 1698.

5

ST. KILDA — FOR THE GEOGRAPHER

THE ISLAND GROUP

St. Kilda lies 180 km (112 miles) west of the Scottish mainland and 64 km (40 miles) W N W of the most westerly headland of the Outer Hebrides, Aird an Runair near Tigharry on North Uist. Leaving the protected waters of the Sound of Harris and passing between the islands of Pabbay and Shillay 80 km (50 miles) of open sea must be negotiated before reaching the main island. St. Kilda is really a group of four islands – Dun, Hirta, Soay and Boreray, which together with their adjacent stacks form a small archipelago. Approaching from Harris by sea the first to come into view is Boreray with its two stacks, Stac an Armin and Stac Lee. Nearing the main cluster you pass the outlying stack of Levenish and enter Village Bay which is bounded by the island of Dun on the left with the main island Hirta ahead and to the right. Soay lies out of sight behind the island mass. The Swedish author, artist and yachtsman, Svensson (1955) described the conflicting emotions experienced on his first visit. "One grey winter's day I saw the barren silhouettes of the islands rise from the sea. They rose above the horizon, changing continually as we approached. The ship hove to outside Village Bay on the eastern side of the island. Through my field-glasses I could discern traces of farmland and could count sixteen dwellings lying in a crescent at the foot of the high hills. It was an overpowering experience, drearily repelling and romantically stimulating. The wide harbour bay is protected from winds from the north and south, but to the east it is open, and the mighty Atlantic waves roll into the bay with undiminished power. Sailors warn visitors to beware of falling winds that rush down from the heights. The North Atlantic is notorious for fogs and strong winds – a dangerous combination."

(1) Levenish

The stac, Levenish, stands as a precipitous pyramid 62 m. high (203 ft.) at the entrance to Village Bay, lying

The St. Kilda Group

Dun   Hirta   Soay   Boreray   Stac An Armin

2.4 km (1½ miles) to the east of Dun. The name is derived from 'livinish', the old British for stream or torrent which well describes the nature of the sea, "the current around it is exceedingly impetuous." (Macaulay, 1764). After a rough and misty crossing in 1896 the Kearton brothers reported that one of the sailors had called out "land ahead" – "The sight was sublime, in front of us loomed a gigantic rock with its summit buried in white mists, and its base surrounded by a fringe of foam left by the broken billows." Morton Boyd, after one of his visits, reported that it was not large enough to have a truly sheltered side; bursting swell curls round it tempestuously, but it is possible to land on the east side. He found about 20 Greater Black-backed Gulls nests, 2 Leach's Petrel burrows, a few Razorbills incubating eggs and 2 Guillemot colonies on the north side with about 20 birds.

Mist over Dun

(2) DUN

The island of Dun is a rocky ridge 1.5 km (1 mile) long, forming the western border of Village Bay and protecting it from the Atlantic. The highest point is at Bioda Mor, 178 m. It was once connected to Hirta but has now been breached by the sea leaving a permanent narrow rocky channel only 50 m. wide. At the eastern end a natural arch has been formed by the pounding of the sea, which in due course is likely to cause its collapse and the formation of another outlying stac. Not far from this arch is the Dun Wall, the remains of a structure once thought to be a hill fort, from which Dun (Celtic – fort) is possibly derived. If it ever existed, most of it must have been lost in a cliff fall, certainly all that is left could only be its outer defences, "though wonderfully well built is made entirely from stones picked up on the spot and not fashioned in any way." (Heathcote, 1900).

The Dun Wall

The site of an ancient altar was known to Sands (1877) although the stones had been removed.

The western edge has been eroded by the ceaseless onslaught of the ocean into a craggy breakwater, while the eastern side has steep grassy slopes which have been honeycombed by thousands of nesting puffins, no fewer than 60-80,000 pairs are on Dun alone. About 7,000 pairs of Fulmars nest on the ledges with 3-4,000 pairs of Guillemots and 1,200 pairs of Razorbills. Other nesting birds are Shags, 150 pairs, Greater, Lesser Black-backed, Herring Gulls and Kittiwakes, 40-50 pairs of Wrens and possibly the largest colony of Leach's Petrels in the British Isles. The St. Kilda Field Mouse also lives on the island.

The good but limited grass was used for wintering lambs and the remains of lazy-bed cultivation are still visible at the north end. The normal place to land today is on the rocks to the east of the beds, but only when there is very little swell. The St. Kildans usually crossed Dun Passage at low tide jumping from rock to rock until they reached the chain, permanently fixed to the cliff, to aid their steep ascent.

On a July afternoon, sit above the landing rocks, on lush tussocky grass surrounded by banks of Common Sorrel and Scentless Mayweed, with clumps of Buttercups and large patches of Sea Campion and watch the thousands of Puffins wheeling overhead. Some carry fish for their young, others stand on rocks like sentinels, small groups pace up and down observing the visitors. Above the rocks greedy Greater Black-backed Gulls call hungrily as they circle over the puffinry where they take some 2,500 Puffins each year on Dun alone. A St. Kilda Wren, brings a green caterpillar, still alive, pauses on a yellow lichen covered rock before flying off to feed her young. Fulmars wheel on short circuits and figures of eight and perform their fluttering display over their sitting partner. Most have a single young one in the nest, squatting like an over-grown grey powder-puff, in a sheltered hollow, often under a rocky ledge, surrounded by Common Sorrel and Scentless Mayweed. Some pairs cackle to each other on their ledges. Below Shags stand, with wings outstretched, on the rocks above the sea.

On the water, surprisingly calm and with little swell, large parties of off-duty Puffins swim around, a few immature Black-backed Gulls peck lazily at a floating jellyfish, three or four Gannets circle round in search of food and leave a long plume of grey bubbles as they dive for fish. The mist slowly rises to give a glimpse of the cliffs of Bioda Mor.

Kearton (1897) recorded a remarkable incident

Razorbills on Dun

which happened in 1892. "Four years ago a girl, whilst watching the men collect eggs on Doon, had her petticoats ballooned by a sudden squall of wind, and was lifted clean over the cliff. She fell 180 feet without a break, and alighted on a ledge which was covered with earth. The cragsmen descended to pick up what they very naturally supposed to be the dead body of the poor child, but was surprised to find that she was still alive. Her head had entered a large Puffin burrow, and the force of the blow had been expended upon her shoulders. This undoubtedly saved her, and although she hung a whole week between life and death in an unconscious condition, she ultimately made a complete recovery, and was a fine buxom lassie at the time of our visit."

(3) Hirta

i Names and Shape

Hirta, the name of the main island, used to be the St. Kildans' name for the whole group. It first appeared as 'Hirtir' in a 13th century Icelandic Saga which referred to an Icelandic ship taking shelter off 'Hirtir' in 1202. This is probably derived from the old Norse word for 'stags', which would be an imaginative description of the islands' stacks and pinnacles. Some have suggested a Gaelic origin. It was sometimes written as "Hirt,

The Village, An Lag, the Gap and Boreray, from Mullach Sgar.

Hirth, Hirta or Hyrtha, a contraction of h-Iar-tir, the Gaelic for west-land or west country." (Seton 1878). In Fordun's 14th century description we have, "The Irte, which is agreed to be under Circius and on the outskirts of the world, beyond which there is no land in these bounds."

Hirta is the largest island in the group, just over 3 km (2 miles) long and the only one to be permanently inhabited. The shape is similar to a distorted 'H' with the cross-piece formed by the ridge of Mullach Sgar (Clefted Summit), Mullach Geal (The White Top), Mullach Mor (The Big Summit); the uprights to the north and east by Glacan Mor (The Big Hollow), Conachair (The Coming together of the Hills), which is the highest point on Hirta at 426 m (1397 ft.), and Oiseval (Norse – East Fell); to the west and south by the Cambir (Norse – Crest or Ridge), Mullach Bi (Pillar Summit) and Ruaival (Norse – Red Hill). Above the ridge to the north Gleann Mor (The Great Glen) is wide and 'U' shaped and has its stream Amhuinn a Ghlinne Mhoir meandering its way to Glen Bay. To the south and east of the ridge, Amhuin Mhor (The Big River) and the Dry Burn, which is far from dry most of the time, takes water from An Lag Bho'n Tuath (The Hollow from the North), both run into the horse-shoe of Village Bay.

Conachair's cliffs are spectacular, falling practically vertically 400 m into the sea and provide nest sites for 6,000 pairs of Fulmars. Mullach Bi. 355 m (1182 ft.) stands like an erect sentinel mid-way along the western cliffs, giving a commanding view along Dun to the south and away to Soay in the north, with the added attraction of Fulmars enjoying their aerial manoeuvres. Ruaival is cone shaped and behind the summit to the south-west is the Mistress Stone where several huge blocks of rock have been piled up, and one of these rests like a lintel on two others. When a man proposed to a girl the whole community went to this rock where he demonstrated his manhood and cliff climbing skill

The Mistress Stone, Ruaival

by placing one foot in front of the other, toe to heel, and then bending forward he placed his clenched fists in front of his feet, with only his heel on the rock. After a successful performance he was "accounted worthy of the finest Mistress in the World." (Martin, 1698).

The Milking Stone

Other rocks also had a special significance, at 'Clach a 'Bhainne', the Milking Stone, their superstitious custom was to pour out some milk into a hollow in the stone on Sundays in the Summer and Autumn to placate a subordinate Divinity they called 'Gruagach'. The custom had died out well before Macaulay reported it in 1764. However, the massive stone still stands on the right of the road, as it bends below the quarry. Sands (1877) recalled another stone, "Close to the churchyard is a stone called the Stone of Knowledge, which is said to have possessed magical properties. He who stood upon it on the first day of the quarter became gifted with second-sight, and was able to foresee all the events that were to occur during that quarter. I tried it on the first day (old style) of the present spring, but saw nothing except three or four women laden with peats, and smiling at my credulity. It does not seem to be much venerated in these sceptical times."

'Tigh an Triar', the House of the Trinity is one of the largest cleitean on the island, with a single chamber and two entrances on the south side, situated among a cluster of cleitean to the right of the road above the quarry. Here in Medieval times they called upon God's blessing on their cattle every time they moved them from one grazing to another; they also sanctified them with salt water and fire. Further up the present road, on the coll of Am Blaid, the St. Kildans had an observation post, and another at 'Tigh na Faire', the Watching House, where in the Dark Ages a watch was kept night and day against pirates who plundered both sheep and cattle; it is situated behind Skull Rock, "Claigeann an Tigh Faire", south west of the summit of Mullach Bi.

The huge rounded, sea washed boulders in Village Bay were notorious for their size and shapes, their fame reaching the mainland. Lachlan MacLean records. "The bay looks to the south east; and is of a semicircular shape. It presents at the curve a pretty sandy beach, where a number of our passengers bathed, and where, at low water, the children might play; but above this shore, at high water mark, as well as round the whole bay, presents ·what is ironically termed 'Doirneagan Hirt', (St. Kilda pebbles) over all the Highlands. These are natives of the abyss profound, and cast up here by the angry waves. The size of some of them I by no means exaggerated in my 'Sketches' when I said twenty-four tons in weight." (MacLean, 1838).

---

ii Springs

Macaulay considered that the fountain water of St. Kilda was "beyond comparison the finest he had ever tasted" and he found no shortage, "one will easily find inexhaustible quantities of it in every corner of the isle!" There are several springs, the 'Tobar Childa' has one main source, but in wet weather can have at least five outlets, and was at the centre of the Medieval Village. 'Tobar Clerich' or 'Tobar Mhinisteir', the Minister's Well is the present source of water for visitors and the Army Camp: it is now covered by the pump house where the water is chlorinated and pumped to the large water tanks by the Head Dyke. To the left of the path from the Glebe to the Feather Store is 'Tobar Gille Chille', the Well of the Servant of the Church, which has its own impressive man made covering. 'Tobar nam Buaidh', the Well of Virtues, rises in the Warrior's Glen close to the Bay, "a low shaped massy stone building, with a stone roof covers the spring which forms a pool in the floor of the cell." (Muir, 1885). The water here is beautiful, cold, clear, light and diuretic, as indeed it is in the Village! 'Tobar na Cille',

The Source of the Tobar Childa

The Well of Virtues in Gleann Mor

the Well of the Church, is very close to the site of St. Brendan's Chapel near Ruaival, and was famous for its alleged power to change the wind. Buchan (1752) also mentions a Well of Youth, which was inaccessible to any but a St. Kildan.

iii Landings

It is just possible to land on the flattish rocks in Glen Bay under certain favourable conditions, Brougham's advance party accomplished it in 1799, and Dr. MacDonald (1823) recorded his first landing on Sept.

16th 1822, "on the north-west side of the island, and in a little loch, or arm of the sea, got the boat under shelter; and leaving it in charge of the crew till the weather would admit of bringing it round, the Master and I stepped ashore, having nearly two miles to walk before reaching the Village." Dun Passage is another alternative; an Irishman once landed in a cave below Mullach Bi, but there is only one normally recognised approach by sea and that is by Village Bay, which can be treacherous in a south easterly wind. Martin writing about his visit in 1697 commented, "It is faced all round with a steep rock, except the bay in the south east, which is not a harbour fit for any vessel, though in time of calm one may land upon the rock, and get up into the island with a little climbing." Everyone visiting St. Kilda is staggered by the steepness and height of the rocks, Sands, who was marooned on Hirta in 1876 described the mountains as "hills, but in reality they are only halves of hills, hills to the interior, but cliffs to the sea." (Sands, 1878).

iv The Village.

The later Village rises from the landing place and forms a crescent along which the Cottages and the Factor's House are built. The Kirk has now been completely restored and refurnished by Allan Aitken and Archie Maynard and their skilled band of helpers

Village Bay and Dun.

and it was rededicated at a memorable service in August 1980. The school is attached to the Kirk, and the Manse is situated on the sea-ward side. In April 1979 Monseigneur John Barry conducted a memorial service and unveiled a plaque to commemorate the crews of three aircraft which had crashed, the Beaufighter on Conachair on June 4th, 1943, the Sunderland in Gleann Mor on June 8th, 1944 and the unidentified aircraft believed to be a Wellington Bomber which crashed on Soay. The Cemetery used by the St. Kildans is in the centre of the Village on the original site of Christ's Church, the only headstones bearing names can be counted on one hand, the others, undressed natural stones taken from the hillside give their own silent witness. Just above the landing point still stand the remains of the Store-house in which the people kept feathers, fish and tweed for export together with their own necessary boating gear.

A surprising object to be seen near the Store-house is the remains of a 4 inch Mark III QF (Quick Firing) Gun with an ammunition store behind, these were installed in August 1918 after a German Submarine had fired 72 shells on May 15th of that year. The shells demolished the Wireless Station, removed the roof off the Store-house and damaged the Kirk, the Manse, two Cottages and two boats, but without any loss of life. Lachlan MacDonald tells the story of how Finlay MacQueen had run out of tobacco at this time, and seeing the strange vessel enter the Bay, launched his boat and began to row out hoping they could help him out, a few gun shots echoing round the hills soon had him heading for the shore in great haste!

On both sides of the street each family had its strip of land reaching from the Head Dyke to the shore on which they cultivated their crops of barley, oats and potatoes. Grazing for the sheep and cattle was normally outside the boundary wall after 1830. However, it was to the cliffs the St. Kildans turned for most of their

The Feather Store and Gun emplacement.

food, collecting vast numbers of sea-birds' eggs and young and adult birds during the spring and summer months.

(4) Soay

Off the north west tip of Hirta, opposite the Cambir, lies the island of Soay, Norse – Sheep Island, the least visited of all Britain's outlying islands. "According to tradition a Viking named Callum brought the first sheep to Soay, but they may well have come much earlier with Neolithic settlers." (MacLean 1972). Viewed from a certain angle Seton noted that it resembled a tiger couching for its prey. The grassy summit is 378 m (1239 ft.) above the sea and is completely surrounded by steep cliffs, making landing extremely hazardous. The only practical landing place is to the south east. School-master Murray visited the island on January 10th, 1887 with a group of men to collect 20 sheep for their New Year feast, and again on May 28th when they snared 500 Fulmars on their nests. For the Keartons it excelled everything they had seen for the sheer numbers of birds, particularly the puffins which were everywhere, dotted all over the sea, sitting out on the rocks and swarming in the air above. Situated on the grassy plateau to the south east is a neatly built altar, 1 m high, which Heathcote

The Altar on Soay,
drawn from a photograph by Heathcote, 1898.

photographed on his visit in 1898, a St. Kildan in the background shows the size.

There is sufficient grass to feed about 500 Soay Sheep, but, being absolutely wild, they pose problems for the catcher. Each year the natives would visit the island with dogs, their fangs previously broken to prevent damaging the sheep when they had been caught or cornered. This exciting exercise, which involved running down the sheep one at a time they called 'Ruagadh' – the 'Pursuit'. The men, assisted by their dogs, would run from rock to rock with great nimbleness and excitement while the sheep ran madly round the island. Kearton (1897) commented, "The way they bounded from crag to crag, and skipped in single file along the dangerous ledges, was simply astonishing."

The island became a prison for one of two sheep stealing brothers from the island of Lewis, Dugan and Fearchar Mor, after their dastardly deeds on Hirta. Having frightened everyone into Christ's Church they set fire to the building and the people, only one woman escaped to tell the true story to the Factor when he arrived in the summer. Fearchar was taken to Stac an Armin where he plunged into the turbulent waters and was never seen again. Dugan was deliberately marooned on Soay to end his days. "He took shelter under a huge stone that springs out of the ground like the chisel of a plane. He deepened the floor with his dirk, and built dry stone walls at the sides and front, leaving a door of about 2 feet square." (Sands, 1877). Outside the cave, which bears his name to this day, Tigh Dugan, was found his dirk stuck into the ground with his bleached bones beside it.

Tigh Dugan, together with three other houses in the vicinity, was used in earlier years by the men on their sheep-shearing visits. MacDonald in his notes for May 30th 1824 wrote, "This day several of the male inhabitants set off for the neighbouring island of Soay, where they will remain eight or ten days at the sheep – fleecing." (MacDonald, 1825). Sands reported that Tigh Dugan, "is still occupied by the six young women who go to this island every summer to catch puffins for the sake of their feathers. They generally remain three weeks at a time, but when the weather is bad, are sometimes detained for six weeks."

Landing on Soay was always treacherous, but getting off could be even worse as Sands described so vividly. "Having caught as many fulmars as he (MacRuaridh) could carry, we descended the rocks where we had landed. The sea had risen considerably since that time. After waiting for about two hours, the boat came round the island heavily laden with fulmars. Some of the crew (there were twelve in all) had got into her on the other side. But four or five came down the rocks to where I was, and cast anxious looks at the waves, that came sweeping along from the west at a right angle with the shore. Two young men sat on the top of the cliff, each holding a rope, by the help of which the others slid into the boat. Then came my turn. A line was fastened to my waist, and a hair rope put into my hand. I was peremptorily requested to take off my shoes, and as I descended, I pushed my toes into any crevice or cranny that offered, until the rock became so smooth that I could find no hold for my feet. Then I was obliged to be passive, and allowed myself to be lowered like a sack until I reached a small limpet-covered shelf on which the waves rose about knee deep. 'Jump! Jump!' shout the crew, and when the boat mounts on the wave, I leap, and fall in a heap among the fulmars – all right. The air was quite calm, but the sea continued to rise, and the boat was in imminent danger of being dashed to pieces against the wall." (Sands, 1877).

From the peak of the Cambir it is possible to look over Soay Sound with binoculars and spot Tigh Dugan and about 20 cleitean nearby and the wreckage of an aircraft which crashed during the Second World War.

Soay Sound

Some 500 m of rough water separate the island of Soay from Hirta, out of which rise three impressive rocks, Stac Biorach (the Pointed Stac) 73 m high (240 ft), one of the most difficult to climb; Soay Stac, 61 m (200 ft) and 300 m long with an archway running through it, and Stac Dona, the Bad Stac on account of the small number of birds which could be caught on it, 27 m high (87 ft). Wilson, who circumnavigated the islands in 1841, noted the changing features of the Stacs. He first described Stac Soay and then Biorach,

Soay Sound from the Cambir
showing Stac Biorach, left, Stac Soay, with the island of Soay behind.

19

Stac Soay gave the "appearance of a gigantic nondescript animal trying to wade across to Soay, while the other assumed a somewhat complex aspect, presenting as it were alternately the characters of an old beggar woman, a Scotch preacher and an Egyptian sphynx." (Wilson, 1842). In stormy weather the depth and darkness of this narrow Sound can be quite awe inspiring, with the clouds sweeping down from the summits meeting the mists arising from far below where the sea is breaking upon the rocks.

Lachlan MacLean informs us that Stac Biorach is the real test of a St. Kilda hero, "The people climb it occasionally, as sweeps do St. Paul's in London, by way of a feat. The man who cannot perform it, never gets a wife in St. Kilda . . . There was just two individuals up since Mr. MacKenzie went to the island 8 years ago. They did it to show their dexterity to an Englishman, and for a quid of tobacco. Mr. MacKenzie, who was present, says, that the attempt was fearful." (MacLean, 1838).

(5) BORERAY AND THE STACS

Boreray and the Stacs rise more or less vertically from the sea 7 km (4½ miles) N.E. of Hirta and form the site of the largest Gannetry in the world. In the breeding season the white of the gannets and the guano give the impression that the peaks are covered with snow. This colony is twice the size of any other and contains about 59,000 nests. The late James Fisher considered it to be the most magnificent and wonderful of all the great gannet colonies of the world. In spite of the difficult landings the St. Kildans made regular visits to Boreray for food, collecting adult birds in March, thousands of eggs in May, and the young gannets or gugas from August to October; they also spent two weeks on the island in the summer to shear the sheep.

BORERAY

i The Island

Boreray (Norse – the Island of the Fortified Place) was often referred to as the 'North Isle' or the 'North Land' by the St. Kildans. Its shape is similar to a huge cathedral roof, pitched much more steeply to the west, with grass covered slopes to the east and south. Puffins by the thousands have burrowed into the steep south-western slopes, and at the height of the breeding season they whirr round in wide circles before peeling off and disappearing underground with beakfuls of small fish for hungry youngsters. It is all coming and going at one of the world's largest puffinries, containing some 100,000 pairs of puffins. On Boreray the jagged

Stac Lee, Stac an Armin and Boreray, left to right.

pinnacles, turrets and towers stand on the top of the west facing cliffs rising to 384 m (1259 ft) above the breaking waves: the ledges provide nest sites for a large part of the gannetry. The lush grass supports over 350 Blackface Sheep. There are the ruined remains of three bothies which the St. Kildans used for their summer stay, each has a single chamber about 1½ x 3 m and 1½ m in height, well let into the steep hillside: the door faces east and is protected from the direct force of the wind by an earth wall. Above the landing place there is a cleitean village where the gannets which they had collected were stored until the relief boat arrived. If they were staying on the lesser islands for any length of time they always carried a fire with them in a pot (Buchan, 1752), in Martin's time, only a few years earlier, they used a steel, flint, and tinder.

ii Tigh Stallar

There used to be a large underground house called 'Tigh Stallar' – the House of Stallar, a man of the rocks. He had rebelled against the steward on Hirta, left the main island and set up residence on Boreray with several of the islanders. It was in this house that ten St. Kildans were forced to spend nine months of the winter of 1759. The only boat the people possessed at this time, having landed the bird-fowling party, was wrecked in Village Bay as the crew were caught in an October gale which raged continually for three days as they returned to Hirta. The marooned men fed on the birds and sheep, and made clothes from the skins of the sheep and the larger sea-birds, tacked together with feathers. They were eventually released when the Factor's boat arrived in June from Skye. They were no worse for wear, but they were "much out of humour." (Macaulay, 1764).

Macaulay has this description of the dwelling, "The house is eighteen feet high, and its top lies almost level with the earth by which it is surrounded; below it is of a circular form, and all its parts are contrived so that a single stone covers the top. If this stone is removed, the house has a very sufficient vent. In the middle of the floor is a large hearth. Round the wall is a paved seat, on which sixteen persons may conveniently sit. Here are four beds roofed with strong flags or stone lintels, every one of which is capable enough to receive four men. To each of these beds is a separate entry; the distance between these different openings, resembling in some degree so many pillars."

A more recent account, 1862, is that given by Euphemia MacCrimmon and recorded by Miss Kennedy, the niece of a former catechist on St. Kilda. It is full of interest but it conflicts in places with some of Macaulay's details. "It was built on pillars . . . quite round inside, with ends of long narrow stones sticking through the wall round about, on which clothes might be hung. There were six croops or beds in the wall; one of them was called Rastalls (Rath-Stallair, the Leading Climber's Cabin), very large, for it would accommodate twenty men or more to sleep in. Next to that was another, named Ralighe (Rath – ?), which was large, but rather less than the first. Next to that was Beran (Bearan – ?) and Shimidaran (?), which would accommodate twelve men each to sleep. Next to that was Leaba nan Con, or the Dog's Bed; next to that was Leaba an Tealaich, or the Fireside Bed. There was an entrance (passage) within the wall round about, by which they might go from one croop to another, without coming to the central chamber. It (the house) was not to be noticed outside, except a small hole in the top of it to allow smoke to get out, and to let in some light. There was a doorway on one side of the house, facing the sea, where they had to bend in going in, and a large hill of ashes near the door would not allow the wind to come in. Bar (Bair) Righ, is the name of the door . . . Euphemia MacCrimmon has seen stones in Tigh a Stallair on which there were writings."

The house had been used up to about 1840 by the inhabitants when they went over to Boreray bird fowling or hunting the sheep. By 1860 the roof had fallen in, but some of the beds could be seen. Now, little of the original house remains as many of the stones have been removed and used in the construction of bothies and cleitean.

Miss Kennedy also recorded, "There was a temple (chapel) in Boreray, built with hewn stones (?) Euphemia MacCrimmon has a mind of seeing it. There is one stone yet, where the teampull was, standing in the ground, upon which there is writings; and the inhabitants of St. Kilda built cleitan or cells with the stones of the temple . . . Also there is an altar in Boreray, and another on the top of Soay." (Thomas, 1867).

iii Spring Harvest of Gannets

Every year the St. Kildans would make several expeditions to Boreray in March and April to take Gannets as they rested on their nesting ledges at night. Schoolmaster George Murray gave this account of his visit in 1887. "On Thursday April 7th. I went with the men to Boreray to kill gannets through the night. We arrived across sometime before dark. When the night began to fall seven went on land and five remained in the boat to cruise round the island to pick up the birds when thrown over the rocks. D.M., W.M. and I went together and had rare work of it. They (the gannets) were sleeping on ledges of rocks which to any but a St. Kildan would be quite inaccesible. There is usually on each ledge a sentinel which thinks that he may refresh himself by a short nap occasionally. When he does so the party must pounce upon them, take hold of as many as possible by the neck and keep them from making a noise lest those in the neighbourhood be scared away, and it was strictly enjoined upon me that though one should take the half of the finger off me I must not make the least noise. They are powerful birds with long powered bills like razors. It is merciless slaughter but as it is one of the means of sustenance in St. Kilda it must be performed and so you must pocket mercy for the night. Being full moon it was much too clear for making what they call 'good work'. I did not complain of the clearness at all as I could, in places where no cat could get, see where I was going. It is very dangerous work on a dark night."

In May they would cross the sea once more, this time to take the Gannets' eggs. Dr. John MacDonald recorded this note in his Journal for May 24th. 1824, "a number of males set off for Borera, in search of eggs, and brought home upwards of 800, besides several hundreds which they left on the island for store, when they should be engaged at the sheep fleecing." These eggs would be mainly, if not entirely, those of the gannet.

iv Summer Visit
A full expedition was mounted in the summer lasting from one to two weeks for the purpose of 'taking the wool' off the sheep, a primitive form of sheep-shearing, using only a pen-knife. Dogs helped to run down the sheep one by one. Before 1880 the women went aswell to snare the puffins and to pluck them for their feathers. The men were never away from home for such a long time unless they were going to the mainland, conse--uently careful preparations were made and the men received a great send-off. School-master Ross (1889) described the scene in his diary. "Those picked for Boreray are easily known on this great day of setting out by the straw basket in the shape of the old Highland 'creel' which each man carries on his back. These 'creels' hold the greater part of their weeks provisions and like wise people they take a 'little more' lest circumstances may detain them longer than expected. Besides the basket each man has his snaring rod and fishing rod, both most useful in adding to the supply of their temporal wants. Very little crockery is required, not being used to it at home, but they take pails with biscuits and other bread as well as kettle and teapot. These latter are placed in the boat by willing hands when there is a farewell scene which to an outsider, would seem more than sufficient should they expect to be away for five years . . . On their return the con-gratulations are as joyful as the parting was sad. They are never happy when any of their friends are absent."

v Autumn Harvest

Between August and October, weather permitting, several trips were made to Boreray to collect the young gannets or gugas. They were hit over the head with a stick and collected up into the boat; sometimes they were plucked and gutted. Wilson was on Hirta in 1841 when the party returned from Boreray. "The boat (they have only one) had gone off with a crew that morning to bring these adventurers home. They arrived while we were still in the island – nineteen stout men and lads, the crew included and we had the opportunity of inspecting their harvest. The large boat was half filled with huge bundles of feathers, and besides those were a great number of smaller bundles of dark red, rather repulsive looking fleshy things, which we found to consist of the hind legs and backs of birds, chiefly young solans. They also brought numerous distended bags (the stomachs of old solan geese) filled with oil, which they extracted nearly pure from the stomach of the fulmar."

vi Communications

While away on Boreray the St. Kildans had developed their own communications system with the main island. They cut pieces of turf on the southern grassy slope to indicate that their work was finished and that they were ready to return home, a piece removed from the left meant they were short of food, one to the right indicated an illness or injury, at one time two patches brought news of injury or death. On one occasion the relief boat was launched only to find that the crew was not needed – nesting gannets had removed the turf! Sands recorded an incident during his stay, an old man had been up on the hill and reported that he had seen two marks cut on the turf on Boreray – the men were over there to pluck the sheep. "He came down in great distress and communicated the intelligence to the rest of the people, who to my surprise were thrown into a state of consternation. The women seated themselves on the ground and chanted lamentations . . . I went up the hill, and with a glass discovered that one of the marks was a number of men building a cleit. I explained this to some of the people who had followed me, but failed to convince them. In the evening, however, when the boat returned from Boreray with the plucking party all well, the sceptics acknowledged with joyful smiles that my glass was better than their eyes." (Sands, 1887).

Martin (1716) reported on the use of fires to contact Hirta on one desperate occasion. "All the men in the isle having gone to the isle of Boreray for purchase, the rope that fastened their boat happened to break, and by this unlucky accident the boat was quite lost, and the poor people confined to the isle from the middle of

March till the latter end of May, without so much a crust of bread; but they had sheep, fuel and fish in abundance. They were at a loss how to acquaint their wives and friends that all of them were alive; but to effect this, they kindled as many fires on the top of an eminence as there were men in number; this was no sooner seen, and the fires counted, than the women understood the signal and were so overjoyed at this unexpected news that they fell to labour the ground with the foot-spade . . . After the stewards arrival in the isle, about the end of May, he sent his galley to bring home all the men confined in the isle."

vi Sea Caves

Below the surface of the sea, west of Sgarbhstac, skin-divers have recently discovered a huge watery cavern with its base 50 m below sea level with a cathedral like arch spanning its roof to a height of 20 m, occupied solely by a party of inquisitive Grey Atlantic seals. Nearby the waves have eroded another large cave, which can be entered by boat. Heathcote and some St. Kildans spent the night sheltering there in 1898 when it was too rough too land. "After their evening meal Norman MacKinnon told us that they were going to 'make worship' (as their custom was) and then followed one of the most impressive services I have ever attended. I could not understand a word, but the earnestness of the men, the intoning of their prayers, the weirdness of the Gaelic tune to which they sang the psalm, and the solemn grandeur of the place, combined to make it a most interesting and impressive ceremony." (Heathcote, 1900).

STAC AN ARMIN

Stac an Armin, the Warrior's Stac, 196 m (644 ft) is the tallest and one of the most impressive sea-stacks in Europe and is home for 9,500 pairs of breeding Gannets. There is no earth or grass, earlier mariners reported a spring running in an easterly direction, recently Mary Harman counted 78 cleitean on the stac, the last one being at about 150 m (500 ft) besides the highest of the colonies. There are also two or three little houses, larger than cleitean on a ledge about 125 m above the sea and not visible from the boat. Martin in 1697 recorded, "here are several stone pyramids, as well for lodging the inhabitants that attend the season of the solan geese, as for those that preserve and dry them and other fowls."

i Landing

Macaulay gives this illuminating account of landing in 1758. "When the weather is fair and the sea smooth, they man their boat with eight of their ablest hands. The Steward's deputy is their sea captain and land officer; he has an indefeasible right to manage the helm and issue out orders. These honours or high privileges expose him to great dangers; he is the first person to land and the last to quit the field . . . After having laid by all incumbrances, his upper cloaths and his shoes, he fastens a string rope round his waist, the other end of it being in the boat; and as soon as the wave rises to a proper height, he springs out toward the rock with all the agility he is master of, and imploys the whole power of his hands and feet, sometimes of his teeth and nails, to settle himself there; if he falls back into the sea, the affront gives him infinitely more pain than the severe drenching; his fellows haul him in, and he repeats the experiment. If he succeeds in the attempt, which is generally the case, he fixes himself in a secure place, makes the rope fast and gives his companions an opportunity of coming ashore. Four of the crew, being left in the boat where they must remain at their oars till the commander and his party return." (Macaulay, 1764).

Wally Wright, the Nature Conservancy Warden in 1980 described the problems of getting a foot-hold on the stac, "Stac an Armin is on a slope where the swell of 10-20 feet is more difficult than on Stac Lee and there is greater danger of capsizing when you go in. There are two landing places, one the St. Kildans used at the corner of the Stac which is vertical, – the one we used the last 5 times is on the main slope. We did it by tying two Gemini's together to make it more stable, making it like a large raft so that it doesn't capsize, and getting on that way. On the Stac you've got 3 main colonies of gannets which you can by-pass so that you can climb the Stac at any time of the year because you are not disturbing the colonies. You've also got great colonies of Fulmars, Razorbills, Guillemots, Puffins as well as even Wren and Rock Pipits. The rocks are smooth to start off for the first 100 ft and then large boulders where all the smaller stuff has been washed or blown away, all the way to the top. Even at the highest point there are nests of Razorbills and Guillemots below the boulders, separate from the Gannets. Another thing that is surprising is to find, on one of the remotest places, so much plastic rubbish that the gannets bring in off the sea, anything that floats at all. This year we had plastic roses, plastic bags, plastic fishing netting and kiddies toy balloons, anything that the gannets can pick up as nest material. There's always a purpose for landing. In 1980 it was to take eggs for analysis and other years to collect lichens or rocks for geologists." The stac has only been climbed 7 times in the 50 years since the Evacuation.

Gannet Landing on Stac an Armin.

ii Harvest of Gannets and Eggs

Adult Gannets were caught in March and April, eggs collected in May and the young between August and October. Macaulay recorded in 1764 "as many as are not required for immediate comsumption are secured within the little houses or barns, without salt or using any other art to preserve them, than opening their backs and washing them clean." Martin writing in 1697 reported, "I remember they brought 800 of the preceeding year's solan geese dried in their pyramids; after our landing, the geese being cast together in one heap upon the ground, the owners fell to share out each man his own, at which I was a little surprised, they being all of a tribe; but having found upon enquiry that every goose carried a distinguishing mark on the foot, peculiar to the owner, I was then satisfied in this piece of singularity."

Lachlan MacDonald, who was evacuated from St. Kilda in 1930 remembers how they visited this Stac in his day. "We would row out from the main island, Hirta, we had a sail but it depended on the wind whether we used it, and we used to land on a narrow ledge. We worked in pairs and had a rope between us; one of us would go for 50-60 yds ahead, and the other fellow would come up to there, walking one at a time for safety. We worked it in bits, zig-zagging our way right up to the top. You had an empty box on your back, and when you got to the top you would start filling up the empty box with gannet's eggs, and the odd guillemot's – not many. There would be half a dozen of us working on the Stac and we would fill up the box on our way down. Then we lowered the box by rope into the boat. Full it would weigh anything from ½ to 1 cwt. (about 50 kg), with layers of nest material to line the box to keep the eggs from breaking. Sometimes there would be a few of them broken. Then we would take them all home, make a hole and blow them; the boys aged about 10 years would sell them for 1d. We would eat the contents – they were great for making pancakes and things like that."

iii A Winter on the Stac

It would be hard to imagine a more inhospitable place to spend a winter than on Stac an Armin, but this was the fate of three men and eight boys who had been landed on the Stac in 1727 in the middle of August to collect feathers and the young solan geese. Normally they would expect to remain there for about 10 days, but during this time an epidemic of small-pox broke out which was to decimate the community causing 94 deaths and leaving only 4 adults and 26 children from 21 families. It struck so quickly that a crew could not be raised to man the boat to collect the party on the rock. They had to remain there until the Factor came in the middle of next May – they were all well. "They lived on fish and fowls, but at times suffered from cold and hunger. They made fish-hooks out of a few rusty nails, and also contrived to stitch together their clothing with feathers and patch them with the skins of birds. They returned mostly to empty houses, crops generally never reaped, and the cattle roaming about half wild." (Mackenzie, 1904).

In 1840 one of the last Great Auks was killed on Stac an Armin, the last survivor of the species was shot off Iceland in 1844.

STAC LEE

Stac Lee, the Blue Stac is 172 m high (564 ft), viewed from the east it rises like a huge fang out of the sea. Wilson (1842) described it from a slightly different angle, from the south west, "the whole presenting the appearance of the mouth of some huge marine monster, of which the upper jaw was raised aloft and the under stretched out horizontally, prepared to snap up a ship or two, or a thousand solan geese at one fell swoop." Kearton (1898) regarded this pillar of rock with the nesting gannets reaching to its summit as "one of the wonders of the world." It has been estimated that about 9,260 pairs nest on the south face. Each year between 5,000-7,000 young gannets would be taken from this Stac alone.

i Landing

Landing on Stac Lee has always been extremely tricky. Heathcote, who climbed it with his sister in 1898 commented, "With the assistance of a rope and a sufficient amount of confidence, any active man could

Landing on Stac Lee,
drawing by Heathcote, 1898.

walk up the side of a house; but it needs a St. Kildan to get a foot-hold on an overhanging rock covered with slippery sea-weed and draw himself up to the top. The first time I landed there the tide was fairly high, and it was possible to get some foot-hold on the upper part of the rock where it is not quite perpendicular, but the next time ten or twelve feet of slimy sea-weed clinging to the absolutely overhanging cliff were exposed. How Finlay MacQueen got up is still a marvel to me." (Heathcote, 1900).

Wally Wright, a skilled cragsman himself, in 1980 made light of getting a toe-hold on the stac, finding it less dangerous than Stac an Armin. "Stac Lee is easier to get on because it is vertical, with the sea going up and down, and you just jump on. There is quite a bit of ledge at the 'blow-hole' where you jump, normally we do it in stocking soles so that you stick to the sea-weed; we are talking about a swell of 10, sometimes 20 feet, you jump and the boat suddenly disappears from you – and you are left!"

ii Harvesting and Casting Lots

It is incredible that the St. Kildans would think nothing of scaling this stac in the dark. Neil Ferguson recalled, "They used to go at night-time and climb the rock at night, when the gannets were roosting. But there was always one bird on watch and that's the one

The Casting Point on Stac Lee
with Hirta behind, Oiseval left, and Conachair right.

they made for first and broke its neck." Martin writing in 1698 described the method to tackle Stac Lee in those days, "One would think it next to impossible to climb . . . but the inhabitants assured me it was practicable, and to convince me of the truth of it, they bid me look up near the top, where I perceived a pyramid house . . . They send a competent number of them to whose share the lots fall . . . and those who are sent act in the public interest, and when they have knocked on the head all that may be reached, they then carry them to a sharp point, called the 'Casting Point', from whence they throw them into the sea . . . until the boatmen cry, 'Enough' – And so by degrees, getting all in, they return home; and after their arrival every man has his share proportionable to his lands."

The method of selection by casting lots was used on many occasions, to make a fair allocation of the cliffs, or of the fish and Fulmars caught, or to choose the boating party to go to the Stacs. Lachlan MacDonald explained the unusual procedure – Each person would place an object, a penny, half-penny, small stone, stick or a piece of paper under a stone; then a St. Kildan, not privy to the arrangement, would point to each stone in turn, thus allocating the person to his share of the catch or his task on the cliff or stac.

Neil Gillies who left the island at the Evacuation, recounted an incident which occured when he was working on the sheer rock face. His fellow worker had crawled along a narrow ledge and had administered the death blow successfully to a number of adult Gannets when one, with its razor sharp bill got the better of him. A distressed cry rang out over the still night air, "The Gannet's got my finger." Neil replied, "Never mind your finger – have you got the Gannet?!"

iii The Summit

In 1969 the Stac was climbed by Morton Boyd and Dick Balharry. As they made their way up the vertical part the birds were 'screaming like an excited crowd at a football match.' The angle lessened, "We were now on a great bevelled roof of gannets and walking up the ledges of slimy guano you sank in at every step. Now and again gannets would reach out and grip your arm in their beaks. However, this was nothing to the top bit, gannets, gannets and more gannets. Even the stones were covered in grey whitewash, so dry and encrusted that your foot broke rather than sank in. We estimated 14,000 gannets were packed together here, and when they rose there was a dust storm which obscured your vision, as happens when a helicopter takes off from dusty ground. There was a wee bothy up there, beautifully dry inside and capable of holding two men, but two fulmars had taken over." (Weir, 1969, quoting Dick Balharry).

GEOLOGY

The four main islands, Hirta, Dun, Soay and Boreray with their adjacent stacs were thrown up from a centre of plutonic activity between Hirta and Boreray around 54-65 million years ago. The Hebrides had been enjoying the sub-tropical climate of the Eocene period when the Tertiary volcanic outburst took place. "There broke out the most prolonged and intense volcanic activity in Britain's history . . . the seven centres of eruption were at St. Kilda, Rhum, Ardnamurchan, Mull, Arran and north-east Ireland. There must have been others near and afar, now hidden under the sea, for the Tertiary igneous province extended north-west across the Arctic Circle to embrace Iceland and Greenland." (Murray, 1973). The Faeroes should also be added to this list. Read and Watson (1966) point out that the Scottish centres of plutonic intrusions "are lined up along a roughly north-south axis that probably marks the course of a deep crustal fracture which served as a conduit for the magma." These intrusions include several gabbros (basic rock) and a number of granites (acidic rock) as well as dykes and cone sheets of dolerite. During this time St. Kilda came into being. Great masses of molten magma were forced up from the earth's crust in four stages. A rock sample taken in 1967 was found to be 57 million years old and therefore

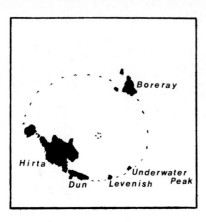

Rim of the extinct volcano

a piece of the oldest known volcano of the Tertiary era. The rim of the volcano is defined by Soay, south and west Hirta, Dun, Levenish and a sub-marine peak E.N.E. of it continuing round towards Boreray. Divers in 1979 reached this sub-marine peak, 38 m below the surface, and beyond it found themselves at 50 m on the outer sloping edge of the rim, angled at 30°. They were on solid rock covered by purple encrustaceans, disappearing into the darkness below.

On approaching Village Bay one is immediately impressed by the contrast between the more rugged skyline of Dun and Ruaival to the south and the more rounded outline of Oiseval and the cone shape of Conachair to the north and east. This difference is caused by the two major rock types, which with a complex central area, give rise to three clear relief zones.

i South and West Zone

This zone includes the underwater peak mentioned, Levenish which is linked to Dun by a sub-marine ridge, also Ruaival, Mullach Bi, the Cambir, Stac Biorach and Soay. The earliest formed rocks are to be found here; they are dark in colour and basic in chemical composition (low in quartz and high in aluminium oxide and magnesium). They are called either Ultrabasic or Eucrite depending on their make-up, and form the main bulk of the rocks in this zone and stand out when other weaker dykes have eroded away. When they do break up they form huge blocks of rock, like the Mistress Stone on Ruaival. Consequently, these basic rocks give rise to the knobbly, jagged formation of the south and west coastline.

ii East and North Zone

This zone is composed of the most recently formed rocks which have crystallised out from a completely different magma to form a light buff coloured granophyre, rich in quartz, which weathers more uniformly to give rise to the more rounded hills of

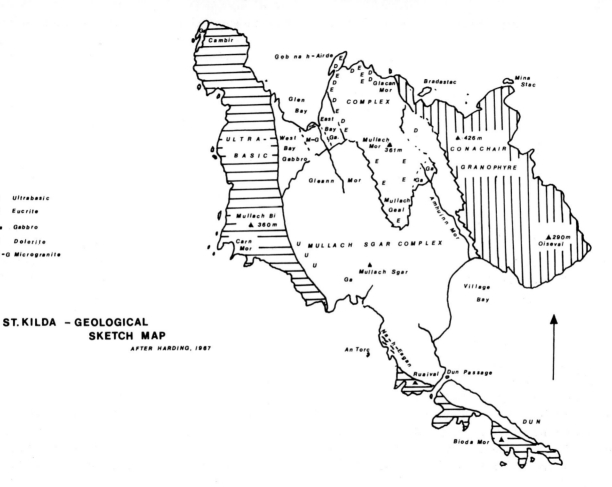

Gob na h-Airde

Cambir

Glen
Bay

West
Bay

Bradastac

Mina
Stac

Glacan
Mor

COMPLEX

East
Bay

M-G

Ga.

Mullach
Mor
361m

▲ 426m

CONACHAIR

GRANOPHYRE

D

ULTRA-
BASIC

Gabbro

Gleann Mor

E

E

Ga

E

E

Ga

E

Mullach
Geal

Mullach Bi
▲ 360m

E

▲290m
Oiseval

Carn
Mor

U MULLACH SGAR COMPLEX

U

U

Ga

▲
Mullach Sgar

Village
Bay

U   Ultrabasic

E   Eucrite

Ga   Gabbro

D   Dolerite

M-G Microgranite

An Torc

Na-h-Eagan

Ruaival

Dun Passage

ST. KILDA – GEOLOGICAL
SKETCH MAP

AFTER HARDING, 1967

DUN

Bioda Mor

▲

D

34

Oiseval and Conachair. Where it is exposed to the elements it tends to disintegrate into great slabs which may be two metres long by one metre thick. Examples can be seen on the cliffs of Conachair which provide splendid nesting ledges for the Fulmar. Thick dark bands of dolerite strike diagonally across the sea cliffs of Oiseval and Conachair having been injected under pressure between the cracks in the rocks at a later date. The contrast between the granophyre and the basic rocks can be seen at Glacan Mor and at the top of the cliffs north of Mullach Mor, near the tracking station, where a little stream runs down a gully opposite Bradastac.

iii Central Zone

The Central Zone is mainly composed of gabbros and dolerites together with other rocks in one great complex, most of the features being visible in the quarry by the road. Many of the thin intrusive sheets cause weaknesses which are accentuated by the elements, a good example is the huge natural arch at Gob na h-Airde which owes its formation to three dykes of dolerite which have been eroded away in more recent times. All round the islands are sea caves which provided shelter for the St. Kildans in times of sudden storms. On the Hirta side of Dun Passage there is an excellent example of a dolerite cone sheet nearly 2 m thick, together with sheets of microgranite. At Na h-Eagan (Norse – Notches) microdiorite enclosed in microgranite can be seen. On the storm beach at Village Bay it is easy to identify boulders formed from the buff granophyre and those of the blue-black dolerite.

Rockall and St. Kilda were probably unaffected by the Quaternary Scottish Ice Sheet which reached the other Hebridean islands, but Hirta may have had its own small ice sheet to the East of Mullach Mor reaching down to the shore of Village Bay and depositing a drift tongue. At the foot of Conachair there is a clearly defined pro-talus ridge formed from rocks which have fallen from the steep face to land in or overshoot the hill foot bed of ice. 'An Lag' above the Village is an example of an ice deepened hollow, which has been terminated by a moraine and then infilled by the downward creep of gravel and stone. (Macgregor D.R., 1960).

iv Boreray and the Stacs

Boreray, Stac Lee and Stac an Armin are of similar composition to each other, being made up of ultra-basics and gabbros with quite a large percentage of dolerite. The centre of plutonic activity occured somewhere between Hirta and Boreray and in 1979 further investigations were made in this area. Several traverses were made in the trawler, the Golden Chance, skippered by Andrew Miller-Mundy, echo soundings of the sea bed were recorded which revealed a gentle undulating floor between 30-40 fathoms. Approximately two thirds of the way over to Boreray was discovered a clearly defined ridge at a depth of 24 fathoms. Skin divers, led by Gordon Ridley, brought up rock samples from the ridge which were identified by Dr. R. R. Harding as gabbro.

The shaping of the islands still continue to this day, millions of years after the original volcanic activity. The continuous onslaught of the sea, the driving wind and rain, and the frost claw away at the basic structure resulting in extensive rock falls and the formation of new sea-caves and sea-stacs.

General outline of the formation of St. Kilda

The formation of the St. Kilda Group of islands has probably developed in four stages:–

(1) The Central Block subsided

In the first stage a plutonic complex of 6-7 kms diameter formed, the centre of which was situated midway between Hirta and Boreray. A central block of ultrabasic, eucritic and gabbroic rock subsided, displacing a certain amount of magma below.

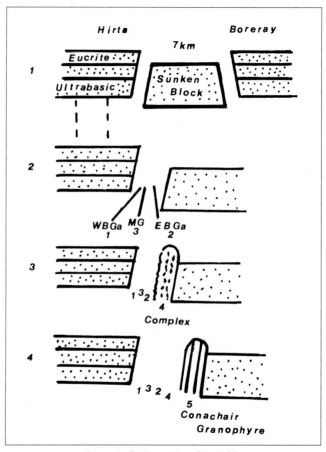

Stages in the Formation of St. Kilda.

(2) Intrusions at Glen Bay

The mass of basic rock forming the periphery was then intruded by:–

i West Glen Bay Gabbro (WBGa)
ii East Glen Bay Gabbro (EBGa)
iii Glen Bay Microgranite (MG)

The eucrites of Mullach Mor and Glacan Mor were intruded by the East Glen Bay Gabbro.

(3) Formation of the Mullach Sgar Complex

A period of time followed in which intrusions of microgranite, dolerites and microdiorites penetrated all the previously described rocks forming the Mullach Sgar Complex.

(4) Conachair Granophyre Intrusion

The final stage was the massive intrusion of a pale buff magma of Conachair Granophyre to form the rounded hills of Conachair and Oiseval and the eastern coastline of Hirta. The junction between these acid masses and the Mullach Sgar Complex can be seen clearly at the Glacan Mor sea cliff to the north of Conachair.

The basic rocks form the rugged west coast and the acid granophyre the more rounded hills to the east and north.

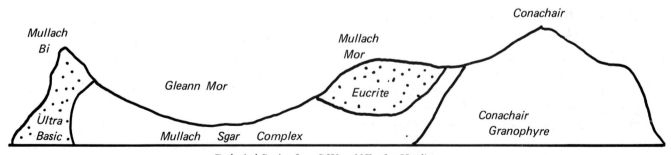

Geological Section from S.W. to N.E. after Harding, 1966.

Key to the rocks of St. Kilda

The key is using fresh, not weathered surfaces.

General appearance	Detailed colour	Features seen with a hand lens	Location	Identification
LIGHT ROCKS (acidic)	Cream	Cream matrix, clear quartz, potassium feldspar crystals, A few black hornblende crystals. Some rocks with crystals in drusy cavities.	Conachair Oiseval Village Bay Shore	Conachair Granophyre
	Light grey + dark flecks	White matrix of quartz, orthoclase, plagioclase; black hornblende.	Mullach Sgar Complex between Glen + Village Bays	Microgranite
	Grey + dark angular blocks	Grey matrix + flat clear crystals of plagioclase. Large, roughly rectangular grains of hornblende.	Quarry	Hornblende Granophyre
GREY ROCKS (intermediate)	Grey-green	Fine texture, light feldspar + dark grey chlorite crystals evenly mixed, with a few small green-black hornblende crystals.	Quarry Dun Passage Na h-Eagan	Microdiorite

Key to the rocks of St. Kilda — continued

General appearance	Detailed colour	Features seen with a hand lens	Location	Identification
DARK ROCKS (basic)	Uniformly dark	Fine grain, mainly dark pyroxenes + few light grey flecks of feldspar. Occasional pink orthoclase.	Dun Passage Na h-Eagan (Cone sheets) Village Bay	Dolerite
	Dark + pale grey streaks	Dolerite as above + grey + white crystals of acid intrusion fill cracks from cooling.	Dun Passage Na h-Eagan	Dolerite + Microgranite
	Mainly black + grey or green flecks	Coarse grain. Large black flat crystals of pyroxene. Olivine, honey coloured on weathered surface. Plagioclase generally white or pale grey.	Glen Bay Cambir (NW) Amhuinn Mor Glacan Mor Mullach Mor Mullach Bi Ruaival Dun	Gabbro Eucrite Ultrabasic

The above descriptions are from collected specimens. There are variations from the above correlation of colour and rock name because identification of rocks on colour alone is not completely reliable. A more detailed study will require more specialised equipment.

ACIDIC ROCKS
(light colour)

Conachair Granophyre

Microgranite

Hornblende Granophyre

INTERMEDIATE

Microdiorite

Dolerite

BASIC ROCKS
(dark colour)

Dolerite with Microgranite

Gabbro or Eucrite or Ultrabasic

ST. KILDA — PLACE NAMES

Several of the major mountains and islands have Norse names, Soay, Boreray, Ruaival and Oiseval, but most are Gaelic and were first recorded by Mathieson, himself a Gaelic speaker, in 1927. Two problems still arise, some of the names seem to have been written down phonetically and although translated back, the meaning in some instances is uncertain. The other difficulty is that the stories behind the names have been lost in so many cases. One can only guess that at 'Geo na Ba Glaise' a Grey Cow slipped over the rocks and ended up in the cave! However, some places have stories or incidents attached to them.

'Geo na Seanig', Little Old Woman's Cave is alleged to be the place where the only survivor lived after Dugan and Ferchar Mor had frightened all the inhabitants into the Church and set fire to it. The old woman hid in the cave until the Factor's boat arrived when she made her unexpected appearance and reported all that had occurred. The culprits were deposited on Stac an Armin and Soay.

'Sgeir Mac Righ Lochlainn', the Skerry of the Son of the King of Norway. This unfortunate gentleman was ship-wrecked off Soay, made his way to the island and while drinking at a water brook the natives "caught him by the back of the neck, and held his head down in the brook until he was drowned." (Seton, 1878). However, they named the rock after him.

'Geo an Eireanach', Irishman's Cave. Some people reach St. Kilda by mistake. One Christmas morning an Irishman was rowing across a bay in his native isle, carrying a keg of whisky to make merry with his friends, when a sudden squall arose and blew him out to sea; over the next few days he was driven across the edge of the Atlantic, all the way to St. Kilda. He set foot at an extraordinary landing place, the entrance of a cave at the foot of Mullach Bi. It was two or three days before the St. Kildans spotted a wrecked boat and to their amazement found the man alive. They lowered a rope and rescued him on the point of collapse. He remained with them for over a year before he could return to Ireland. The sea cave was named after him!

'Geo nan Plaidean', Blanket or Plaid Cave. In this particular cave the natives would wait all night, covered by a thick blanket to protect them from the oceans' spray as they hid until the birds returned to their ledges, and the slaughter began.

'Sgeir Dhomhnuill', Donald's Rock. Lachlan MacDonald recalled the story behind this rock. In the 1920's the men often went shooting shags, to supplement their diet, on Rubha an Uisge. After firing the first shot the birds had the habit of flying around to another rock where they would rest in safety. To

prevent this happening they first settled Donald MacQueen (son of Finlay) on the rock, now the birds would not land there, but circled round and flew back allowing the hunters a second shot, hence, 'Sgeir Dhomhnuill' – Donald's Rock.

The natives never spoke of the Lover's Stone, but they called it 'Bearradh na cloiche moire' – the Ridge of the Big Rock; the Gap between Conachair and Oiseval was known as 'Bearradh na h-Eige' – The Ridge or Cliff of the Gap.

There must be many lost stories behind the fascinating place names.

The following list is taken from the 6 inch Ordnance Survey Maps and begins at the north point of each island, circling the coastline in a clockwise direction, before doing the same inland.

'Geo' comes from the Norse 'gja', a creek, but it is used in north and west Scotland to denote a long narrow, tide filled gully or sea-cave.

HIRTA

a. Coastline – Hirta

Cambir – bent, crooked or (Norse) – Crest or Ridge.
Geo Chalum McMhuirich – Callum Murchison's Cave.
Geo Sgeir Chaise – Cheese Rock Cave.

Mol Carn na Liana – Shingle beach of the cairn of the green sward.
Geo Crubaidh – Stooping Cave.
Sgeir na Cairaidh – Rock of the fish weir or pond.
Geo Chruadalian – Hardship Cave.
Leacan an Eitheir – Flat Boat Rocks.
Geo nan Ron – Seals Cave.
Gob na h-Airde – Point of the High Ground.
Geo Oscar – Oscar's Cave.
Geo an t-Samh – Bad Smell Cave.
Na Cleitean – The Cleitean.
Bradastac (Norse) – Steep Stac.
Geo na Mol – Shingle Cave.
Geo nan Plaidean – Blanket or Plaid Cave.
Minastac (Norse) – Lesser Stac.
Leac Mhina Stac – Minastac Rock.
Sgeir Dhomhnuill – Donald's Rock.
Mol Ghiasgar (Gaelic + Norse) – Shingle of the Skerry.
Stac a' Langa – Ling Stac (fish).
Am Broig – The Boot.
Geo na Eige – Cleft Cave.
Rubha Gill – Gill's Point.
Geo na Muirbhuaile – Bream Cave (fish).
Sgeir nan Sgarbh (Norse) – Cormorant Rock.
Rubha an Uisge – Point of the Waters (water spout).

Geo Brababy – Brababy's Cave.
Geo Glann Neill – MacNeill's Anchorage.
Rubha Challa – Harbour Point or Point of Loss.
Abhainn Ilishgil (Norse) – Deep Stream of the Spring.
Geo Chille Brianan – Cave of St. Brendan's Church.
Geo Leibli – Leibli's Cave.
Giasgeir (Norse) – Skerry of the Cove.
Caolas an Duin – Dun Channel.
Sgeir Mhor (Norse + Gaelic) – Big Skerry.
Geo na Seanaig – Little Old Woman's Cave.
Geo Gharran Bhuidhe – Yellow Guelding Cave.
An Torc – The Boar.
Abhainn Gleshgil (Norse) – Shining Gully Stream.
Geo Rubha Mhuirich – Cave of Murchison's Point.
Laimrig nam Gal – Stranger's Anchorage.
Geo na Ba' Glaise – Cave of the Grey Cow.
Geo na Capuill – Mare or Horse's Cave.
Gob Chathaill – Cathelu's Point.
Geo Creag an Arpaid – Cave of Arpaig's Rock.
Geo an Eireanach – Irishman's Cave.
Sgeir Mhor (Norse + Gaelic) – Big Skerry.
Geo na Lashulaich – Sparkling Cave (Sparkling water inside).
Geo na Stacan – Stac Cave.
Poll a' Choire – Kettle or Chauldron Bay.
Baghan – Little Bay.

Beul na Geo – Mouth of the Cave.
Geo Chaimbir – Cambir's Cave.

b. *Inland Hirta*
Leacan an t-Sluic Mhoir – Rocks of the Big Hollow.
Leathad a'Ghlinne – Glen Brae.
Leathad na Guiltichean – Brae of Weeping.
Tobar nam Buaidh – Well of Virtues.
Gleann Mor – Great Glen.
Abhainn a' Ghlinne Mhoir – The River of the great Glen.
Airigh Mhor – Big Sheiling.
Mullach Mor – Big Summit, Big Hill Top.
Conachair – Coming together of the hills.
Aird Uachdarachd – Top of the High Ground.
An Lag Bho'n Tuath – The Hollow in the North.
Oiseval (Norse) – East Fell.
Glacan Conachair – Conachair's Hollow.
Tobar Gille Chille – Well of the Servant of the Church.
Tobar Childa – Kilder's Well or Well in both Gaelic and Norse or Childa Chalda (Norse) – Cold Well.
Lag Aitimir – Sloping Rock of the People.
Gearraidh Ard – High Grazing.
Mullach Geal – White Top.
Creagan Breac – Spotted Rocks.

Creagan Dubh – Dark Rocks.
Tigh an Triar – House of the Trinity.
Cnoc Bhaennaichta – Hill of Blessing.
Am Blaid – Flat-land.
Mullach Sgar – Clefted Hill Summit or (Norse) –
    Bare Hill Top.
Cnoc Sgar – Divided or Clefted Hill or (Norse) –
    Bare Hill.
Ruaival (Norse) – Red Fell.
Clas na Bearnaich – Limpet Rock.
Na h Eagan (Norse) – Notches.
Tobar na Cille – Well of the Church (St.
    Brendan's).
Leathaid Sgithoil Chaoil – Steep Slope of the
    Tiresome Narrow Hill.
Claigeann Mor – Big Skull (rock).
Claigeann an Tigh Faire – Skull of the Watching
    House.
Mullach Bi – Pillar Summit.
Carn Mor – Big Rocks.
Na Mullichean Mor – The Big Tops.

DUN – Fort
Seilg Geo – Hunter's Cave (hunting puffins) or
    (Norse) – Seals Cave.
Geo na Ruideig – Kittiwake Cave.

Na Sgarain – The Fissures or Divide (Tunnel at the
    Arch).
Gob an Dun – Point of Dun.
Gob na Muce – Point of the Pig (often used of
    the sea-pig or whale).
Hamalan (Norse) – The Way Home (Seafarer's).
Giumachsgor – Lobster Rock.
Sgeir Cul an Rubha – Skerry at the back of the
    Point.
Bioda Mor – Big Hill Top.
Geo Ghiasgeir (Norse) – Skerry Cave.
An Fhaing – The Fank (sheep).
A' Chlaisir – The Harp.
Cul Cleite – Back of the Cleit or Back of the Rocky
    Hillside.

STACS IN SOAY SOUND
Soay Stac – Sheep Stac.
Stac Biorach – Pointed Stac.
Stac Dona – Bad Stac (poor for birds).

SOAY (Norse) – Sheep Isle
Geo Ruadh – Red Cave.
Glamisgeo – Large Mouth Cave or (Norse) – Noisy
    Cave or Cleft in the Cliff.
Mol Shoay – Soay Shingle.
Laimhrig na Sroine – Nose Landing Place.

Geo nan Ron – Seals Cave.

A'Chala – The Harbour.

Scarpalin (Norse) – Sharp Projecting Rock.

Sgeir Mac Righ Lochlainn – Skerry of the Son of the King of Norway.

Gob Phursan – Phursan's Point.

Geo Phursan – Phursan's Cave.

Gob na h-Airde – Point of the High Ground.

Lianish (Norse) – Ness of the Slope.

Gob a'Ghaill – Headland of the Strangers.

Creagan – Little Rock.

Am Plastair – ? Place of Splashing – ? The Rascal.

Laimhrig Adinet – Adinet's Landing.

Poll Adinet – Adinet's Bay.

Cnoc Glas – Grey Hill.

Bearraidh na Craige Chaise – Cliff of the Steep Rock.

Tigh Dugan – Dugan's House.

Pursan a' Chaim – ?

BORERAY (Norse) – Island of the Fortified Place.

An t-Sail – The Beam.

Gearrgeo – Short Steep Cave.

Udraclete – Stony Ridge or (Norse) Outer Cliff.

Geo Shunadal (Norse) – Sunadal's Cave.

Creagan na Rubhaig Bana – Rock of the Little White Headland.

Creagan Fharspeig – Gull Rock.

Coinneag – Frothy Bay or (Norse) – Bay of the Woman.

Rubha Bhrengadal (Gaelic + Norse) – Headland of the Dale of the Breast or Headland of the Dale of the Grassy Slope.

Laimhail (Root-hand) – ?

Gob Scapanish (Norse) – Ness of the Caves or Ness of the Hollow Places.

Geo Sgarbhstac (Norse) – Cormorant Rock Cave.

Geo na Leachan Moire – Mary's Rock Cave.

Geo an Araich – Cave of Ruin.

Geo an Fheachdaire – Watchman's Cave.

Clesgor (Norse) – Rift in the Cliff.

Geo na Tarnanach – Thunder Cave.

Sunadal (Norse) – South Dale or Sun Dale.

Mullach an Tuamail – Top of Tuamail (Tuam – root for a tomb).

Cleitean McPhaidein – MacFayden's Cleitean.

Clagan na Rusgachan – The Shearer's Bell.

Clais na Runaich – Hollow of Resolve.

Na Roachan – ?

Mullach an Eilein – Island Summit.

Tigh Staller – Staller's House.

STAC AN ARMIN – The Warrior's Stac.

Am Biran – The Stick.

Rubha Briste – Broken Headland (loose rocks).

STAC LEE – *The Blue Stac.*
Rubha Langa – Ling Point (fish).

CLIMATE, CURRENTS AND CROSSING

(1) CLIMATE

"The general climate can be summarised as being rapidly changeable and permanently humid!" (Campbell in Jewell, Milner, Boyd, 1974). St. Kilda has an Atlantic climate but the high land mass causes clouds to form and increases the rainfall and the blusteriness of the wind. The islands lie close to the track of the most vigorous Atlantic depressions with dominant winds between south and west. Gales are recorded from all quarters throughout the autumn and winter. With gusts of 209 km per hour (130 mph) it is the windiest place in the British Isles. Sometimes it rains for 2-3 weeks without stopping, and quiet spells of more than a few hours are rare; in summer the winds are often strong. Warm moist air often reaches the islands in a northerly flow and cools to form sea fog which, on reaching the hills, turns to drizzle and rain. However, in late spring and summer there are quiet days and sunny spells which can last for a week or so, and long dry periods have been recorded. Rainfall is much the same as in the Outer Hebrides. about 125 cm (50 inches) a year.

Martin Martin (1698) said of Hirta, "The hills are often covered with ambient white mists." The late James Fisher commented, "He was right. St. Kilda is the home of clouds; it is a cloudmaker in a part of the Atlantic where there is plenty of material to make clouds from. Soay, Hirta and Boreray comb and rake the sky with their rugged fangs, and the weather spills out of it. On a fine day they have crowns of cloud, blowing away with the wind, and making as they blow. Gusts of dark clouds and showers come out of nothing. When Boreray makes black clouds it looks like a smoking anvil." (Fisher, 1948).

The winters are harsh and in the past special practical precautions were taken to preserve their equipment. "The St. Kilda community have no more than a single boat, which must lie idle all the winter, and is filled up with stones and earth in a secure place, to prevent the greatest of all public calamities, that of its being swept into the sea, or dashed against a rock by a violent gust of wind." (Macaulay, 1764). A similar tragedy can happen at any time of the year, even in the summer of 1981 the trawler, 'Golden Chance' dragged anchor in a squall and was smashed to pieces on the rocks in Village Bay.

Nowadays, few people are present to experience the severity of the winters, however, Captain Alasdair Cameron, R.A., the Officer Commanding the Unit on

St. Kilda will never forget one of the worst periods in the early months of 1979. "Perhaps my most vivid memory of a St. Kildan winter is the ceaseless wind that howls and whines its unpredictable way round the bay. Many times I sat at the Mess window half expecting to see a sheep sweep past at 100 mph, 6 feet off the ground. The first week in January saw the arrival of six feet of snow on the hills . . . St. Kilda is certainly an island of extremes. Its brown chameleon appearance of winter turned almost overnight in early May to a more lush green, which enshrouded it for most of the summer. The harsh boulders on the beach of the nocturnal months were suddenly covered, within a fortnight, by a soft Caribbean sand." (St. Kilda Mail, March 1980).

(2) SEA CURRENTS

The main factor influencing the waters off St. Kilda and all the Western Isles is the relatively warm and saline water which flows eastwards across the Atlantic in the North Atlantic Current. On reaching the Scottish Continental shelf some of the water from the Rockall Channel passes on north east through the Faroe-Shetland Channel to enter the Norwegian Sea (Ellett, 1979).

To the south of St. Kilda the Atlantic water reaches the edge of the shelf west of the Hebrides from the east side of the Rockall Channel. Once on the shelf the waters mix with that from the Clyde and the Irish Sea; some of this flows northwards through the Little Minch, and some southwards to Barra Head, then northwards along the west coast of the Outer Hebrides. The other factor influencing the surface circulation is the high rainfall run off in the local coastal waters.

In winter the water on the Hebridean shelf is stirred up throughout its depth by the frequent gales and invades the larger part of the western islands. By April less dense water begins to spread westwards on the surface and occupies the larger part of the outer shelf north of Barra Head. From April to October there is considerable variation. In the summer there are weak currents to the west of St. Kilda with cold saline bottom water on the shelf until summer and early autumn; this indicates a lack of horizontal flow on this part of the shelf and this would tend to generate cyclonic movements of air.

The upwelling currents on the edge of the shelf bring up the nutrients from the bottom waters and supply food for the plant and animal plankton, and subsequently the larger fish and seabirds.

(3) THE CROSSING

The voyage to St. Kilda has always acted as a deterrent to the casual visitor and a challenge to the determined island goer! Martin Martin soon ran into trouble when he left Harris on May 19th 1697 with the wind and tide against him. The party struggled on, "Our crew became extremely fatigued and discouraged without the sight of land for sixteen hours . . . until one of our number espied the Isle of Borera . . . this was a joyful sight." However, they had to ride out another violent storm throughout the next day sheltering under the towering northern cliffs, "The storm did almost drive us to the ocean . . . our men laid aside all hopes of life." The next day June 1st was calm and the men rowed to St. Kilda and they were able to make a safe landing in Village Bay.

Macaulay described in some detail his experiences on his voyage to St. Kilda in 1758, The day was quiet and sultry when he left Harris on June 6th. By 10 p.m. "the wind was at first extremely favourable, as it blew from the south east, and was little more than a gentle gale. It began to freshen at the end of half an hour and was gathering new strength every moment; before we had proceeded above four leagues (12 miles), the whole face of the sky was over-cast with clouds; which after the severest threatenings, bursted asunder and tumbled down upon us in violent torrents of rain, accompanied with flashes of lightning and peals of thunder extremely terrible. All this was succeeded by a hurricane which would have alarmed the most insensible, and did greatly confound the stoutest

seamen among us . . . To me it was a matter of astonishment that a vessel so small and frail, a six-oared highland boat, could have struggled for any time against such enormous billows, without either being overset or dashed to pieces. The storm continued to rage for about six hours . . . we dropped anchor before the Saddle and made a shift to stand there for five hours more in a most distressful condition, drenched all over, and under dreadful apprehension of being swallowed up every moment." They did land safely, thanks to the courage of the St. Kildans who formed a double human chain in the raging sea!

My first visit was memorable. Our party left Oban in a converted trawler 15 m long (50 ft) at 4.30 p.m. – we were well protected in the Sound of Mull but entered a heavy swell off Ardnamurchan which continued most of the way. The sun set into a bank of cloud before we reached the Sound of Canna, with the mountains of Rhum hidden under a thick cloud cap. At first light we saw gannets diving for mackerel as we manoeuvred our way through the tricky waters of the Sound of Harris. The skipper stated, "According to the echo-sounder we have been on dry land for the last half mile!" The weather forecast was poor – "Gale force 9, decreasing gale force 5-6, locally 8." Shillay stayed in the same place for over an hour as we bobbed up and down like a cork. "It may take us 10 hours at this rate, we may not be able to land, and we would have to do the whole journey again to-morrow." commented the skipper. We turned back and sheltered in the still waters of West Loch Tarbert, until we left at 2 a.m. the next morning. We emerged from the calm of the Loch into the swell of the ocean. Our leader apologised for his uncomfortable state – "I'll be all right when we get there. Last time I was sick 9 times on the way out, but I had a good return trip – I was only sick 5 times." The outward voyage from Oban took 44 hours, which

Approaching Village Bay on the 'Charna' – Dun ahead.

surprised us all, particularly an American Woman who thought the scheduled 22 hrs. was a misprint by the typist for 2-3 hours!

The ship's Visitors' Book had a few interesting comments, "Too sick to sign!" "St. Kilda is an experience for the eyes and the stomach!" But when you set your feet on the jetty in Village Bay – it is worth it all! The forecast for our return journey sounded ominous, "Low 990 over Rockall, Gale 6-7, locally 8, cyclonic. Depression moving slowly S.E.!"

Nevertheless, many share the feelings of Fraser Darling when he wrote, "The only thing which can dull the enthusiasm for reaching little islands must be the stiffening joints which may prevent one from getting ashore in the moment of the slackening swell. Sea-sickness is certainly not enough to keep the naturalist on the mainland, and neither is the thought of holing the boat and swimming for one's life. There are certain situations which arouse a tremendous feeling of exhilaration and physical wellbeing. We know of none to beat the approach in a launch to a remote and uninhabited island where the swell is whitening the foot of the cliff . . . The island is still remote till your foot touches down, and sometimes the swell will beat you, and you will make the long journey home unrewarded, only to return again." (Darling, 1964).

ST. KILDA — FOR THE ARCHAEOLOGIST

St. Kilda is rich archaeologically, having the remains of man made structures and buildings from most stages of civilisation to the present day, all preserved within a closely confined area. The first settlers appear to have reached the islands around 2,000 B.C. and left behind them their 'boat shaped settings' and 'cairns' on An Lag above the present Village. In the early centuries of the Christian era other settlers used stone to build their hut circles, enclosures and the earth-house near the Tobar Childa. Cottam (1979, see Small 1979) believes that at the same time further colonists introduced the art of corbelling to the Village, unfortunately, none of the original structures remain there but excellent examples can be seen in Gleann Mor. At this time the hut became divided into living and sleeping quarters, the inhabitants squeezing their way through a small opening into a corbelled cell to their beds. Possible increases in the colony may have led to pressure on the land in Village Bay during the first three centuries A.D. and the formation of the settlement in Gleann Mor. Two settlements probably flourished at the same time during this stage, although few remains can be seen in Village Bay due to the re-use of stones in new building operations. Cottam considers Gleann Mor to have been occupied from 6-8 centuries A.D. until it was abandoned perhaps in the 14th. century, and apart from some buildings which have been adapted to form cleitean, and others suffering damage from the elements, the structures remain unchanged. In the Village Bay area examples of varying shapes and sizes, developed from these prototype houses are to be found, some with sleeping quarters and provisions for storage.

Norse settlers probably reached St. Kilda in the 10th. century and founded a small colony, but none of their buildings have survived. Their only legacies are a couple of beautiful tortoise brooches, one of which has been lost, the other resides in the National Museum in Copenhagen, and the Norse place-names which have been passed down orally through the centuries before being entered onto modern maps.

The more recent structures in the Village underwent considerable changes at certain periods; one surge forward was between 1834-38 when the whole Village was rebuilt and the land re-allocated. Further modernisation took place in the early 1860's with the construction of the 16 New Cottages. Apart from the addition of the school, the Post Office, the gun emplacement in 1918, and the Army Camp from 1957, and improvements to the jetty very little has changed since the 1860's.

An Lag – 'Boat shaped settings' left; 'Cairn' right – After Cottam, 1973.

(1) AN LAG BHO'N TUATH

The oldest monuments on St. Kilda are to be found in An Lag Bho'n Tuath (the Hollow from the North) above the Village. In 1973 Cottam surveyed 20 ancient monuments in detail on An Lag and others have been found since. Some are quite complicated structures whereas others have been reduced to only four or five standing stones. Cottam found four clear examples of 'boat shaped settings' of stones all of similar size and shape; he also identified four cairns on mounds of about the same size. Other structures had features associated with 'boat settings' and 'cairns'; a further group of nine showed certain characteristics of 'boat settings'.

i Boat Shaped Settings

These monuments are composed of several large stones set on edge, some have one side convex, others both, and all are longer than they are wide and come to a point at both ends, this gives the structure a definite boat shaped appearance. Well over half of each stone is embedded below ground level and most of them are 'pegged' with smaller stones to keep them upright. The infill often differs from the nature of the surrounding material indicating disturbances below the surface. Many of the structures have their long axis pointing in line with Dun passage, a few at the apparent visual conjunction of Oiseval and the southern tip of Dun.

The 'boat shaped setting' illustrated is situated on the steep slope above the Head Dyke, several of the stones are clearly set and pegged in position, with external measurements of 3.5 x 1.5 m. When excavated it was found to have a layer of stone on compacted gravel at a depth of 40 cm, and the infill was of a black sticky nature, differing from the surrounding material and implying disturbances. A soil sample was taken and carbon dated and found to be approximately 1850 B.C.

The purpose of the structure is uncertain being too small for any domestic or agricultural use. Cottam believes it most likely to be a funerary monument. Although it is large enough to accommodate an extended inhumation burial there is no evidence for this use. If cremation had been practised it is possible that the ashes would have been interred in a vessel or urn but none has been found.

ii Cairns

The few cairns on An Lag have certain characteristics in common, all being of similar size and on their own mound which may be between 30-60 cm in height and roughly circular. They have some stones set on edge and the rest form a circular scatter with a stone free centre, and no kerb. Probing has revealed a considerable amount of sub-surface stone below 20

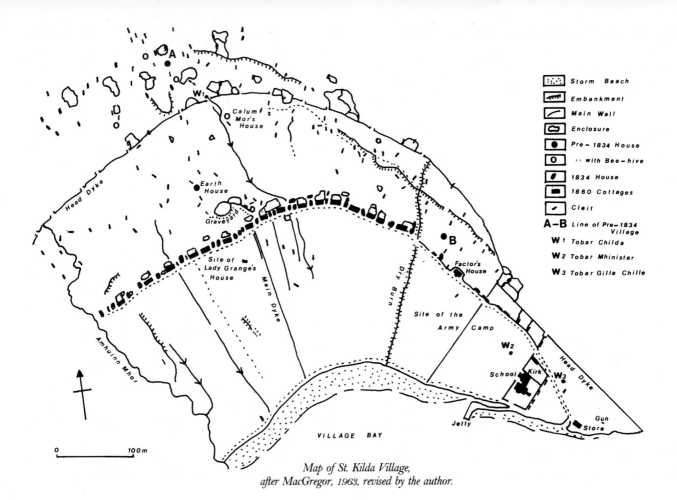

Legend:

- Storm Beach
- Embankment
- Main Wall
- Enclosure
- Pre – 1834 House
- " with Bee-hive
- 1834 House
- 1860 Cottages
- Cleit
- **A–B** Line of Pre–1834 Village
- **W¹** Tobar Childa
- **W²** Tobar Mhinister
- **W³** Tobar Gille Chille

Head Dyke

Calum Mor's House

Earth House

Graveyard

Site of Lady Grange's House

Amhuinn Mhor

Main Dyke

Dry Burn

Factor's House

Site of the Army Camp

School

Kirk

Head Dyke

Jetty

Gun Store

VILLAGE BAY

0   100m

Map of St. Kilda Village,
after MacGregor, 1963, revised by the author.

cm, a diagnostic feature of a cairn. Some show distinct evidence of disturbance in the form of material which differs from the surrounding area.

The ruined cairn illustrated is on the shoulder of An Lag, well above the Head Dyke overlooking the Village at about 85 m above sea level. The mound reaches a maximum height of 32 cms, with a stone free centre and a broad scatter of stones in a roughly circular arrangement. There is sub-surface stone below 20 cm and its long axis is aligned approximately N/S with its external measurements of 4.5 x 4.0 m.

(2) THE VILLAGE AREA

THE EARLIEST BUILDINGS

i The Earth-house

This structure is possibly the earliest in the Village dating back to around 500 B.C.-300 A.D. It is simply a long narrow underground tunnel 11 m long (36 ft) walled on each side, with a flagstone floor and drain below. In the east wall is a small annexe which is 2 m in length, and probably two others just outside the present entrance. The roof is made of huge flat stones at ground level, and it is in no place more tham 1 m high. After examining the area to the N.W., Cottam concluded that it may have been continued in a curve beyond its

present limit to approximately 18 m. It was discovered in 1844 but was not opened up until 1876 when Sands found "a large quantity of limpet shells bearing the marks of fire, bones of sheep and cattle, seafowl chiefly those of the Fulmar and the Solan Goose."

The St. Kildans called it "Tigh an t'sithiche" or the "House of Fairies." It was thought to have been a house or hide-out, but recent theories suggest an ice house for the storage of food. Another earth-house was discovered by Mackenzie in 1830 in the small central area behind the glebe but he walled it up again.

ii Calum Mor's House and other domed houses

Calum Mor's House is thought to date back to around 600 A.D., its oval floor size is 4 x 3 m. With greater head room it shows an intermediate stage between the earth-house and the oldest of the Medieval houses. Whereas the earth-house was entirely sub-terranean, this is only partly underground. To enter, it is necessary to stoop low under the lintel, before stepping down into a single room with a domed roof, high enough to stand in the centre. It is made from enormous unhewn stones, some weighing half a tonne, and is well corbelled into the roof, with earth piled up to keep out the wind. The immense size of the stones has led to the story that it was built by a local strong man or

Development of the Houses on Hirta

1. *Earth-house*   2. *Calum Mor's House*

3. *Medieval House with Bee-hive Annexe*   4. *Pre 1834 Thatched House*

giant who had not been permitted to go with the fowlers to Boreray. To demonstrate his strength he used massive stones to erect his house in one day!

There are signs of bee-hive annexes but the connecting tunnels have been blocked and only a few peripheral stones remain today.

The Rev. N. Mackenzie has this interesting description of how he found similar houses in 1830. "Of their most ancient houses several still remain. They are circular or nearly so, and roughly built. The walls are six or seven feet thick, with spaces for beds left in them. These bed spaces are roofed with long slabs, and the entrance from the interior of the house is about three feet by two feet. The walls are not arched, but contracted gradually by the overlapping of the stones to nearly a point. The entrance door is about three feet by two and a half feet. The outside is covered with earth and rubbish and appears like a green hillock. In some places they are almost entirely underground. The furniture of these houses, so far as I can ascertain from tradition and what still remains, was a quern, a hollow stone for a lamp called 'clach shoilse', which was filled with oil, and a cinder of peat was the wick; a vessel made of badly-burned clay called 'cragan', which was used for a pot; a water-pitcher, a dish to drink out of and a rope made of hide."

THE OLD VILLAGE

i Medieval House with Bee-hive Annexe

Only one house with a complete bee-hive annexe remains, but this is in excellent condition, situated 70 m west of the Tobar Childa, outside the 1830 Head Dyke. To obtain greater head room the walls were built higher, and having dispensed with turf to keep out the wind the walls had to be thicker, but turf was retained on the roof to absorb and keep out the rain. In corbelling, the stones were not laid horizontally, but at a slight slope outwards to deflect the rain. Williamson and Boyd (1963) studied it carefully and described it in this way. "The walls were of rough granite stones taken from the fields or pro-talus ridge beneath Conachair, the ceilings were formed of granite slabs laid across the tops of the walls; and so that the structure might have greater breadth, the long walls were cleverly corbelled, narrowing inwards from 7 ft. apart at the floor to less than one yard at the top. The bed chambers were not hollowed out of the enormously thick walls as in the Hebridean black-houses, but were tiny bee-hive shaped cells tacked on to the house, with a low connecting tunnel through which the inmates wriggled to their rest." Some of these cells had a lintelled window built in and this particular house shows this structure well.

Another complete house with two roofless bee-hive annexes can be seen, approximately 100 m E.N.E. from the above, built into the wall of one of the small enclosures. This shows the lintels of both the exit tunnels leading to the bee-hive compartments and a few peripheral stones. A third house can also be seen nearby, on higher ground with the lintel of the tunnel and some roofing stones still in position and all the basal stones, giving the clear outline of the cell on the north east wall of the house.

ii Thatched Houses – 'Pre 1834 Houses'

When Martin visited the islands in 1697 the people were living in thatched houses built in two rows facing one another with a stone causeway which was unique among the Highlands, and which they called the High Street. He described them in this way, "their houses are low built, of stone, and a cement of dry earth; they have couples and ribs of wood covered with thin earthen turf, thatched over with straw and the roof secured on each side with double ropes of straw or heath, poised at the end with many stones: their beds are commonly made in the wall of their houses, and they lie on straw, but never on feathers or down." The reason he gives for having the bed in the wall is to make room for their cows. One thing that struck Macaulay in 1758 was that the roofs were nearly flat, similar to those of oriental nations, "were their houses raised higher than at present they believe the first winter storm would bring them down about their ears."

A century after Martin landed, in 1799 Brougham's party arrived and landed an advance group with considerable difficulty on the rocks in Glen Bay. They explored the Glen before climbing up onto the shoulder of Am Blaid where they saw the Village for the first time. "In the centre of a small bay surrounded by an immense amphitheatre of mountains lies the village of St. Kilda which from the height where we stood looked like a cluster of bee-hives, nor should we have recognised them as houses but for the smoke which arose from them in thick columns . . . and from the noise of the dogs." (Anonymous, 1799).

The Basic Pattern

The original community was probably centred on the Tobar Childa, but the later buildings and vestiges lie on a crescent between the Tobar Childa and the Factor's House (A-B on the map), on an embankment of rising drier ground, which had a sunny aspect and a ready water supply. Two examples of the Medieval thatched houses remain, one 60 m N.W. of the Tobar Childa and the other 40 m N.N.W. of the Factor's House. Both measure approximately $3\frac{1}{2}$ x $2\frac{1}{2}$ m internally, with corners at right angles and low, east

'Pre 1834 House' near the Factor's House.

facing doorways. On the outside, the corners were rounded to cut down the wind resistance, giving an oval shaped exterior, whereas the earlier houses had been practically circular. For better insulation they had doubled walls, infilled with earth to the eaves, and no windows or chimneys. To obtain greater width they used wood resting on the inner walls, instead of corbelled stones, and then thatched the roof with heather and turf and secured them with twisted heath, weighed down with stones or pegged with the beaks of gannets to prevent the whole structure from being lifted off in the frequent gales. The doubled walls were 1½ m thick and 2½ at the gables into which the bunk bed or 'crub' was built. Captain Thomas crawled into

one on his visit in 1860. (Thomas, 1867), "a hole in the wall, two feet from the floor, enters to a large boot shaped cell, which is highest at the broad end or head, decreasing and narrowing towards the foot. The roof was formed by overlapping, or at the end by lintels. I was supplied with a light and boldly crawled in, and sketched, measured etc., not without a consciousness of that stern joy which the prospect of becoming a victim to archaeology must ever produce." The door of the house was made of wood and was only 1m in height. Between the two remaining buildings there are vestiges of middens and ash pits lying on the natural embankment and forming the 'Old Village' street.

Mackenzie's Description in 1830's
These were the houses in use when Mackenzie began his work in 1830. He described them in the following way. "The walls were seven or eight feet thick, about six or seven feet high, and the same height all round. The beds were in the thickness of the wall as before. There was also the absence of a window. The only opening for light was a small circular opening at one end, where the thatch joined the wall, left for the exit of smoke. The door aperture was near the end and faced the east. It was higher than in the former houses, and had a wooden door with wooden hinges and lock. A partition of rough stones about four feet high, called

'fallen' divided the abode of man and dog from that of the cattle. There was a light wooden roof resting on the inner edge of the wall, covered with a thickness of about eighteen inches of straw, simply laid on, and not in layers as ordinary thatch. When beaten flat and uniform it was secured by numerous straw ropes called 'siman'. The straw used was that of barley. As the wood of the roof was supported not on the outer but on the inner edge of the thick double wall, when the thatching was finished there was left a broad walk along the top of the wall outside of the thatch. The walls were formed on an inner and outer facing of stone about four feet apart, and it was in this space that the beds were left, the remaining space being filled up with earth . . . The furniture of these houses consisted of an iron pot or two, a chest or two, a wooden dish called 'buta' and a smaller called 'cuman', a large straw tub like a bee-hive and called 'loban', an iron lamp called 'cruisgean', a quern and a few old barrels. Some of these latter were held together, not by hoops but by a rope made from twisted stems of a kind of ground willow." (Mackenzie, 1911 from notes written in the 1830's). When MacDonald visited the island in 1822 he noted that they had no chairs or tables, their place was taken by wooden stools or stones. (MacDonald, 1823).

Lachlan MacLean's visit in 1838
Lachlan MacLean visited the islands for two days in July 1838, he described the general view of the village and entered one of these old houses. "You naturally look for the houses of the natives, but you over-look them, till someone tells you that 'those are they', like a cluster of bee-skeps, 200 yards westward (from the Chapel) in the centre of the glen, and rising up from the shore . . . We entered one of the older houses; the door is five spans high of my spans, which I find to be three feet; in entering, the stone lintel took off one of my coat buttons, not a front one. Not a ray of light was in, except what entered by the door or sluice. The shape of the hut is oval, divided in the centre by loose stones, and each apartment about nine feet crescent ways. Opposite the door I observed a pit, cave or grave, about five feet into the wall and considerably below the level of the floor. This is the only bed in the house. The host and his daughter crept in at its contracted stone entrance, at my request, to show how they slept, and laughed heartily at our surprise. An elderly woman sat on the centre of the floor with her legs bare to the knee, grinding barley with the 'Bra', or hand-mill. I could see nothing in the shape of furniture, except a small pot and an old box. I took upon me to reprove them for excluding day so completely, when they explained that the roof of the hut being applied annually for manure, they confine the smoke on purpose to make soot."

MacLean continues, "This house, indeed, may be

taken as a sample of all the houses in the island, which are twenty-six in number, all in one confused cluster, with these two exceptions, namely that in the more modern houses, the cave is exchanged for the floor, and in the widows' houses there is but one circular apartment, like a pig-stye. The outside of the houses are ornamented with solan geese, stuck into the wall – which is about five feet high – by the bill, in order to dry the feathers previous to being plucked; and on the ground, on every hand, their mangled carcases meet the eye, emitting effluvia the reverse of ambrosial. It was rather a ludicrous sight to see our passengers every one with his nose in his hand, as if acting in a pantomime. Here I was very much affected by the tremulous but musical voice of an old woman, Margaret MacLean, who sat on a stone by the side of her house, with the distaff stuck down her side, twirling the spindle, and singing an elegiac song, composed by a mother to an only son, who fell down the rock 'Soa', and was killed." (MacLean, 1838).

Dr. John MacDonald's Visit in 1824

Dr. John MacDonald paid several visits to St. Kilda, originally concerned for the people's spiritual welfare, but seeing their lack of basic creature comforts raised money for practical relief. In his Journal he recorded the method of thatching these houses – the date of his note is Friday 26th. May 1824. "During the day the people were busiest thatching their houses. For the winter half of the year their huts have generally two coats of thatch; but about this season of the year they remove the lower, by this time sufficiently smoked and sooty, for the benefit of their fields, and lay the other in its place. In October again, they lay a new cover of thatch over the old; and in May thereafter, remove the old as formerly; thus repeating the operation every year." (MacDonald J., 1825).

Wilson's Visit in 1841

Wilson, on his visit in 1841 adds further details about the wall beds. "These inner rooms, though small, were free from the incumbrance of beds, for the latter were placed in, or were formed by deep recesses of the wall, like low and horizontal open presses, into which they crept at night, their scanty bedding being placed (in imitation of the puffin) upon stones. There seems to have been only two of these dormitories in each habitation, however numerous the family may have been." He also illustrates other aspects of their way of life. "Another peculiar habit, connected with their slight agricultural resources, must have rendered these small inner apartments still more incommodious. Of course they had no windows, and light and air could find admittance only through the same opening in the roof

61

through which the smoke ascended. But with a view to the collection of manure in spring, the ashes of every fire were daily spread on the floor, moistened and trod upon, so as to form a compact substance, which increased so rapidly, that after a time the flooring was several feet higher than at the commencement of the season, so that at last not only was it impossible to stand upright, but the inhabitants were obliged to dive into their sleeping dens at night like rats or rabbits, – for the middle portion of the flooring was by this time far above the opening of the so called beds . . . When the due season arrived these floors were broken up, and carried out of doors, and after being mingled with manure collected from the cattle in the ante-room, and with the remnants of birds and other offal from an odoriferous pit opposite the front door, were spread upon the ground to increase its scanty and precariously productive powers." (Wilson, 1842).

Carruthers writing about the early 1830's underlined the urgent need for modernisation, "Every hut is nearly inaccessible from the filth which lies before its door, consisting of putrid sea fowl and refuse of all disgusting kinds. The interior is scarcely better, consisting generally of 2 apartments; within one is the dunghill, gradually growing into a pile of manure, which is removed once a year to the tilled ground adjoining. The stench, both inside and outside is intolerable." (Carruthers, 1843).

THE NEW VILLAGE

1830's RECONSTRUCTION

The Transition

After his third visit to St. Kilda in 1827, Dr. John MacDonald of Urquhart, the Apostle of the North, began collecting money to build a new church and manse. The actual work was completed in 1830, ready for the arrival of the Rev. Neil Mackenzie. (Kennedy, 1866). At this time the houses were in a deplorable state.

The stimulus for change and improvement eventually came from Sir Thomas Dyke Acland sometime M.P. for Devon, who visited the island on his yacht in 1834 and was horrified by the primitive and unhealthy state of their dwellings. As an incentive he left a gift of twenty guineas with the Minister to be presented to "the first person or persons who should demolish their old house and erect a new one on a more proper and convenient plan." (Wilson, 1842). As there was a strong feeling of uniformity, no-one desired to step out of line or appear to give the impression of stealing a march on his neighbours, consequently, "it was some time before any one was bold enough to advance beyond the habits of his ancestors and contemporaries, although at last a spirit bolder than the rest made up his mind to proceed in accordance with the plan prescribed. Every obstacle, however, was thrown in his way by his more indolent or less aspiring neighbours. However, at length the individual alluded to proceeded to the work of demolition and reconstruction, and was followed almost simultaneously by about half a dozen others. A general masonic movement then took place, after which the worthy clergyman, who may be regarded, under the Divine Master whom he serves so faithfully, as the presiding genius of the island, contrived to prevent undue haste, and that incompleteness of work which might result from hurried labour as it was now obvious that whoever might have the merit of commencing, all were likely to come to a quick conclusion at one and the same time, it was arranged that the great prize should be shared in equal portions by the heads of the house in the whole community." (Wilson, 1842)

The Plan

The work was carried out under the inspiration and leadership of the Rev. Neil Mackenzie, the Minister on St. Kilda from 1830-44. He was a remarkable man. After his theological training he offered to go to Labrador, but the place was taken by someone else so he "volunteered to go to any place for which no one else could be got, and it was this that eventually led to his being asked to go to St. Kilda." (Mackenzie, 1911). He had many gifts and had a great concern for the physical and spiritual needs of the people; nothing was too much trouble for him and he was willing to tackle any practical job. The outcome of his work "resulted in the appearance of an entirely new planned settlement." (Macgregor, 1960). The Village was enclosed by the Head Dyke, built at the same time and extending for 1½km enclosing an area of 20 hectares (50 acres). The Church and Manse were erected first, the work was completed by 1830, and they were given their own triangular enclosure. Between the Dry Burn and the Amhuinn Mhor the 'New Village' was laid out in an open crescent, the houses regularly spaced, each with a field strip of about 25m width stretching from the beach to the Head Dyke.

The thirty houses, now known as the '1834 Houses' had their narrow end to the sea and were built on a standard plan with the byre, living area and sleeping quarters all under one roof. The byre was situated at the low side with a drain to the cultivation plot; one or two small windows let in a little light, the stone hearth was kept in the centre, and the double walls were infilled with gravel or peat, the inner wall supporting the wooden beams and the turf or thatched roof. "The roof shed its water down into the cavity where it filtered down to the ground . . . so that it kept the cavity material moist and consolidated and thus sealed out the

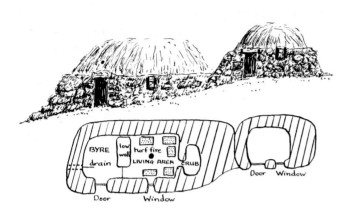

1834 Improved Thatched House.

vicious wind which would have otherwise penetrated the dry stone walls." (Rutherford, 1970).

When the houses were nearly completed in 1838 the Rev. Neil Mackenzie recalled that, "it was necessary that I should go south to purchase with the money left by Sir Thomas the windows and other things needed for their completion. I soon found that the money which I had was not nearly sufficient to purchase the things of which they stood in immediate need. I therefore went to Dr. MacLeod of St. Columba's, and some other kind friends, and they entered so heartily into the matter that in a short time I had a good supply of windows, tables, bedsteads, kitchen dressers, chairs, stools, and crockery ready for shipment." (Mackenzie, 1911). It so happened that Lachlan MacLean was on the same boat, the steamship 'Vulcan', as Neil Mackenzie who was returning to St. Kilda with the windows and other gifts he had been to Glasgow to purchase. The ship reached Village Bay on Saturday, 28th July 1838. "The natives by this time had launched their boat, and were alongside us, asking if the minister was on board of us. I answered in the affirmative, when they with one voice exclaimed, "Taing do Dhia," i.e. thank God!"

The passengers also included two ministers – the Rev. Dr. Dickson of Edinburgh and the Rev. Dr. MacLeod of Glasgow. Dr. Dickson was returning to the Vulcan by rowing boat, "When but one of his legs had entered the small boat a retiring wave unceremoniously swept her away, when the Doctor played a somerset into the water . . . this circumstance gave rise to the name 'Dickson's Bay'." Dr. MacLeod preached many sermons during his short stay. He also brought with him and distributed 47 bedsteads, making two for every house paying rent, and one for each of the poor widows; also 24 chairs, 21 stools, 21 tables, 21 dressers, 21 glass windows, together with pieces of delft-ware. Sir Thomas Acland had contributed £20 towards this endowment. At the same time Dr. Dickson was "equally busy in landing barrels of lime, and a quantity of slate, with a view, I believe to the extension of the manse." In recognition of the endeavours of Dr. MacLeod they named Glen Bay, 'MacLeod's Bay".

On disembarking Lachlan MacLeod was immediately taken by Mr. Donald Mackenzie, the sub-tacksman "to a hut where he had two live Solan Geese in their wild state, and fully grown, with which he presented me." MacLean goes on to describe the manse, the chapel and the new school. "The first thing that strikes the eye is the manse, which is a neat one-storey slated house, of four apartments, I think, about 100 yards from the beach, on the N.E. side of the bay. End-ways to it, and forming the letter T, is the chapel in tasteful keeping. This remote Bethel was built at an expense of about £600, mostly collected by the Rev. Mr. MacDonald of Urquhart, and partly contributed by the Society in Scotland for the Propagating Christian Knowledge . . . On our way (towards the village) we entered the academy or school-house. It is a new building of one apartment, about nine feet by eight, where the clergyman, as a free-will offering instructs a few. It has one window looking towards the bay, with canvas for glass, and a wooden tube of about three inches square, thrust through the roof by way of chimney, or ventilator. A ram's horn, twisted and stuck into the wall, served for a shelf." (MacLean, 1838).

Wilson's Description in 1841

By the time Wilson visited St. Kilda in 1841 the new village had been completed, "The houses, or at least the front ones, form a pretty regular line, though some are placed farther back or behind the others, so, as in these parts to make the line double. They run rather inwards and upwards than along the Bay, and have the appearance of being detached from each other, though sometimes two small dwellings join together. As stones are plenty in the island, the walls are of great thickness, or rather each wall is double, there being built, first of all, a couple of very strong dykes within a foot or two of each other, and then the intermediate space is crammed with earth, which fills up all the interstices, and produces a comfortable dwelling. The door-way is very low, and the great thickness of these double walls produces a space as you enter, which may be called a passage. There are generally two rooms together, each apartment being covered by a separate roof, although there are smaller single tenements for widow women and old maids." Wilson continued with some interesting observations concerning the roof, "They have circular or somewhat rounded roofs of thatch, well fastened down with ropes or stretches of the same material, and instead of the straw overhanging the walls, as is usual in the low countries, and affording an effectual purchase for the wind to lay hold of, the edge

1834 Houses and Dun, Wilson, 1842.

of the thatch springs from the inner side of the thick wall, and so the wind blowing up its outside, and there finding nothing else to act upon, instead of carrying off the roof as it would otherwise be apt to do, simply slips over this cupola kind of covering, and then sughs itself away into the clouds."

Around each house there was, and still is today in some cases, "a double or triple row of large stones which must form dry stepping places nearly all the seasons of the year . . . There are covered outhouses for such collections of fuel, while animal garbage, such as viscera, and heads of birds, are thrown into a circular open pit, of which one is attached to (we should rather say dug in the vicinity of) each little group of houses. It was near these pits as well as elsewhere, that we were struck by the presence of several grey crows (Corvus cornix), which sat so close upon the house tops as we were passing, that none of us doubted that they were pets. On mentioning this to the Minister, we thought at first that he agreed they were, but we soon found he meant and said that they were 'pests', for they tear off the thatch in search of either grain or insects, and are extremely injurious before the setting in of winter, in loosening these otherwise firm and convenient roofs." He also mentions the Kiln, "in which the people of this 'distant island of the sea' dry their corn. It consisted of two dark apartments, one within and of considerably higher level than the other, and a hole runs from a corner of the lower floor under that of the upper, in which a man sits to tend the fire. The grain is dried in the sheaf, and then threshed out on the lower floor." (Wilson, 1842).

Today – The remains of the '1834' houses.

Three types of houses are still distinguishable, probably belonging to this building phase:–

Large Houses – 18 Large houses, 7 x 3m with a single low doorway and small east facing window, a cattle stall at the southern end, some with a drain, and no chimney.

Smaller Houses – 7 similar but smaller houses, 5 x 2m, close to the larger ones either facing them or set end to end on the landward side, to house elderly couples or single persons.

Tiny Houses – 5 smaller houses still, built on the land end of the larger houses, two with windows and three without.

These houses stand in pairs and close to them are small walled gardens, tiny fuel huts and pit middens. There were 18 households with perhaps 20 single or old folk in addition. These improved thatched houses had stood only 27 years when they were replaced in the 1860's by the New Cottages.

The Completion of the New Village with the '1834 Houses'.

By the time that the Rev. Neil Mackenzie left in 1844 the whole Village had taken on a completely new look. The operation was carried out in the following order:–

1. The Church and Manse were built first and the Glebe laid out.
2. The arable land and house plots were divided out as equally as possible, first by an outsider, but finally by the St. Kildans, and then apportioned by the casting of lots.
3. The '1834' houses were started, probably in the winter of 1835 and completed in 1838. The beds were no longer built into the walls, there was an opening for a window, they agreed to stop covering their floors with all kinds of rubbish and they abolished the rubbish pit in front of the door.
4. The arable land was cleared of stones, drained and the natural water-courses were deepened and straightened.
5. The Ring Fence or Head Dyke was built, using large stones, round the arable land, and was continued between the land and the sea. This part of the wall was at an even greater height than the rest and proved invaluable in protecting the crops and in preventing the gales from blowing away the seed and from carrying the cut grass into the sea.
6. The massive stone wall was built round the Grave-yard in an oval form. Mackenzie adds poignantly, "It was the portion of our work in which I took the greatest personal interest, as there I buried three of my children who died in infancy."

1860's NEW COTTAGES

On the 3rd of October 1860 a dreadful storm swept across St. Kilda. Captain Otter, his crew and the 'Porcupine' the Admiralty Service Vessel were very nearly lost and the roofs of a number of the '1834 houses' were carried away by the gale. In Glasgow a large sum of money was raised to relieve the distressed St. Kildans, some being allocated to build new houses. However, apparently the proprietor, John Mac-Pherson, was opposed to the scheme. Instead, in 1861, he sent out John Ross, a master-mason and some carpenters to erect the first 4 New Cottages, with the help of the island labour force. In the following year others were built to give a row of 16 modern cottages.

In the construction of the cottages, hewn stone was used at the corners and the much thinner walls were harled with a lime-sand shingle mix, the chimneys were situated at both gables and the two windows were glazed (three windows were included in Cottage No 1 and one other). Imported wood was used to line the

The Village in 1884 showing the 1860 New Cottages.
Photo by G. W. Whyte.

The Village with the slopes of Conachair, Hirta.

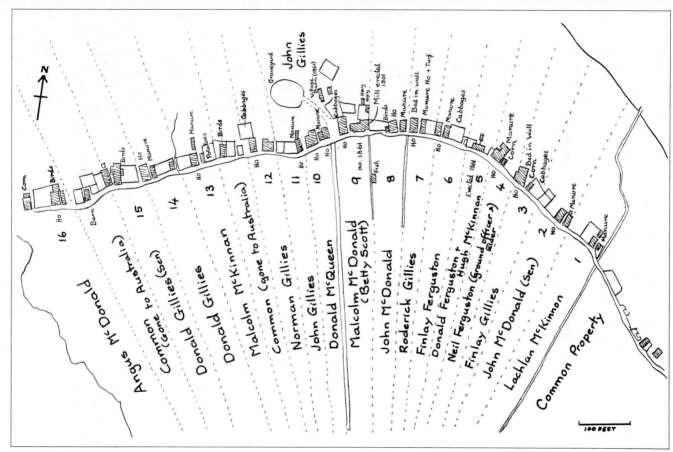

Within the map, the following labels appear:

N

Corn
Birds
Ho
Birds
Ho
Manure
Barns
Manure
Potatoes
Birds
Cabbages
Manure
Ho
Ho
Graveyard
John Gillies
Village Hall (1801)
Manure
Cabbages
Manure
Ho
Ho
Ho. 1861
Fish
Ho
Ho Hay
Birds
Ho
Manure
Mill erected 1861
Bed in wall
Manure Ho + Turf
Ho
Manure
Cabbages
Ho
Manure
Corn
Bed in Wall
Erected 1861
Elder
Ho
Cabbages
Corn
Ho
Manure
Ho
Manure

16 15 14 13 12 11 10 9 8 7 6 5 4 3 2 1

Angus McDonald
Common to Australia
Common Gillies (Sen)
(gone to Australia)
Donald Gillies
Donald McKinnan
Malcolm (gone to Australia)
Common
Norman Gillies
John Gillies
Donald McQueen
Malcolm McDonald (Betty Scott)
John McDonald
Roderick Gillies
Finlay Ferguston
Donald Ferguston
Neil Ferguston + Hugh McKinnan (ground officer »)
Finlay Gillies
John McDonald (Sen)
Lachlan McKinnon
Common Property

100 FEET

Sharban's Map of the Village in 1860, redrawn.

71

walls and to make two or three rooms, usually a kitchen and a bedroom; the floors were simply hard beaten earth. Cottage No. 16 has a recess in the wall where Lachlan MacDonald's father had designed his own built-in cupboard. There were soon problems with the new zinc roofs which had to be renewed with zinc plates nailed over the boards as security against the winds. The Rev. J. MacKay the resident Minister said that zinc was a complete failure, "since it rained inside whenever it rained outside." The zinc was later to be replaced by felt painted with pitch and held down with metal straps on battens which passed over the roof and attached to a spike driven into the wall. The '1834 thatched houses' were now used as store-houses for birds, corn and peat and as byres for the cattle. On the landward side each cottage had its own ash pit and a walled garden for keeping the stacks of corn stalks for the cattle's winter food. Some cottages had their own little stone built fuel store with a turf roof. Stone slabs were also laid down along the Village "Street".

These New Cottages were very smart when they were first erected, but few inhabitants painted the walls in later years. Other problems arose, the window walls faced the sea and the storms, the chimneys caused severe draughts, and the thin walls and roofs gave poor insulation and were very cold compared with the thatched houses in a climate so severe and where fuel

The Mill today, marked on Sharban's Map of 1860.

was in short supply.

Sharban's Map, dated 1860, which has a number of later additions, shows the site of a "Mill erected 1861" between Cottages No. 8 and 9. On this site now are the remains of two thatched houses between which is part of a raised floor with one large flat slab still in situ. It is probably the last vestige of a winnowing floor as the wall immediately behind has a gap, designed to allow the wind free access for the disposal of the chaff. Sharban also named the occupants of the houses and marks those which still had a crub in the wall. He also indicated the contents of the store houses in the Village which included, fish, birds, corn, hay, turf and peat.

When MacDiarmid visited St. Kilda in 1877, he was impressed by the conditions he found within the New Cottages. "Every house I entered contained a fair assortment of domestic utensils and furniture – kitchen dresser with plates, bowls etc., pots, kettles, pans etc., wooden beds, chairs, seats, tables, tin lamps etc. The old dwellings were used to keep the cattle during the winter."

OTHER BUILDINGS AND ARTEFACTS

Christian Churches

Some of the earliest buildings may well have been Christian Churches. Steel (1975) wrote, "Hirta was in all likelihood made Christian long before much of mainland Scotland. It seems likely that during the migration of the monks from Ireland to Iceland in the sixth century many of them may have settled on St. Kilda to convert the people living there, or perhaps even to form a nucleus of a community themselves."

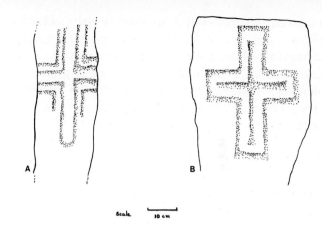

Incised Crosses from Cleit 74 (a) and Cottage 16 (b), Harman, 1976-77.

Perhaps the simple incised cross, known to Sands in 1875 and believed to be from the original Christ's Church, rediscovered in 1956 when some plaster fell off the outside wall of Cottage No. 16, may date back to the sixth or seventh centuries. At present it is built into the wall near the window, lying in a horizontal position, but it could have been the central stone of an arch or altar in an early chapel. Another cross was found by Mary Harman in 1977 on a roof lintel in Cleit No. 74, between Amhuinn Mhor and the graveyard. No crosses with similar outline shape have so far been found or noted in the Western Isles.

There have been three churches in the Village

vicinity, but little is left to indicate their existence. There was Columba's, 100m to the west of the stream Amhuinn Mhor, 170m from the beach and between two existing cleitean on a raised patch of ground. St. Brendan's was on the way over to Ruaival on a small promontary, situated in the north corner of the most southerly sheep-fold, 500m north of the Dun Passage. It has its own little spring a few metres to the north. Christ's Church was stone built and measured 24 x 14

The Church, centre; School, right; with the Manse behind; Dun Passage in the background, 1980.

feet and stood within the present graveyard in the Village: its roof was similar to the old houses. It fell into disrepair and was rebuilt on its present site near the jetty around 1830. The manse was built nearby at the same time and the school room attached to it in 1899. Ross (1884) included this description of the Church. "The Church is a plain, barn-like building standing north-east and south-west. You enter by a door in the north-east gable. A bit of very rough causeway leads up the centre to the pulpit and presentor's box at the remote end. Other than this causeway, which is only the breadth of a narrow pavement, there is no floor to cover the cold, damp, black earth. Nine heavy coarse wooden benches without backs are placed on each side of the causeway, and these give ample accommodation for all the worshippers. Above your head are the bare rafters, with numerous spiders performing profane somersaults in the air while divine service is going on." The walls at this time were whitewashed but deteriorating due to damp and mildew with patches crumbling away. The Church was renovated by the carpenters who came to build the school room in 1898, work included the boarding of the walls and the laying of a wooden floor.

Cleitean

In a moist climate with frequent mists and high rainfall it is necessary to devise ways of drying the peats and grass as well as keeping food from going mouldy. The St. Kildans were ingenious enough to develop their own method by modifying the cells of their earlier houses. Most buildings attempt to keep out the wind, the cleitean were designed to give it free access and to use it to desiccate the contents and to keep out the rain. They kept the stone wall and slab roof with turf design to absorb most of the rain water, and each had either a wooden or stone slab door. The prototypes were circular, later followed an oval plan with the door on the long side and a window on the short lee wall. As the art of corbelling was lost the cleitean became narrow and increased in length with almost vertical walls with a small window above the door on the lee side. The increased length provided greater drying and storage space. The wind passed through the dry stone walls drying out the stored crops of oats and barley, as well as their clothes, rope, peat and turf (which would not stand exposure to the elements). In fact some families would have as many as 20 cleitean full of peat and a score of little stacks outside. (Mackenzie). Ross describes the contents of the cleitean in 1889, "Those on the inside of the wall which surrounds the Village were used for drying and keeping hay, also for drying and keeping birds and those on the outside of the wall for drying and keeping peats or what goes under the name of peats from both wind and weather . . . the peats are simply parings off the hill sides and are so light that a gale of wind might blow most of them over the rocks." Captain Thomas (1867), made the point that, "A bird or piece of meat hung up in them undergoes an unpleasant change at first, but afterwards dries, and is cured; and it is probable that fish or meat preserved in this manner will be more wholesome than if salted."

One of these structures was known as the 'coffin cleit', a long building with a door at each end, situated near the Kirk, in the wall above the bell. It took its name from the custom of storing wood in it for the manufacture of coffins: they were actually constructed in the open in dry weather or in the main Store-house if it was too wet.

To their ingenuity they added industry, not only in the size of the stones used, but in the number of buildings they erected. Mary Harman has recorded over 1,000 on Hirta alone dotted like mole hills all over the island. She also reported over 40 on Soay, 50-60 on Boreray, one on the summit of Stac Lee with a gannet nesting on its roof and 78 on Stac an Armin. On Mulloch Geal some still have dried peats inside, another had a nesting fulmar and many have a collection of the bones of the Soay Sheep which have died there. Emerging from one cleit, just outside the Head Dyke, no fewer than 14 Soays ran out in a long line from their protected resting place. Some of the cleitean provide nesting places for the St. Kilda Wren and safe homes for the St. Kilda Field Mouse.

MacCulloch (1819) visited the islands in 1815 and was most impressed by the cleitean and felt "the practice worthy of imitation to those inhabitants of the rainy parts of the Highlands whose peats and crops are frequently rendered useless by the continuance of the rainy season. The grass and corn are thrown loosely into the dome as soon as they are cut and are thus secured from all future risk."

Site of Lady Grange's House

No description of dwellings within the Village would be complete without mentioning Lady Grange's House. One looks in vain for an imposing residence to suit the titled lady and one wonders how she could possibly have survived her seven years exile on the site of the existing large stone walled, turf covered cleit in the meadow. This unfortunate lady was the wife of James Erskine of Grange, brother of the Earl of Mar, one of the Lords of Session. He was a Jacobite and feared that she had overheard too much intrigue, so he had her "spirited away to the isle of St. Kilda, gave out that she was dead and celebrated her funeral." She remained on the island from 1734-42.

When Lachlan MacLean visited the islands in 1838 the remains of the house were still to be seen, "I went up to the village once more, and visited the ruin of the hut in which the celebrated Lady Grange spent seven years of her tragical existence. I was led by a grandson of the native Finlay MacDonald, who attended her in exile. The house is seven paces long, of my paces, and three and a-half wide, which is about 20 feet by 10. Like the rest of the houses it is divided in the centre by a partition of rude loose stone. In one of these apartments sat Finlay MacDonald every night for seven years, and Lady Grange in the other, – for she never slept at night, whatever the reason, – thus making the entire of her Ladyship's accommodation 'ten feet semilunar'. She had acquired the Gaelic, my guide said, tolerably well, and took pleasure in listening to the native tales and romances of Finlay. Through the day she slept, except when she took a solitary ramble to converse with grief and the roaring ocean. Finlay made for her a seat of twisted straw – a luxury in St. Kilda. This seat she carried with her when she went, leaving 12s in silver with Finlay in lieu." (MacLean, 1838).

Hut Circles

Iron Age hut circles have been found near the Tobar Childa with diameters of 3.5-4.0m, made of boulders and small stones indicating that there was a very early settlement in the Village Bay vicinity. Others have been found in Gleann Mor (see below).

Artefacts

During the rebuilding of the Village in the 1830's several Bronze Age stone cists were found, and in a mound on the glebe an iron sword, a spearhead, a long and narrow whetstone and other pieces of iron were unearthed. When Sands excavated the earth-house in 1876 he made the following report. "Amongst the debris on the floor I found numerous stone axes, knives, and fragments of a lamp, as well as pieces of rude pottery. As there was no tradition concerning this house, and as it was assigned to the fairies, it may be very old; but I am inclined to think that the stone period

The lost St. Kilda Viking Brooch of the 10th. Century.

extended to a very recent date on St. Kilda." (Sands, 1877).

In the past Viking tortoise brooches and a Viking sword have been discovered on Hirta. Unfortunately, both brooches have been lost, one was almost certainly a Rygh 652/4 of the 10th Century, very beautiful with a double shell and open work on the top, with five impressive bosses with holes in them and four simple and plain. It was first described and drawn by the Danish antiquary J. J. A. Worsaae who visited Scotland in 1846-47 and wrote "The Norwegians must even have visited the little island of St. Kilda . . . At least two of the often mentioned brooches have been discovered on the island; one of them I have seen in the Andersonian Museum in Glasgow." Taylor (1969) concludes that, "the find suggests Norse settlement as early as the tenth century, and indicates that one of the settlers had a female relative who had an expensive set of brooches and who was given a heathen burial."

(3) GLEANN MOR

In Gleann Mor, the Great Glen, there are many indications of human activity and habitation on both sides of the wide valley. There are 'Horned structures', Hut Circles, Cairns and a Circle of Stones possibly of Bronze Age times, also boulder dykes, enclosures, sheilings,

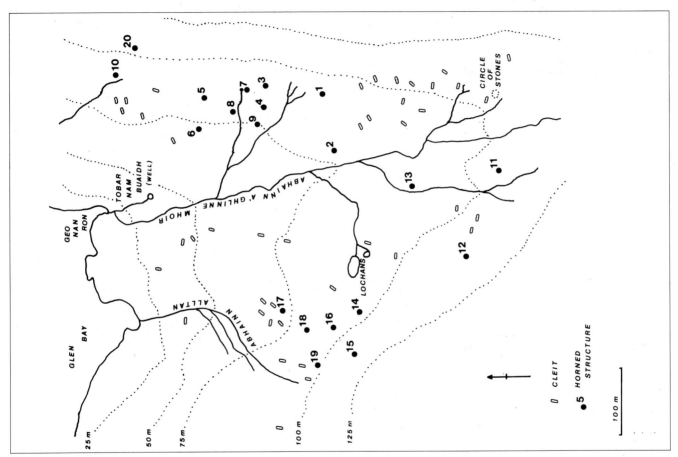

Labels visible on map:

20, 10, 5, 17, 3, 8, 4, 1, 9, 6, 2, 11, 13, 12, 17, 18, 16, 14, 15, 19

CIRCLE OF STONES

TOBAR NAM BUAIDH (WELL)

GEO NAN RON

ABHAINN A' GHLINNE MHOIR

LOCHANS

ALLTAN

ABHAINN

GLEN BAY

25 m
50 m
75 m
100 m
125 m

CLEIT
HORNED STRUCTURE
5
100 m

Map of the Horned Structures in Gleann Mor, after Cottam, 1979.

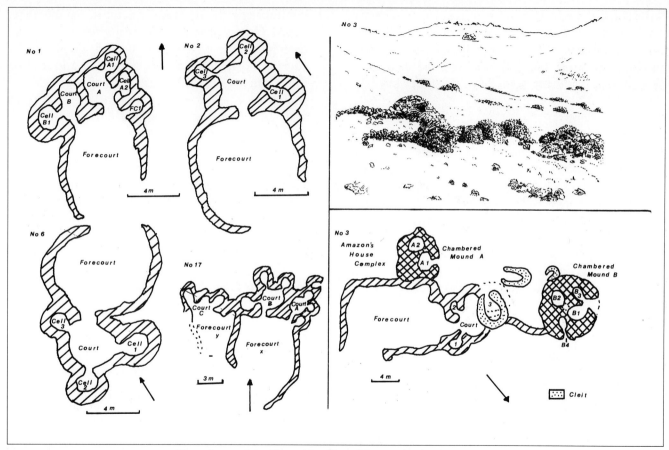

Plans of some of the Gleann Mor Horned Structures, after Cottam, 1974.

wells and lazy beds. The lazy beds and Hut Circles are on the west side of the Glen. At least 5 Hut Circles are on a natural terrace site where a boulder dyke passes through the area; four of these are on their own scooped out platforms, some have no stonework left.

Horned Structures

A total of 20 Horned Structures are to be found in Gleann Mor and nowhere else in Britain or Europe and are thought to have evolved locally on St. Kilda. The shape consists basically of a Forecourt formed by two horned shaped walls leading into a main Court (around 3 x 3m) with two or three cells (about 1.2 x 1.6m) branching outwards. The entrance into the cells is well above ground level but only measures about 50 x 50cms. The whole structure is made of dry stone, the walls are corbelled and each cell had a turf covering. Cottam (1974) estimates that they were probably inhabited between the 6-14th century A.D. Later generations of St. Kildans used them as sheilings in the summer. Schoolmaster Murray in his diary for May 28th, 1887 records, "On Thursday the ewes and lambs were brought to the glen and folded there, where they are milked daily. The lambs are shut in at night, and the ewes are milked early in the morning. There is a fold for each family, and it is the women's part to herd them all day keeping them separate."

For numbering the separate structures, see the map.

i Simple Horned Structures. There are several splendid examples of these, No. 6 is particularly good with the curving horns forming the Forecourt and leading into a single Court with three cells off the enclosing wall. No. 2, 5, 6, 7 are all simple structures; No. 11, 13 and 16 have been modified for re-use. Two chambered mounds have been developed at No. 3, the Amazon's House and at 19.

ii Complex Horned Structures. These show considerable variation on the basic scheme. No. 1 is a good example with a Forecourt and two Courts with four cells. No. 17 has been modified but is by far the most complex structure with three Courts and ten cells (one is out of the diagram to the left).

The Amazon's House No. 3.

The best known building in the Glen is the Amazon's or Female Warrior's House. The notable owner featured widely in St. Kilda folk lore, the stories about her impressed Martin in 1697 but unfortunately he recorded none of them, however, he did describe the house in the following way. "The whole is built of stone, without any wood, earth or mortar to cement it, and it is built in the form of a circle pyramidwise towards the top, having a vent in it, the fire always being in the centre of the floor; the stones are long and thin, which supplies the defect of wood; The body of this house contains not above nine persons sitting, there are three beds or low vaults that go off the sides of the wall, a pillar betwixt each bed, which contains five men apiece; at the entry to one of these low vaults is a stone standing upon one end fixed; upon this they say she (the Female Warrior) ordinarily laid her helmet; there are two stones on the other side, upon which she is reported to

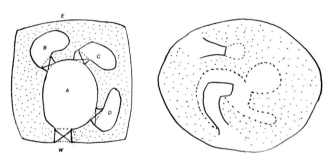

Plans of the Amazon's House
Left, by Thomas in 1861   *Right, by Mathieson in 1927*
when complete.   *after damage.*

have laid her sword; she is said to have been much addicted to hunting . . ."

The house was still intact when Muir and Captain Thomas visited the Glen in the 1850's, both have illuminating descriptions. Muir pointed out that, "There is a square aperture on the ground at the west end, but so narrow as hardly deserving the name of a doorway; and there is another through the middle of the roof of somewhat more ample dimensions, which has all the appearance of a chimney. On the west side of the doorway is a short rough pillar, and there are three square-set niches, or 'beds', in the thickness of the walls, two near to each other on the west side, and one directly opposite to the doorway in the east end." Thomas adds the following notes, "In plan it is an irregular square, the wall in front being built perpendicularly for three feet (and two feet behind), and thence sloping rapidly to the top. The house is built of moor-stones, such as were most conveniently near, and the stones are not remarkable for size. The doorway faces the line of the valley, is about 3ft. high, with inclined jambs. The central chamber is 9 x 11 feet, and 8 feet high, irregularly oval; and the arch is formed by overlapping stones in the usual way. There has always been a hole (farleus) at the apex, to allow the smoke to escape and to admit light; the farleus would be closed with a flagstone or turf in bad weather. Around the central chamber are three doorways entering to irregular beehive chambers . . . These chambers are in the thickness of the wall, are irregular ovals, about 5 feet high." (Muir, 1861, with notes by Thomas).

The building was partly destroyed between 1875-76, Sands described what had happened. "In Glen Mor is a curious old building, which was almost entire on my first visit, but has been much damaged since by two men who wanted the stones because they were 'briagh' (pretty) to build claetyan . . . Internally it is circular in form, and about 9 feet in diameter, and at the top the stones overlap to form a dome. It contains three beds in the wall. It was occupied, according to Martin, by an Amazon who used to hunt . . . Outside it resembles a little green hill." (Sands, 1878). By 1927 when Mathieson surveyed it further deterioration had taken place, accompanying his plan he made the comment, "It is now so delapidated that my interpretation of the plan may not in all particulars agree with the original. What is now the entrance appears as if it at one time formed one of the apartments." (Mathieson, 1927-28).

Today the Amazon's House Complex consists of a large horned Forecourt leading into a single Court with three cells. To this has been added two Chambered Mounds, and in more recent times three cleitean have been constructed using some of the stones from the Mounds. Mound 'A' is higher up the hillside, and contains two chambers, A1 is in a delapidated state but leads into A2 which is well corbelled and roofed. Mound 'B' is larger with either four chambers or a central chamber with three leading off. Chamber B1 is the largest but the roof has fallen in; it leads into B2 which is slightly smaller, "but is beautifully preserved and is the best example of a corbelled chamber in Gleann Mor. It is completely roofed and turfed." (Cottam, 1973-74). Chamber B3 is small but well corbelled and B4 is in a poor state and is open to the exterior but shows signs of corbelling.

A comparison of the plans of Thomas, Mathieson and Cottam clearly points to the lower Mound 'B' in the Complex as the site of the original Amazon's House.

ST. KILDA —
FOR THE HISTORIAN

OWNERS

One of the earliest documents referring to the ownership of St. Kilda dates from January 1373 when a Charter was ratified by King Robert II enabling John, Lord of the Isles, a MacDonald, to present St. Kilda and a number of Hebridean Islands to his son Reginald. Later this group was transferred to the MacDonalds of Sleat, on Skye. From this family it was to pass in the mid-15th century to the MacLeods of Harris who had their seat at Dunvegan on Skye. Tradition records great rivalry at this time between the people of Harris and those of Uist. Lachlan MacLean (1838) recounts the story, "The question was soon to be put at rest by an expedient worthy of the times. It was mutually agreed upon that two currachs, one from Uist, and one from Harries, should start at the same time, and that the boat that first made out the island should be declared for. Off set the two currachs, buffeting the astonished main with their yielding oars – each man was silent – each face lowered defiance – each heart, we may conceive, was the sport of fear and hope by alternations, on nearing the new empire. Towards evening, on approaching the goal, the Uist boat was a few strokes ahead, and ready to seize the prize; which, when Colla 'Cloud, or MacLeod, master of the Harries currach, saw, he seized his scian-dhu, and, with one determined stroke, cut off his left hand from the wrist, flung it ashore, and was unanimously declared the rightful possessor, and lord of St. Kilda, as to this day! The point on which he landed is called Rudha-Cholla, and the well of which the bleeding hero first drunk, Tobar-Cholla."

Thompson (1970) completes the brief summary of the history of the ownership "In 1799 St. Kilda, with Harris was sold to Captain Alexander MacLeod for £15,000. During the next century the island changed hands twice, but always within the MacLeod family. In 1871 St. Kilda was sold back again for £3,000 to Norman, twenty-second Chief of MacLeod, in whose family, the senior branch of the clan, the island group remained until Sir Reginald MacLeod sold it to the fifth Marquis of Bute in 1934." He was to bequeath it to the National Trust for Scotland in 1956.

OUTLAWS

In 1615 St. Kilda was visited by one of infamous character, Coll MacDonald, or MacGillespie, or, as he was later known, Coll Ciotach, the head of the MacDonalds of Colonsay at the period of the final extinction of the family's power in the western isles. In the spring of 1614 there began the first of the Islay or MacDonald rebellions. The castle of Dunnyveg on Islay was seized and held as a bargaining counter against the government. The castle eventually surrendered, but Coll Coitach escaped on the night of Thursday 2nd of February 1615. He reached North Uist via Canna and was moved on by Donald Gorm Mac-Donald the owner. Stevenson (1980) takes up the story, "To get rid of their unwelcome guests they suggested that these outlaws might be safe from the long arm of the government if they sailed to the remote island of Hirta or St. Kilda, lying thirty miles out to the west of the Outer Hebrides. After about eight days Coll took the hint and, having been provided with guides, set sail westwards. Not surprisingly this aroused the fury of Sir Rorie MacLeod of Dunvegan, who owned St. Kilda; according to his account Coll's men killed all the cows, sheep and horses on St. Kilda and carried off all the spoil they could, leaving some in North Uist with the guides to reward the islanders for their help. By Robert Williamson's account St. Kilda had only about twenty inhabitants at this time, and Coll took from them a great store of barley and about thirty sheep. He stayed about a month on the main island of the group, Hirta, and then sailed three and a half miles north-east to the great stack of Boreray; 'there Coll had a purpose to keep to himself, for it is of such strength as not to be gained but by famine' . . . On this great rock Coll the outlaw dreamed of establishing an impregnable pirates' lair, where he could live safe from the enemies who had driven him from Islay and Colonsay, preying on Hirta and other islands and on shipping. Though Boreray had probably been inhabited from time to time (rebels from the authority of MacLeod's steward on Hirta are said to have withdrawn there on one occasion), it was not really suitable for Coll's purpose, lacking both a harbour and a beach for drawing up boats. That Coll considered such a plan even for a moment indicates his desperation, and perhaps his awed reaction to Boreray's towering peaks and pinnacles; the stack looks as if it ought to be a grim fortress."

Other imposters and outlaws left their scars on St. Kilda. The notorious sheep stealing brothers from Lewis, Dugan and Fearchar Mor, having done irreparable damage were eventually trapped down. They were exiled to the outlying islands – the incident is recorded under the island of Soay.

THE PEOPLE

'SAVAGES' ?

When Henry Lord Brougham (1778-1868) landed on St. Kilda in 1799 he was horrified by the primitive and squalid appearance of the inhabitants and their dwellings, as well as by their fears, laziness and ignorance that he felt the only suitable description was to call them 'savages'. He had come from a very different background, "a charmed circle of extremely able young men . . ." in Edinburgh before going on to greater things. He became Attorney General, M.P. for Winchester, Knaresborough and Yorkshire, and Lord Chancellor. When he visited St. Kilda he was on his planned voyage to the Faroes and Iceland, but the last part had to be abandoned and the tour continued to Denmark and Scandinavia. His party consisted of the following members:

Mr. Henry (the fitter out of it) a nephew of Ld. Moira.

Physician – Dr. Jas. Miller of Paisley.

Draughtsman – Mr. Saunders.

Harper – Le Sieur Revellet.

Steward – Mr. Fortune – Captain Stuart.

Company:

Capt. Stroud of New York – a very well informed and excellent man.

Lieut. O'Harva of New York.

Robert Campbell of Shawfield (also Skipness) – Advocate and almost certainly the author of the Anonymous Account of the voyage.

Chas Stuart (son of Sir C. ye General) – and a most excellent fellow, also well travelled and read.

And your humble servant.

The boat soon became known as the 'mad brig'. Brougham makes many interesting and amusing comments about his time on St. Kilda. At first he could not understand why they were slow to welcome the party ashore. "We afterwards found that we were taken for a French privateer, and avoided as such, all the inhabitants preparing their all for a flight to the mountains . . . At last came two boats, one belonging to the place and ours besides, but both manned by the savages. This alarmed us: we thought that our party must be lost or taken, and the armschest was instantly opened; but the boats approaching we found the natives quite pacific, and several came on board – among others their priest, without whom nothing would induce them to venture near us . . . They live in constant dread of invasion as if all the wealth of London and Liverpool were stored up in St. Kilda."

That evening the party set off in the St. Kildan boat to go across to Boreray. "Our crew talked most infernally, and rowed very ill. Seeing that this proceeded from laziness and loquacity, I desired the first (who alone could speak a word of English) to promise them a dram if they rowed better, and to bid them be more quiet. The effect was instantaneous, and immediately the song arose, extempore in composition and far from unmusical in execution; of course pleasing in point of effect . . . We now weathered the gigantic rocks of Boreray, which surrounded St. Kilda to the north and north-east; and as it was past eleven, I allowed myself to be lulled asleep by the cadence of the chorus and the oars. About half-past twelve I heard a little confusion, and found the steersman quitting the helm to give place to a more experienced one. Upon looking round, the scene presented itself which beggars all description. We were roughly and rapidly rolling through such a frightful pass as you cannot form any idea of. On each side huge masses of broken and impending rock stretched up to a terrible height above our heads. These were towards their bases pierced with large, dark, rough caves, into which the sea dashed with stunning noise. Around our crazy overloaded bark lay huge masses of broken rocks, which rendered our course very serpentine, and every instant the keel grazed with a heavy and petrifying noise along the sunken rocks." One of the party called out, "Mr. Brougham, sir – sir, I am just looking where we shall leap out, for a last chance, when the boat is dashed to pieces!"

The party returned from Boreray and landed in Village Bay at about 1 a.m. and entered the priest's house, "A more wretched hovel never sheltered beast from the storm than this; and yet it is the only thing tenantable in the island, except the tacksman's. We refreshed ourselves a little, with his wife and mother." Brougham describes the Village and the people. "And now for the first time we had a view of the city. Conceive, if you can, a sort of green bosom, at a quarter of a mile's distance, with steep green mountains, and on one side with a fine bay opening into rocky scenery; at one corner the dreadful pass, which I described before, and which appeared almost as bad by daylight. The rest of the scene is ludicrous. The green bosom is divided into 400 'rip' or fields of barley and oats and potatoes – 25 feet by 3! in the centre several green tufts of grassy sod, upon heaps of loose stones – these we at last discovered to be the houses, twenty-six in number: on the hills, more such molehills, rather smaller, for cutting peats. This is the town or city of Hirta, or St. Kilda. It contains 100 inhabitants; and the rest of the island is only browsed by some sheep, horses and cows. The view of this village is truly unique. Nothing in Captain Cook's voyages comes half so low. The natives are savage in due proportion; the air is infected by a stench almost insupportable – a compound of rotten fish, filth of all sorts and stinking sea-fowl. Their dress is chiefly composed of a coarse stuff made by themselves, somewhat like a tartan. They wear this chiefly in trousers and jackets, with coarse brogies, also made by themselves. They make brooches of clumsy iron rings, with pins across: these are worn by the women to tuck up their plaids. Needles coarse in proportion; thong-ropes for ascending the rocks in quest of nests and birds; fish-hooks finer than the other articles; thread and horn-spoons are the remaining manufactures of this place – infinitely coarser and more clumsy, and made in smaller quantity and less variety, than those which navigators have found in any of the Pacific islands, New Holland in the south excepted. A total want of curiosity, a stupid gaze of wonder, an excessive eagerness for spirits and tobacco, a laziness only to be conquered by the hope of the above-mentioned cordials, and a beastly degree of filth, the natural consequence of this, render the St. Kildian character truly savage." (Brougham, 1871).

Brougham goes on to quote the proverb "One half the world don't know how the other lives." In these remote Outer Isles life at this time was basically a struggle for survival – a struggle against the elements, disaster and disease. Like all animals and plants man is adaptable and consequently in these situations he develops certain skills and patterns of life which enable him to exploit all the resources of his environment to the full. On St. Kilda he was also alert to the needs of his environment, and on the whole, he was careful not to destroy it.

LIFE IN THE VILLAGE

CHARACTERISTICS

Until the evacuation in 1930 St. Kilda had probably been inhabited for about 4,000 years. We know very little about the earliest settlers who left behind them only their "boat shaped settings" of stones on An Lag, or of those who lived in their hut circles around the Tobar Childa, or indeed of the community in the Great Glen. But we know that the influence on later generations of the isolation and the battle against the elements brought out certain qualities and characteristics. The men had to be able to put their hand to any task in order to survive. Connell writing about his visits in 1885 and 1886 makes the point that, "Every man follows five or six different callings. He is at once crofter, cragsman, fisherman, weaver, tailor and cobbler."

Another mark was their strong community life. Neil Ferguson, the postmaster recalled how "Everybody helped each other. You ran short of anything, if your neighbour had it, you would get it. That's how it went on." The Missionary's daughter, Mary Cameron who was on Hirta from 1919-26 related, "They were people of very strong character, kind and hospitable folk. Their lives were upright in every way. There was no insobriety or anything like that. No dishonesty. People didn't lock their doors. They would be coming in and

The Natives – a drawing by Sands, 1878.

out of each other's houses at any time, and the people themselves were just like one family. What was one family's sorrow or joy was sorrow or joy to the rest." (Cameron, 1979).

Each day except the sabbath, men shared their ideas and plans in what became known as their 'Parliament' where they would discuss the business of the day. "Here questions such as whether potatoes are to be weeded or sheep caught occupy perhaps two hours; here one has to wait if one wants to know whether a boat is going to Boreray or whether sheep are to be sheared; here perhaps one hears arguments in favour of collecting crotol (to dye wool brown) or mending the boat, or of catching fulmars, if it be after the 12th. of August." (Gladstone, 1927). Often the talking went on until well after mid-day, but when the decision was made everyone settled down to the job in hand until it was finished. They shared out the rocks from which they fished, the cliffs with their nesting birds, as well as their corn and their grass. Having collected the fulmars, gannets and fish they divided them out, not forgetting to provide for the elderly and the sick. Connell records "The gannet, like the fulmar, is the common property of the 16 families, each of whom occupies a croft in St. Kilda. Every carcase, every feather and every egg is divided equally among them. Those are the only two birds which appear to be treated on socialist principles.

Some of the Inhabitants in 1884
showing on the left, Schoolmaster, Mr. Campbell, and in the centre, Nurse A. McKinlay. Photo G. W. Whyte.

The puffin is anybody's property, and so also are the guillemot and the razorbill." (Connell, 1887). Within the family Martin Martin records his observations in 1697, "It is ordinary with a Fowler, after he had got his purchase of fowls, to pluck the fattest, and carry it home to his wife as a mark of his affection." The Parliament had no Cabinet and no Prime Minister, each voice carried equal weight; the spacial extent of their concern was considerably limited as A. A. MacGregor (1969) points out, "Outside St. Kilda, its members had no interest excepting, perhaps, the welfare of any relatives who happened to live elsewhere than home. Neighbouring Boreray was the limit of their foreign policy; and, even then, that policy was concerned solely with sheep, with seabirds and their eggs."

Most of the inhabitants had not been further than Boreray, but a few had visited friends in Lewis, Harris and Uist and returned with surprising accounts of what they had seen; Sands commented that a man with a wooden leg created the greatest interest while he was on the island. The daily meeting of 'Parliament' not only conducted the business of the island but also gave an opportunity to share their experiences and to keep them cheerful in spite of their isolated position. Sands commented (1877), "Man is a gregarious animal, and there are no people more so than the St. Kildans. In work every one follows his neighbour. If one puts a new thatch on his barn, a man is to be seen on the top of every barn in the village. If the voice of praise is heard at the door of one house, all, you may be sure, are engaged in worship, and so on." In the 1690's the women also had their meetings, "The women have their Assemblies in the middle of the Village where they discourse their affairs; but in the meantime employing their distaff, and spinning in order to make their blankets; they sing and jest for diversion, and in their way understand poetry, and make rhymes in their own language, both have a genius heretofore." (Martin, 1698).

ROUTINES

For the human community to survive in these isolated islands the St. Kildans had evolved their own yearly routines which depended mainly on the vagaries of the weather and the breeding activities of the seabird population. MacGregor (1960) has admirably summarised the pattern in this St. Kildan Calendar.

St. Kildan Calendar

Nov	Spinning and Weaving	Turf carrying
Dec	Spinning and Weaving	Turf carrying

Jan	Spinning and Weaving	Turf carrying		
Feb	Weaving	Turf carrying	Food scarce	
Mar	Cattle infield	Turf scarce	Catch Guillemots	
Apr	Cattle outfield Prepare land	Turf cutting	Catch Gannets and Puffins	Prepare boat
May	Prepare land	Turf cutting	Fulmars, Gannets and Puffin eggs	Strip old thatch for manure
June	Cattle to shieling	Turf cutting	Puffins. Eggs. Sheep clip and killing	Fishing and Fish curing
July	Cattle to shieling. Ewes to shieling.	Turf cutting	Puffins	Fishing and curing
Aug	Return from shieling. Harvesting.	Turf cutting	Young Fulmars	Fishing and curing
Sep	Hay-making. Feather storing.	Dry corn	Young Fulmars. Young Gannets.	Building repairs
Oct	Cattle infield. Wool preparation.	Grind corn	Young Gannets. Sheep killing.	Thatching repairs

Meals were taken at unusual times and lacked both variety and balance resulting in a good deal of indigestion!

Breakfast: Between 9-10. Porridge and milk with the flesh of the Fulmar occasionally, the bird being boiled in the porridge.

Dinner: Around 4 p.m. Mutton or the flesh of the Fulmar or Gannet with potatoes when they had any.

Tea: Around 9 p.m. in the summer; 11 p.m. in the winter when they worked on into the night. Tea with bread and cheese, and the flesh of the Fulmar occasionally, and sometimes porridge.

Eggs, fresh or decaying, were considered a great delicacy by the St. Kildans and they would collect thousands of them during the breeding season. In the 17th century they preserved them "for 3 or 4 months with moist earth and brayed peats, three gang spread above other ye earth being spread betwixt every gang or layer of eggs." (Sir Robert Sibbald, 1641-1722). Visitors to the islands did not share the local's enthusiasm.

Macaulay (1764) pointed out how fortunate the St. Kildans were in having such an abundant supply of free fresh food. "The Lavie (Guillemot) visits them most seasonally in the month of February, when their fresh mutton and bread are perhaps nearly exhausted, and continues to furnish plentiful repast till the Solan Geese appear in March. These supply their wants till they begin to lay. Then are these succeeded by the Puffins and a variety of eggs. When their appetites are cloyed by a frequent use of this food, the salubrious Fulmar, and their favourite young Solan Goose, crown their humble boards with grander entertainments, and hold out all autumn over. In winter they have generally a greater stock of bread, mutton and salted fowl, than they are able to consume."

In 1840 MacGillivray visited St. Kilda and recorded the menu, it consisted of "Fulmar, Auk (Razorbill), Guillemot, one of each boiled; two Puffins, roasted; barley cakes, ewes cheese and milk; and by way of dessert, raw dulse and roasted limpets 'ad-lib'." His visit was in July when food was varied and plentiful; in the winter it often became very scarce indeed. It has been said that the winter held no attractions whatsoever and life was near to hibernation. Certainly, School-master Ross (1889) dreaded the thought of a winter on St. Kilda where "the medicine chest contained little but fulmar oil, castor oil, mustard and whisky!" During those long nights the men worked at their looms or made straw baskets for bringing down the turf from the hillsides; at other times they made ropes and special sacks for storing their feathers and grain.

Although surrounded by sea water, salt was a rare commodity. In the 17th. century Sibbald wrote, "They have no salt but what they make by burning the sea tangle which is very black. They rub their cheese with it which maketh it black." This was another regular occupation, the seaweed being burnt in a small kiln; in more recent years it was bought from the Factor, but even in 1799 the visitors recorded, "The fish and their gannets they cure with salt manufactured by themselves in a species of small kiln underground." Some of the fish they dried out in the cleitean on the ridge of Mullach Mor at about 250m because the wind was so much more effective at that altitude. They carried the fish up there but Professor Heddle of St. Andrews University could not pursuade them to cut their peats from there, they preferred to take the inferior turf from a lower level, all he could get out of them was "It would not dry up there . . . peats are not fish; we will not carry peat down that distance." (Smith, 1879).

Seasonal Foods

January	Fulmar and Gannet (salted).
February	Food scarce.
March	Guillemots, caught at night.
	Gannets from Stac Lee at night.
April	Gannets and some Puffins.
May	Fulmars – a few adults.
	Gannets and Puffins eggs.
June	Puffin eggs.
July	Puffin adults.
August	Young Fulmars harvested.
September	Young Fulmars and Gannets.
October	Young Gannets.
	Sheep killed.
November	Fulmar and Gannet salted.
December	Fulmar and Gannet salted.

COMPENSATION AND FINES

Accidents happen, sometimes through carelessness and the St. Kildans had developed their own codes of conduct and methods of compensating losses. An example is given by Buchan in the early 1700's, "If a man leave the door of his cleit half open, and a sheep of his neighbour's goes in thereat, and die therein, the owner of the cleit must make it good, in paying the sheep. If the door be quite open, and access be had out, as well as in, he is free, or if he has Witness that he closed the door, he is free, tho' several sheep died in his cleit."

Martin (1698) wrote about more serious situations, "If any man is guilty of beating his neighbour, he is liable to a fine not exceeding the value of two shillings sterling; if any has beat his neighbour so as to draw blood from him; he is liable to a fine, but it must not exceed four shillings and six pence; these crimes are complained of by the officer to the steward on his arrival, who either exacts the whole, or dispenses with the fines, as he judges convenient for their future quiet and peace." Some of these stewards received a bad press, no doubt deservedly, one was described by the visitors of 1799 as being Lawgiver, Judge and Executioner, as well as Shopkeeper.

The people were law abiding and fines were rarely imposed. However, when they were necessary payment was usually in kind. In the 1830's a fine of £100 would be paid with 100 full grown Fulmars, 50 gugas (young Gannets) and a hair rope. In fact, the rope was the most valuable possession held by anyone, and was the first article mentioned in a father's will to his eldest son, equivalent to two of the best cows on the island. (Macaulay, 1764).

The St. Kildans from early history were aware of the need to conserve their limited resources; they were particularly fond of a certain seaweed growing on the rocks, called Laver, which they were all permitted to pick but one man or more was over zealous or over greedy and "scraped away the Laver from off the face of the rock with a shell. This high crime and misdemeanor coming to light, the community was greatly alarmed. The chief men of the state met immediately in council, and fearing that this invaluable seaweed would be entirely exterminated, unless proper precautions should be taken, as the roots of some parts of it had in their frightened imaginations been totally destroyed by the shell, conjured the parson to excommunicate the guilty; but I did not hear that the 'Anathema' was actually pronounced." (Macaulay, 1764).

WEAVING

The most pressing and time consuming occupation during the long winter evenings was the preparation of the wool and the weaving of the cloth which was to provide clothing for the inhabitants and tweed in lieu of rent to the Factor. A visitor in 1799 commented, "The women spin upon the distaffs, the use of the common wheel being unknown to them. They also weave, for which purpose they have 3 looms of the rudest kind." 'Waulking' was done by the women by laying down the tweed on ropes made of hay, a fatiguing labour which they relieved with a song composed for the purpose. He continued, "The only colours are white, black, red or grey. White and black from the sheep, grey a mixture, red is produced by boiling the culbeard, a species of lichen which grows in great quantities on the rocks."

Mackenzie described the process as it had developed by the 1830's, "All their clothing is woollen and manufactured by themselves . . . In the evenings the women tease out and card the wool in rolls for spinning. Much of the spinning is done by them on the distaff at odd times; the remainder of the wool is spun during the winter evenings on the ordinary small wheel. The men are the weavers and the cloth they make is coarse, but strong and durable . . . with the exception of the reed they make their own primitive looms. All are able to act as tailors, dressmakers and shoemakers for their own families. The men's clothes are fairly well made after the fashion which prevails in Harris, but when dressmaking for the women they are not so particular, and absolutely refuse to make any changes in the ancient simple fashion."

Writing some 50 years later Connell (1887) adds detail to the picture, "His loom is in operation for only 2 months of the year, when the nights are at their longest and outdoor work is suspended. The loom is set up in one of the two apartments into which every house (1860's Cottages) is divided, generally the kitchen. It is a primitive looking machine, every portion of it is

Lachlan MacDonald at his St. Kilda spinning wheel in 1980.

home-made, and displaying much ingenuity and dexterity. The most heterogeneous and unpromising materials have been utilized. A little 'bit of timber thrown up on the shore has been scooped out with a pocket-knife into a shuttle; for a spindle there is the quill of a goose (solan goose), and a bobbin has been shaped out of the stalk of a common weed – the dockin!" He continued, "For two months the sound of the shuttle is heard in nearly every house. The work is carried on with astonishing zeal, the men often sleeping in their clothes, and sometimes for but a few hours each night. The dawn of day finds them at the loom, which they do not leave till an hour or two past midnight. It is the same every winter."

Callum MacDonald left St. Kilda in 1924 and in his reminiscences he recalled the evenings preparing the wool and washing the tweed. "All the tweeds made on St. Kilda were of three shades, light blue, light grey and brown. The brown is a colour derived from boiling stone moss, the resulting mixture was used as a dye, into which the wool was dipped until the tweed was the required reddish brown. One winter event I always looked forward to was the night of the Big Carding . . . The kitchen would be cleared of everything except chairs which were set out in a circle. One person from each of the other families on the island would come and take his or her place in a chair. There would be anything up to twenty five persons present including the grown up children of the family concerned seated in the kitchen . . . Each person was given a bundle of plain wool which was set beside him, then he was given some dyed wool. The cards were pieces of wood with short wire teeth like a brush, onto this you placed the white wool with some of the dyed wool. These were stroked between the two cards until the required tone and colour of the wool was derived. It took about five minutes to complete one cardful of wool. The finished mixture was thrown in a heap on the floor until a small hillock amassed in the centre, which would eventually reach up to the ceiling. Carding would start around midday by the family themselves. Around 6 o'clock the neighbours would start to appear one by one and carding would go on till the early hours. The children who were too young to card could only look on from the back and listen to the conversation, jokes and stories that were being told. Some of the stories had been handed down from ancient times, some concerned life on the mainland. At 1 a.m. everybody stopped work for the night. the wool was stacked into canvas bags. The tables were brought back into the kitchen and layed out with a meal for all those who had taken part in the work. The high light of the meal was the huge dumpling set in the middle of the table. Grace was said and the feasting went on till around 2 a.m."

Another great occasion was the washing of the tweed to remove the oil. Callum recalled, "Half a dozen wooden tubs were placed in the middle of the kitchen floor. A huge boiling pot was suspended over a fire by a hook and chain hanging from the chimney. Into this pot was placed the next best thing to ammonia that the islanders could obtain . . . The boiling mixture was placed by the women, for this was women's work, into the tubs. Washing soda and soft soap were added and the whole lot allowed to cool to a certain temperature. The smell was horrendous! The women then tucked up their dresses to knee length and stepped into the tubs. They put so much tweed in as they required and began treading it, very much in grape treading fashion. All the time they danced, they chanted some Gaelic rhythm, which I could never make out . . . They kept this activity going for ages, sweating, laughing and shouting until all the tweed had been through the tub. When they had finished dancing in the tub the tweed was then spread across a long wooden table. Two women would get on each side of the table and pound the tweed for all they were worth. It was then thrown into the air to fall back onto the table. As this process was carried out the tweed began to get thicker and thicker in texture. This action was called 'waulking the tweed' and was very arduous as the tweed was soaking wet. It was a great body exercise! The tweed was then taken out to a running stream and my father and us boys went through the same process but with a certain relief that we were out in the open. Finally, when the water was running clean and clear, the tweed was taken to a stone dyke. Here it was spread out and left to dry. When dried it was measured, rolled up and was now ready for selling."

EDUCATION

Schooling on St. Kilda was always a haphazard business with limited equipment and discouraging results. It depended almost entirely on school-masters who only stayed for a short period of time or on the resident minister. Alexander Buchan, who was on St. Kilda from 1705-30 was the first to start a mission school under the auspices of the S.S.P.C.K., lessons were held from 7-11 a.m. and 1-5 p.m. from February to October – daylight hours dictated the times throughout the winter. He also built up a free library of 56 books, but in 1728 only two people had learnt to read. For practically the next 100 years teaching was carried out by the resident catechist or missionary. In 1811 the Gaelic School Society was founded and took over the responsibility of educating the St. Kildans until 1884. In 1821 they received a report that out of the 110 inhabitants only one person could read and continued, "The people being so poor it would be requisite to allow

them all the books necessary gratis, as they have not a coin in circulation among them." (Gaelic Sch.Soc., 1822). They quickly responded and sent out Alexander Mackenzie in June 1822. He was to stay until 1829, and he found the people eager to learn. During the 1830's and early 40's the Rev. Neil Mackenzie and his wife made a great effort to improve the standards with daily lessons which included reading, writing and arithmetic, with a Sunday School for religious instruction. They also found a readiness to learn and often all three generations of a family would be present in the lessons which were still in Gaelic. After Mackenzie's departure there was practically a 10 year inter-regnum during which time things once again came to a halt.

In 1846 the Free Church took over the care of St. Kilda, although their first Catechist was unable to arrive until 1853, others followed until the Rev. John Mackay came as resident minister in 1865, staying until 1889. In 1884 the Ladies Association of the Highland Society raised money to send teachers over the next few years. Mr. Campbell was the first of these and he was given a room in the Factor's House, so began formal teaching on St. Kilda with English, geography, history, arithmetic and composition. Most of these teachers were young men who only stayed a year which resulted in minimal continuity. However, Connell commented

School at St. Kilda in 1927. Photo by Cockburn.

Back Row: Neil MacKinnon, Donald Ewan MacKinnon.
Middle Row: Donald Gillies, Cathie Gillies, Flora Gillies, Mary Ann Gillies, Rachel MacKinnon, Alick J. MacLeod.
Front Row: Ewan Gillies, Kenneth Macleod.
The Schoolmaster and Missionary – John MacLeod with his two sons above.

after his visits in 1885 and 86, "The masters of this and similar schools are usually divinity students who let their regular studies stand for a year. It hardly needs to be pointed out that the student who allows himself to be sent to train the young St. Kildian, even if only for a twelvemonth, does a heroic thing and is quite entitled to the gratitude of his church as the missionary who goes to Old Calabar or the Cannibal Islands." (Connell, 1887). However, progress was made, and many teachers like Murray and Ross left behind them detailed and illuminating accounts of their time on "the island on the edge of the world."

Masons and carpenters from Dunvegan began work on the new school room adjoining the Church in 1898, which was finally completed and opened in 1899. The school was now under the Inverness County Council and was run as a 'side' school under the supervision of a teacher from Obbe School, Harris (now Leverburgh), and was visited annually by H.M. Inspector of Schools. From 1906 most of the teaching was undertaken by the Missionary or his wife. The School Log was started in 1900 and makes fascinating reading, reflecting the problems and frustrations of the teachers and the many events which affected the life of the community. Some extracts from the Log for 1918 indicate the difficulties of a school on this lonely outpost.

1918

Jan. 11 "Intensely cold and heavy snow. No school in the afternoon."

Jan. 15 "One scholar, Rachel MacDonald, has now been absent for over two weeks with chilblains." Jan. 22 "Still absent."

Mar. 6 "Every house in the island washing tweed today, scholars assisting, so no school was held."

Apr. 8 "School closed for 3 weeks – bad attack of influenza."

Apr. 30 "No school – people gathering birds eggs."

June 24 "School re-opened today. No school has been held since the island was bombarded on 15th. May. During most of that time the school has been occupied by a party from the Naval Station while their own premises have been repaired." (The bombardment was by a German submarine).

July 31 "No school for the last 2 days as Mrs. MacKinnon's baby is sick and her husband is at present absent from the island."

Aug. 16 "No school . . . for a week as all will be engaged in killing and salting fulmars for the winter."

Oct. 25 "No school . . . children bringing peats from the hill for the school fire."

Alick J. MacLeod on his return visit to St. Kilda in 1979. Now a retired schoolmaster from Harris, appears in the School photo for 1927.

Nov. 8   "Great storm raging. No school held as it is unsafe to enter the building for danger from falling stones or slates from the church which has never been repaired since the bombardment six months ago."

Nov. 12   "A boat came today with the news that the terrible war was over. Children given a holiday in honour of the great event."

Dec. 6   "No school this afternoon as the school and church are being cleaned for a marriage next week."

Dec. 10   "Marriage today, a lad from the Naval Station and a girl from the Village." (Malcolm MacLean and Mary MacDonald).

In spite of the limited scope of the educational fascilities on St. Kilda, on leaving the islands, although some understandably became disillusioned by the lack of opportunities, others were able to make the best of it and obtained interesting jobs varying from a ship's wheelwright to employment with the Forestry Commission. Individuals acquired such diverse positions as a prosperous tweed merchant in Glasgow, a Presbyterian Minister in Canada, and one ending up as a valet at the Grosvenor House Hotel, Park Lane, London.

WORSHIP
i Sunday Worship.

Martin in 1697 mentions 3 chapels, Christ's Church, St. Columba's and St. Brendan's, all aligned east-west, and each with an altar at the east end covered with thatch after the pattern of their houses. Christ's Church was on the present cemetery site and was the main place of worship, but being only 6 x 4m (20 x 14ft) it could not hold the whole congregation so the Sunday

Services were held in the church-yard which was surrounded by a low stone wall in 1697. On Sunday mornings young and old would attend and say the Lord's Prayer, the Creed and the 10 Commandments. By 1758 Macaulay could report that, "The St. Kildans were devout, they attend Divine Worship very regularly and strictly observe the Lord's Day."

By the late 1700's Christ's Church had fallen into disrepair and the services were held in the Minister's house. A member of Brougham's party went to a service on his visit in 1799. "This being Sunday, immediately after breakfast the Bellman, if he may be so called, was sent to summon the inhabitants to church which he did by retiring to the end of the house and emitting a kind of piercing howl, which he had borrowed from some of the seals which frequent the neighbouring rocks. In a few minutes the whole congregation was assembled in the Parson's kitchen, men, women and children. The Parson, himself, was seated upon a large bag of feathers with a barrel of oil before him by way of reading desk – the psalm being read out, the whole party proceeded to sing it, accompanying it with every species of gesticulation and grimace, the melody was not a little heightened by the snoring of some of the party which enraged the Bellman so much that getting up, he struck one of them over the back with a species of boat hook which he carried by way of mace or badge of office – with this exception the whole of the service was conducted with utmost decency." (Anonymous, 1799).

John Gladstone attended a Sunday morning service in the Kirk and gave this account in his diaries for 1927. "As a mere formality Norman MacKinnon gave six pulls at the bell rope although everyone on the island had collected. We went in putting our money in a little box on a pedestal. Callum MacDonald began to read through the metrical psalm which the congregation was to sing. This being over Norman stood up and 'led the praise', singing each line first, the congregation repeating it after him . . . The Psalm ended Callum read a chapter of 40 verses from St. John . . . after he had finished reading the New Testament, he put up his hands and prayed. The women sprawled over the desk in front of them and the men stood up; for this is the custom of St. Kilda . . . Another Psalm was then sung; and the Old Testament lesson, the last chapter of Ecclesiastes was read. Old Callum's address followed . . . we then sung the 23rd. Psalm to the tune 'Covenanters'. Finally, Callum called on John Gillies to pray – for everyone in St. Kilda prays in turn – with beautiful rythmical lowerings and risings of the voices, and we were struck by the beauty of the sound."

On his visit to St. Kilda in 1838 Lachlan MacLean joined in the worship in the Chapel and jotted down notes and recorded the prayer. "As we entered they were all standing up, and one of the natives praying. The scene was interesting and highly edifying. He was barefoot with a coarse jacket on, a pair of shapeless trousers out at the knees, and a curly shaggy head of hair that might be mistaken for a cap of their own peculiar sheep-skin; his voice was firm, his delivery slow, his Gaelic select, his manner solemn and expressive: prayer seemed to him not a matter of rote, but the emanation of a mind imbued with the spirit of prayer. His eyes being closed he had not observed us entering, I took out my journal, and, whilst I trust I joined him and the rest of the humble suppliants, I took down what was before us of his prayer . . . I shall translate:–

> Thou art the fountain of living water, and the rock of our hope.
> It is boldness in us to take Thy great name into our lips,
> But we have no alternative, there is none other to whom we may go.
> Poor and solitary as we are, we are Thy own creatures.
> Was not Thine own Son poor? Take pity upon us therefore,
> And vouchsafe us Thy Holy Ghost.
> Bless those into whose hearts Thou hast put it to come and visit us –
> Not to mock us, but with hearts running over with love –
> With the message of the Lamb who taketh away the sin of the world.
> This we seek for Thy sake. Amen'."

ii Family Worship

They were on the whole a simple God fearing people. Family worship would be held in the morning and evening when the head of the household would open 'the Books' and read from a Psalm or another part of the Gaelic Bible and lead in prayer. This continued even when they were out at night in their boats fishing, or over on Boreray shearing the sheep or collecting the gannets. They would stop whatever they were engaged in and pause for a time of worship. School-master Murray described his experiences in 1887. "On Thursday April 7th. I went with the men to Boreray to kill Gannets through the night. We arrived sometime before dark. When the night began to fall seven went on land and five remained in the boat to cruise round the island to pick up the birds when thrown over the rocks . . . Being full moon it was much too clear for making what they call 'good work'. I did not complain of the clearness at all as I could, in places where no cat could get, see where I was going. It is very dangerous work on a dark night. After working for an hour or two we rested and had Family Worship. The scene to me was very impressive. The three of us sat down on the bare rocks with the ropes about our middle, the cloudless sky our canopy, the moon our lamp, and the ocean still and quiet far below, and offered praise and prayer to Him who was able to preserve us in such dangerous work".

Worship on St. Kilda over the years reflected the Christian climate on the mainland varying from the Church of Scotland from 1705 and earlier, to the Free Church in 1846 and the United Free Church from 1900 to the evacuation. The St. Kildans greatly valued the spiritual help and leadership from Ministers like the Rev. Neil Mackenzie who worked with them and cared so much for their complete welfare. In spite of all the criticism in the past the Reverend Donald John Gillies, himself born on the island, could say at the rededication service in 1980 "The most important building on Hirta is the House of God. This particular spot where we find ourselves gathered today is sacred to the memory of many. It is here that they received their early education and religious training and have since gone forth to other parts of the Empire, and for that matter, other parts of the world and have made a mark for themselves in their new homes."

LIFE ON THE LAND — CROFTING

Land

Before the introduction of the New Village Plan in the 1830's, each family on the island had about two acres of ground which was called a 'farthing land'. This was a term associated with the Norse naval defence system based upon ouncelands and pennylands land divisions, which was later converted to a means of taxation. In the Western Highlands, one ounceland = 20 pennylands, one farthingland = a quarterpennyland. St. Kilda would be equivalent to 5 pennylands. It was used for rental purposes as a unit of landholding, although it was not a fixed acreage. The portions of land on Hirta were carefully marked out with stones and each one was known by its old Norse name in use at that time. Macaulay (1764) gives us some examples, "Among the best of these are the divisions called Multum agria, Multum taurus, Multum favere, or Multum fodere, Queen o Scot, Land dotteros, . . . Lanphalin, or Paul's division." Every three years these plots would pass by lots from one to another.

After the replanning of the Village in the 1830's each family had its own permanent field strip reaching from the sea wall to the Head Dyke, and every crofter had his own gate in the Head Dyke so that when all the crops had been lifted in the autumn the cattle and sheep were allowed on to the field strips to graze and add manure to the ground. If a neighbour's crops had not been harvested he could let his cattle onto his own croft provided it was tethered. As the weather deteriorated the milking cows were brought into the byres; from 1860 they used the old thatched houses. Here they were fed with hay which had been dried in the cleitean, and the stalks of barley and oats which had been stored in sheaves and ricks in the garden enclosures at the back of the houses where the cattle could not reach them. These were brought into the byres as the need arose.

Preparing the Ground

The cattle and sheep were allowed to feed off the remaining crops and grass within the Village until the spring when the grass began to grow outside the Head Dyke, at this time they would be put out and the gates in the wall would be closed up again. In April, with the approach of spring, the two acre field strips would be prepared for planting. In the early days the soil was turned over with the 'caschrom' or crooked spade which had a wooden pin at the junction with the shaft on which the foot could get a purchase. The normal practice was to give two powerful jerks before turning the clod, first to the right and then to the left, walking backwards as the successive clods were turned. The task was executed quickly, 12 labourers could turn over one acre in a single day, but it did not reach a great depth and the large clods had to be broken up with a 'caibe', an instrument shaped like a hoe, similar to a carpenter's adze, but much heavier. They also used the caibe to destroy weeds and to 'earth up' and dig their potatoes. Mackenzie introduced the English spade in the 1830's and together with his system of drainage the crop yield was doubled. Having broken up the soil, the ground was carefully raked over with a heavy, short handled wooden 'racan' with wooden teeth, "and all the rest supplied with Tangles of seaware (seaweed) tied to the harrow by the small ends, the root hanging lose behind, scatter the clods broken by the wooden teeth." (Buchan, 1752). Stones and weeds were meticulously removed. The ground was now ready for the manure which consisted of the midden from the byres (in the old thatched houses there was a hole in the wall to allow the liquid to drain through onto the cultivation plot), the inedible remains of birds and sheep and occasionally seaweed. Mackenzie made the following observations in the 1830's, "The manure is carried to the fields by the women in ordinary wicker creels, which the men, as their share of the work, fill and put upon their backs. While they are absent the men rest, smoke and talk, for they are everlasting talkers. The manure is spread over the fields with their hands, and in this work both men and women take their part."

The two acres of ground for each household were now ready for sowing. They were usually subdivided into little fields, in 1799 Brougham reported about 400 rips or fields of oats and barley, each measuring about 25 x 3ft. The men sowed the seed, both oats and barley were spread very thickly to help the plants to support each other in the severe winds, while the women threw handfuls of soil to cover the seed from the marauding birds and the south-easterly gales. When the barley reached about 5cm or so they stripped the thatch from the roofs of their houses and used the inner, soot impregnated layers as a top dressing.

Harvesting the Crops

The time for harvesting the crops usually fell between the Fulmar and Gannet harvest and involved everyone in the village. In Mackenzie's time in the 1830's the ripe barley was pulled up by the roots (later generations used the scythe) and tied into sheaves and left lying for a few days before being built up into small stacks. The family would then cut the sheaves, separating the heads, which were built up again into little stacks, the stalks were tied up ready to rethatch the houses. This work was finished in one day. Mackenzie paints the picture, "The women of this particular family will not remain long with the workers, but as soon as the ears are cut from a few sheaves they carry them home. There they are spread out and set fire to the straw, which is allowed to burn till the straw is consumed and the grain left, dry and hard enough to grind. It is then freed from the dust and rubbish, ground into meal in the quern, and cooked for the supper of the workers. Supper is at all times the principal meal of the day. In about two months these ears, except that portion which is reserved for seed, are taken by each family in turn to the kiln, and spread out to dry and harden. When this is done they beat off the grain from the straw, and winnow it from the chaff in the breeze. The grain is now stored, and ground in the quern as required, which is generally only a few days-supply at a time. As by keeping, some of the effect of kiln-drying is lost, it is restored by placing a portion of grain in a straw tub, and with it a hot stone, which is moved about among the grain till it is again suitable for grinding. this may be done every week or two, with about a bushel each time."

Buchan (in 1752) and MacDiarmid in 1878 noted that each house had its own hand-grinding mill, "This consists of two circular granite stones, about 15 or 18 inches in diameter, laid flat upon each other. In the centre on the under one is an iron pivot, upon which the upper one is turned by grasping a wooden handle. The corn is allowed to drop into a hole in the centre of the upper stone, find its way between the stones as the

105

upper is kept revolving, and by the time it comes out at the edge between the stones it is supposed to be sufficiently ground. The meal makes a very fair porridge and bread." (MacDiarmid, 1878). From the mid 1800's some oatmeal was regularly imported as the crops were never adequate for the needs of the people.

The St. Kildans had no conception of crop rotation so that potatoes were grown on the same plot year after year, and produced a very poor yield. MacDiarmid recalled, "The return it gives is miserable. From a barrel of potatoes (about 2 cwt) scarcely three barrels will be lifted . . . with oats the return is never above two and a half times the quantity of the seed sown; formerly it used to be five or six times."

Shepherding

"The pasture is excellent and forms as fine a sheep run of its size as can be seen anywhere." commented MacDiarmid. Surprisingly, the sheep were not held in common, each crofter owned and looked after his own and they occupied a good deal of his time at certain seasons. At the lambing the young and sickly needed special attention: when they were old enough some of them were put into walled enclosures near the Head Dyke where they had a ready supply of good ungrazed grass to help to bring them on. Rounding up the sheep in May for the clipping and in October for slaughtering

for winter food was always a time of great excitement which they called the "Ruagadh" – the Chase. Everyone was involved and expended a tremendous amount of energy. Each sheep had to be extracted from every nook and cranny of the island and often it was necessary to chase them down in small numbers, or one at a time, to get them into the sheep fanks. Dogs were used to help in this operation, their teeth having been broken previously to avoid damaging the sheep. Dr. MacDonald (1825) records his observations on May 26th. "This morning . . . the men proceeded to the rocks to fleece the sheep. I took a walk about mid-day to see this operation, it is certainly hazardous to man and beast. The animals are driven together to a precipice on the summit of a high perpendicular rock, and are there hemmed in on all sides by the men and their dogs till every one of them is got at, and stripped of its fleecy mantle. I saw one poor animal fall headlong into the sea, from a height of about 300 feet and completely disappear. I am told however, that few accidents of this kind happen."

School-master Murray in his diary for May 28th 1887 recorded, "Yesterday was a great day. All the sheep along the north side of the island had to be driven to the Cambir. This was accomplished in the same way as sportsmen beat the hills for game. The men and boys were extended along a line on the hill tops while two or

St. Kildans sheep shearing in 1927. Photo by Cockburn.
From left to right: *Donald Hugh MacKinnon*   *Donald Gillies*   *Norman MacQueen*   *Lachlan MacDonald*   *Donald MacDonald*

three were driving them up from among the rocks below. What shouting on the part of the men! Nor did the dogs, eager for the chase, diminish the noise with their barking. There was racing and chasing on Conachair's side. Several times a number of the flock would make a rush back, through men, women and dogs and then every one was in full pursuit. Of course I was in the midst of all this excitement. The Cambir was reached about two o'clock, when the girls came with our dinner."

The method of shearing the sheep was very primitive and entailed removing the fleece in bits and pieces with a pen-knife, leaving the animal in an extremely ugly state. Murray encouraged them to use the modern shears but they were not convinced about the idea. "Today the sheep are to be clipped. I clipped seven yesterday and learned them the way to use the shears. Their shearing instrument is the common knife which of course makes work. One man last year got a pair of shears in a present and on my making use of it yesterday it became an object of wonder and was called a 'great invention'. There was a crowd of about forty men and women in a circle round about me with eyes full wide with astonishment at the strange operation which the beast was undergoing. Remarks such as the following were made: "O graidh! na gearr an sgornan." (O Love don't cut the throat). "Na toir as a' grudhan" (Don't take out the liver). While the owner of the beast said it would not stay on that side of the island after hearing such "Ghogadaich" noise about its ears, meaning the sound of the shears. All this was very amusing to me." In October the sheep were killed and salted for the winter and later around November, they would kill off the sickly looking animals which would not have survived until the spring. They also made excellent candles from the tallow of the sheep.

Fishing was resorted to in the summer with the long lines, mainly for ling, and occasionally in the winter, in order to help to pay the rent, as most of the St. Kildans "disliked the taste of fish, claiming that it was not oily enough for their palate." (Steel, 1975). Each householder had to pay rent to the owners, the MacLeods of Skye through his Steward, for his croft and for each of his sheep and each head of cattle on the island. (See section on Rent).

St. Kilda Sheep Song
Margaret Shaw (1977) in her book of Folksongs, included this St. Kilda Sheep Song, which in the original is in Gaelic and describes some of the characteristics of Hirta's lively sheep.

Chorus: The foot of the Hirta sheep, o !
    Hirta, Hirta, Hirta o !
    The foot of the Hirta sheep, o !
      That was the nimble foot.

1. That was the elegant sheep,
   The colour would grow on her back,
   She would require neither lichen nor soot
                              (for dyeing),
      But to spin the wool for trousers.

2. That was the sheep that was swift,
   Whenever she would come around
   Not one on the north country
      Could 'pull a feather out of her'.
                        (keep up with her).

3. The lamb went by himself
   Over yonder with the cattle,
   That is when she became violent,
      When her chain began to rattle.

4. That is the sheep that was angry,
   She was not accustomed to be on the hill.
   She was always at home
      And lovely would be the grass she would
                                          eat.

LIFE ON THE ROCKS AND SEA — FISHING

To support the huge numbers of seals and seabirds the waters around the island group abound with fish.

Visiting trawlers shelter in Village Bay.
Drawn from an old photograph.

The Dutch and French for centuries have obtained good catches of hake, ling, halibut and herring and more recently the Norwegians and Swedes as well as the British have also fished these waters. One of the earliest memories of Alick MacLeod (son of the Missionary Teacher from 1927-29) as a boy was on a winter's night seeing Village Bay fully illuminated with the lights of the Fleetwood trawlers sheltering from a storm. Fishing was never looked upon by the St. Kildans as a viable proposition: the birds were comparatively easy to take, in their estimation, and in abundant supply, whereas fishing in small open boats was fraught with far too many dangers.

Macaulay (1764) recorded that men would fish from

the rocks. The fish-hooks used in the early history were either made from nails extracted from pieces of wood washed up on the shore or hooks removed from fish or the stomachs of gannets which had swallowed the ones which had escaped from the long lines. There were only two suitable places for fishing, each had ten sittings where two men would work in shifts to stand or sit. "They catch a variety of excellent fishes, cod, ling, turbot, pollacks, perches, lithes and some other kinds." However, in spring and early summer there was a ban placed on fishing from the rocks in case it disturbed the nesting birds. By 1875 Sands wrote that while he was on the island, "Two boats, with crews of eight and nine men respectively went to sea frequently in the evenings to fish for ling with long lines baited with conger-eel. Each boat would return in the morning with perhaps on average 35 ling with a few cod, besides other fish (lithe, halibut, blackmouths and skate). The ling were salted and stored for the Factor, who pays 7d each. The cod are sold for 3d each. The men provide their own lines, but are supplied with salt. They themselves keep no note of the fish exported but MacLeod incidentally acknowledged receipt of 1,080 marketable fish. A number of elderly men sit on the rocks near the Village and angle for bream in the July evenings. For each of these they receive a penny."

At times risks were taken, even in the winter, as this entry in School Master George Murray's diary for New Year's Day 1887 clearly illustrates. "The men had the lines set last night for the ling and this morning they went to lift them . . . There was a terrible swell on and really it was a job to get them landed. Everyone that was able to walk was at the shore assisting as best they could. I thought several times that the boat would be swamped with them amongst the breakers or dashed on the rocks. First the lines, fish and oars were landed by means of ropes, then, when all on the shore were ready to pull and an opportunity was affored by the waves, the nine men in the boat held fast clinging to the sides and let it run with the waves on the rocks. The united effort of all of us on the shore, hauled it right up clear of the rocks . . . Really it is a dangerous shore. They got about 20 ling and as many yesterday."

In the 1920's fish were still being caught to help to pay the rent. Lachlan MacDonald, "Fishing with the big lines, mostly ling we used to go for, and you would take it ashore, split it and clean it and take the big bones out of it, salt it and put it out on the stones to dry in the sun. It used to be lovely fish, right enough. Then you would make it into 1 cwt (50kg) packets and send it to Glasgow."

The St. Kilda Maid's Song is recorded by Seton (1878) and goes back to the mid 1700's. It has many interesting allusions to St. Kilda life and the refrain is an imitation of the loud "discordant clamour of a flock of sea-fowl over a shoal of fish."

"Over the rocks, steadily, steadily;
  Down to the clefts with a shout and a shove, O !
Warily tend the rope, shifting it readily;
  Eagerly, actively, watch from above, O !
    Brave, O brave my lover true, he's worth a
                              maiden's love;
    (And the sea below is still as deep as the sky
                          is high above !)

Sweet 'tis to sleep on a well-feathered pillow;
  Sweet from the embers the fulmar's red egg, O !
Bounteous our store from the rock and the billow;
  Fish and the birds in good store, we need never
                                  beg, O !
    Brave, O brave . . .

Hark to the fulmar and guillemot screaming,
  Hark to the kittiwake, puffin and gull, O !
See the white wings of the solan goose gleaming;
  Steadily, men, on the rope gently pull, O ! . . .

Deftly my love can hook torsc, ling and conger,
  The grey fish and hake with the net and the
                              creel, O !
Far from our island be plague and be hunger;
  And sweet our last sleep in the quiet of the
                          keel, O ! . . .

Pull on the rope, men! pull it up steadily;
  There's storm on the deep, see the skart claps
                          his wings, O !
Cunningly guide the rope, shifting it steadily;
  Welcome my true love, and all that he
                          brings, O !
    Now God be praised, my lover's safe, he's
                      worth a maiden's love;
    And the sea below is still as deep as the sky is
                          high above ! "

LIFE ON THE CLIFFS —
BIRD FOWLING

The St. Kildan style of bird fowling brought together
many different skills. It involved a working knowledge
of bird behaviour learnt over the centuries, together
with the evolution of ingenious bird catching methods
and the remarkable development of rock climbing
feats which brought wide recognition to the
community. Some individuals, like Finlay MacQueen,
became legendary figures within their own life time.

The rocks or cliffs had such food resources that these
were regularly divided out by the casting of lots. "These
exalted rocks are more carefully divided among the
inhabitants of this solitary isle than their very corn

111

fields." wrote Buchanan in 1793. The actual harvest of young Fulmars was shared equally by the whole population but the casting of lots meant that during some years a family would be working the cliffs of Oiseval, near to home, whilst in other years be out on the Cambir necessitating a long trudge back with a heavy load of birds. The allocation of the cliffs gave families an area to work at the time of the harvest and the freedom to take adults and eggs at other times. Casting lots eliminated any arguments.

Learning the Art

It was the ambition of most of the boys to be lowered down over the cliffs by rope to take the young Fulmars. Martin commented that "The young boys of three years old begin to climb the walls of their houses." Lachlan MacDonald related, "If it wasn't in yourself, you still had to go! If you didn't want to go, a rope would be put round your waist, you'd be shown a bird, and off you went, or you'd be pushed off!"

Callum MacDonald wrote about a frightening incident which happened to him when he was very young. Having pestered his brother to let him down over the cliff by rope his brother became irritated because he was so slow in taking the Fulmar. Callum continued, "It was difficult to get a foot-hold with my bare feet. I tried several times but the bird defended itself admirably. Everyone above kept shouting 'go on, catch it', my brother meanwhile was becoming impatient at my antics; he gave a sharp tug of the rope and before I could retrieve my position I was hanging upside down. From my upright position I was now looking onto the bottom rocks and the foaming sea . . . I now began slipping through the noose . . . the rope slipped round my knees and tightened around my ankles before I finally felt my brothers strong hands pull me clear of danger. When he had pulled me to safety he said, 'That is the last time I will ever lower you down!'."

The men only wore shoes in the winter, they found bare feet gave them a much better grip on the rocks which were often wet with rain or spray, or slippery with seaweed. The feet of both men and women became extremely tough and well developed, Connell visited St. Kilda in 1885 and 86 and described his landlady as having "ankles and feet like a rhinoceros."

The rope used in the 18th century was about 30 fathoms in length, "made of strong, raw cow-hide, salted for that very purpose, and cut circularly into three thongs, all of equal length. These thongs being twisted together form a threefold cord, able to sustain a great weight and durable enough to last about two generations." (Macaulay, 1764). A more costly horse-hair rope was also used, 9-10 fathoms in length for more accessible places, and to prevent damage by the rocks, the ropes were lined with sheep-skin or salted cow hide. By 1870 Manilla hemp rope was used.

Fulmars

The men usually worked in pairs on the cliffs. "One man stands on the verge of the precipice, and the rope which he holds in his hands is fastened round the body and beneath the arms of him who descends, while another rope is pressed by the foot of the upper man, and is held in the hand of the lower . . . thus they dart downwards, just as spiders drop from the top of a wall." (Wilson, 1842). Once on the ledge, "a long stick, resembling a fishing rod with a noose at the extremity, was let down to him from above, which he cautiously extended, making the noose fall rapidly over the head of the bird, the fluttering victim being immediately captured. Several (adult) fulmars and puffins were secured . . . To any one who has witnessed the daring proceedure of the St. Kilda cragsman, the most startling feats of a Blondin, or a Leotard appear utterly insignificant!" (Seton, 1878). Stac Biorach in Soay Sound was regarded as the crucial test of the fowlers skill. Here a rope was of no avail, the rock could only be climbed in the fashion of a steeple jack. The young fulmars were easy to take from the nest and were killed with a quick twist of the neck. Then they were tied in

Fulmar cliffs of Oiseval from near the Gap.

113

bundles and hauled up to the top of the cliff where the valuable oil was extracted, and the birds carried back to the Village.

Puffins

To catch the puffins the St. Kildans would use a 5m long pole onto which was attached a curved stick with a sliding noose of horse hair on a gannet's quill. The long handle was held firmly and slipped along the ground, supported by the curved stick, in front of the puffin, the noose being at 'puffin head level'. The inquisitive birds would watch as the noose came nearer until with a sudden twist it was lowered over the head of the unsuspecting bird. Kearton in 1896 recorded no fewer than 620 taken by Angus Gillies in a single day. When the party visited Boreray in the summer the girls spent their time over there catching and plucking the puffins. They had dogs with them which were trained to catch the adults as they fluttered away from the nest burrows. However most of them were caught in a very simple way recounted by Sands (1877). "The girls also place hair ropes on the ground held down at the ends by stones. Nooses of horse-hair are affixed to the rope, into which the birds (which frequent the island in incredible numbers) push their feet. In this way some of the girls catch as many as four hundred puffins in a day."

Guillemots

Guillemots were taken at night by an ingenious method which required considerable daring and skill. Macaulay describes the method in the 1750's. "As soon as the Lavie is discovered on the coast, the heroes who have formerly distinguished themselves by such feats, go down, with the help of their ropes, into the well known shelves of those rocks, each having a broad piece of linnen, or anything remarkably white, fixed on his breast. This operation is done in the night time; the bird mistaking an object so conspicuous for a part of the rock, endeavours to cling to it, and is immediately caught and dispatched. In this posture the fowler continues till about dawn. Then, and not till then, whatever his success may be, he makes the wonted signal, that is, he pulls the rope at which his life hangs. His companion who stands above, takes care in the first place to secure the prey, which sometimes consists of no less than four hundred Lavies; and once that is done, helps or hauls up the adventurer."

Gannets

The St. Kildans visited Boreray and the Stacs on three separate occasions in connection with the gannets, taking adults in April, their eggs in May and the young between August and October. The visits in April were during the night, Buchanan gives this account in his book of 1793. "The fowler, thus let down by one or more men, who hold the rope lest he should fall over the impending rocks into the sea, with a white towel about his breast, calmly slides over the face of the rocks till he has a full view of the sentinel. Then he gently moves along on his hands and feet, creeping very silently to the spot where the sentinel stands on guard. If he cries bir, bir, the sign of alarm, he stands back: but if he cries grog, grog, that of confidence, he advances without fear of giving an alarm because the goose takes the fowler for one of the straggling geese coming into the camp, and suffers him to advance. Then the fowler very gently tickles one of his legs which he lifts and places on the palm of his hand; he then as gently tickles the other, which in like manner is lifted and placed on the hand. He then no less artfully than insensibly moves the sentinel near the first sleeping goose, which he pushes with his fingers; on which he awakes, and finding the sentinel standing above him, he immediately fall a fighting him for his supposed insolence. This alarms the whole camp, and instead of flying off they all begin to fight through the whole company: while in the meantime the common enemy, unsuspected, begins in good earnest to twist their necks, and never gives up till the whole are left dead on the spot . . . a man told me he was one of four men that catched four itts or pens, being 300 each, in the whole 1200 solan geese in one night." Dr. MacDonald (1823) recorded the return of the boats from the stacs in Sept. 1822, "On one of the days I was on the island, the people brought home in their boats deeply laden with 1200 (young solans) and left 400 more to be sent for afterwards. When the booty was brought ashore, it was immediately divided by lot, into 20 equal parts, according to the number of the families."

Even in daylight these cliffs were terrifying to any but a St. Kildan. School-master Murray expressed his feelings when he went on Boreray on August 11th 1886 to take the young gannets, the gugas, and some fulmars. "At 11.15 a.m. I suddenly dismissed the school and set out with the men and Mr. MacLeod for Boreray. A terrible sight to see the men go over the rocks in quest of birds! A strange life indeed and one fraught with great danger. I would not be satisfied till I should try the rope myself, so on I got and over. Hanging between sky and earth on a strong rope I set to and performed the part of a fowler. Over cliffs and along ledges I and the other two went until, I am sure, we went down about 1,000ft. The birds were plentiful and we did well. I shouldered twenty Fulmars and two Solan Geese and began the ascent, which was no easy matter. A terrible shower of rain fell as we were getting into the boat, in which Mr. MacLeod and Norman Gillies sat fishing all day and caught one mullet. Got home at 9.30 a.m. pretty tired!" The young Solans were dispatched by being hit over the head with a club.

Team-work was essential for all these activities on the cliffs, occasionally selfishness reared its ugly head as in this instance recorded by Lachlan MacLean. "Some years ago, a circumstance took place in St. Kilda, which is now become a universally known proverb in the Highlands . . . The man, who went down upon the rope having succeeded in killing an extraordinary number of fowls, his covetous heart suggested to him that if they were all his own undivided property, what a fortune! Dreaming thus of golden times he cried to the one holding the rope above, 'Let every man take birds from the rocks for himself.' The one above, indignant at this courier, cried back, 'Then let everyman hold a rope for himself,' suiting the action to the word. It is unnecessary to add that the poor fellow below never caught another bird in St. Kilda. The proverb is applied when one of two parties refuse to act in concert." (MacLean, 1838).

Going over the cliffs for the birds was such an integral part of St. Kilda life that it is said that in olden days a man had to demonstrate his rock-climbing skills at the time he proposed to his prospective wife. The whole village community would make its way over to the Mistress Stone on Ruaival where he would perform his balancing act. This was apparently taken in his stride. However, in the course of work accidents did occasionally happen, caused by a slip on wet turf, a dislodged rock, or a fall in the dark while catching Guillemots or Gannets at night. Some of these were fatal and work would cease for a considerable time and a great gloom was cast over the whole community for many days.

During the 19th Century poetry and singing were practically non-existent, but earlier generations had natural gifts in this direction. "The subject of their songs are the accomplishment of their fair friends among the female sex, and the heroic actions of their fowlers in climbing rocks, catching fowls, and fishing, and melancholy deaths over the rocks." (Buchanan, 1793).

An 18th. Century Elegy

An anonymous visitor, one of Brougham's party, landed on St. Kilda in 1799 and in his fascinating account of his stay on the islands recorded this delightful elegy about one of Hirta's sons who had been lost in a recent tragedy. It is full of lovely allusions to the way of life of the people and delicate descriptions of the landscape.

"Isabella the blue eyed, why stands that tear within
                                                            its cell

Isabella, thou daughter of beauty, why are thine
eyes fixed upon vacancy?
And what sounds dost thou listen for in the
breezes of the mountain?

Iver was the pride of our isle, firm he trod the
rock,
The crimson of the starfish shone on his cheek
And the yellow ringlets shaded his dark eye.
When we sailed for the island of the north
He was the first to plunge into the sea.
Alone he dared to climb the rugged steep
And in vain the precipice, slippery with the
ooze of the ocean,
Protects the young gannet.
His step was rapid as the petrels
And his voice was like the breezes of summer.
But the spirit of Iver fled,
No longer he joined the dance
And the music of his voice was hushed.
White the sun shone, his door was closed,
But the passer by heard from within the voice of
sorrow
The maidens gathered round him and would
have assuaged his sorrow.

Isabella the blue eyed alone laughed at his woe,
she only refused the tear of pity.

When the storm howled and the ghosts danced
in the air,
We have often seen him alone sitting upon the
high rock,
We have marked him speaking to the white
moon,
And caught his notes in the breezes of the night.

Gravestones.

117

But when the sun rose or the storm was at an
end
We have seen him returning wet with the spray
of the ocean.
The maidens gathered around him and
endeavoured to assuage his sorrows.

Isabella the blue eyed, alone laughed at his woe
But why does the tear stand within its cell, why are
her eyes fixed upon vacancy?
Or what sounds does she listen for on the breezes
of the mountain.

The cliffs of Soa are high and green sea washes
their feet,
The sharp rocks entered his bosom and the
white waves shrouded his limbs,
The green turf was stretched over him and the
grey stone raised to make his head.
The yellow weed now decks his sod,
The maidens gathered round, each dropped a
tear of pity.

Isabella the blue eyed alone laughed at his fate, but
his ghost now visits her in the storm
And she hears his groans in the pauses of the gale.
For this it is Isabella, the blue eyed, that the tear
stands within its cell,

For this it is thou daughter of beauty that thine
eyes are fixed upon vacancy,
And these are the sounds that thou listenest for in
the breezes of the mountain."

LIFE AND THE OUTSIDE WORLD

Rent

Until the 20th. Century very little money ever changed hands. In the 1830's money was of little use and not coveted, in fact, the total currency of the island 50 years later was only 17s 6d. (Ross, 1884). Everything was paid for in kind. Milner writing about his visit in 1847 related, "The people pay their rent in kind. Each family contributes seven stone of feathers (1 St. Kilda Stone = 24lbs = 10.9kg), valued at five shillings a stone; these are procured from the fulmar, gannet and puffin. It requires the feathers of 80 fulmars to make a stone, the same number of gannets, and 800 puffins. Each family has also to contribute 20 pecks of barley (bere) at a shilling a peck; and from most families the proprietor receives rent, for a cow's grass 7 shillings, for a sheep's grass 1 shilling, and for a lamb's grass 6d. per annum. The average number of sheep possessed by each family is 8, some have two cows. In addition to exporting wool and feathers the people send out 32 barrels of bird-oil, principally obtained from the fulmar, which sells at £3 the barrel. The average number in each family is four, one man and one only has 5 children. The houses are 28 in number, of which 21 have land attached to them, and are inhabited by married men and widowers. The remaining 7 are occupied by old maids and widows."

The Rev. N. Mackenzie tells us that the proprietor's agent also took away and marketed for them any surplus feathers, oil and home spun cloth, bringing back the next year any goods they required in exchange. Exports at other times have included tweed, blanketing, cheese, tallow and fish.

The Account book for MacLeod of Skye records the debts and discharges of the tenants of St. Kilda, following is one extract for 1883.

Lachlan MacKinnon No. 1.

Charge	£	s.	d.	Discharges	£	s.	d.
Rent of lot	2	0	0	Cash	3	5	9
Grazing of Cattle	5	3	6	Cattle	3	10	0
Goods–Stock book	13	8	9	Oil	2	0	6
Cash Paid	–	–	–	Tweed	12	3	0
Balance due Whit 1883	3	0	0	Tallow		14	7
Total Debt	23	12	3	Cheese		7	0
				Fish	–	–	–
				Feathers	1	11	5
				Blankets	–	–	–
				Arrears	–	–	–
				Credit	23	12	3

The total income from St. Kilda in 1883 was £489-6-5¼

Communications

The 80 km of rough Atlantic Ocean between the mainland and St. Kilda has always caused problems of communication, cutting the islands off completely in the winter time. For many years the only regular contact was the Factor's yearly visit from Skye to collect the rent and to bring any goods ordered the previous year. The Rev. Neil Mackenzie explained the extraordinary situation in the 1830's. "It was at this time that we got our letters and newspapers and small supplies of necessaries. This was our only regular way of maintaining intercourse with the outside world, but at times we got items of news from passing vessels: In 1837 we heard in this way of the death of William IV., and I was not a little horrified to find that I had been praying for him some months after his death. I consequently altered my style of praying, not for any one by name, but for His Majesty the King. When the packet came in autumn, 1838, I found I was not yet right, and that I should have been praying for Her Majesty the Queen. It was very seldom that passing vessels paid us a visit, only indeed when they found themselves out of their course or wanted water. Occasionally a yacht would pay us a visit. At times we had to provide for shipwrecked sailors."

The factor also brought a year's supply of newspapers. Mackenzie recorded his method of reading them. "At this time most newspapers were published only once a week, and it was my custom, after I had heard all the more recent news from our visitors, to take the paper of the corresponding week in the past year, and so on week by week, and in this way spread out my interest in the events recorded as much as possible. One year we had a succession of gales at the time when the yearly packet was on its way to the island, which lasted so long that the crew began to run short of water and provisions, and at last had to return without having been able to effect a landing. As it was getting late in the season they did not attempt to return that year. Consequently we had to do without our usual supply of groceries for the next year."

The isolation was sometimes unbearable. Sands became marooned on the island in 1876 because the vessel which was to return him to the mainland failed to appear. The long winter days dragged on; he was joined by some shipwrecked Austrians, off the Peti Dabrovacki, who in desperation launched the first St. Kilda mail-boat made from a life buoy, a small sail and a bottle enclosing a letter to the Austrian Consul. Surprisingly, the letter reached its destination via the Orkney Islands and the relief ship arrived within 3 weeks of the launching. This was a method of communication which was to be used on several occasions, especially in times of dire need.

The situation was to change with the advent of the steam ships which gave the opportunity for more people to travel. In 1877 the Dunara Castle ran the first Summer Cruise to the Western Isles and St. Kilda, arriving in Village Bay on July 2nd. with about 30 passengers on board. From 1898 the Dunara Castle and the S.S. Hebrides both paid regular visits until 1939, giving the opportunity for the St. Kildans to receive news and to increase their export of eggs, socks, gloves and tweed.

The attempt in 1877 to persuade the Government to provide a regular postal service for St. Kilda failed. Instead small subsidies were paid for services rendered to the trawler skippers from Aberdeen and Fleetwood who sometimes managed to get through in the winter when weather permitted. On the island the minister normally distributed the letters and sent off the mail in an unofficial capacity. However in 1900 the Rev. Angus Fiddes was appointed the first sub-postmaster and subsequently the task was taken over by the resident missionary until Neil Ferguson took the job in 1906 until the Evacuation.

After the desperate winter and spring of 1912 when no mail or supplies could be landed until May, moves were made to acquire a wireless transmitter. One was eventually installed in the Factor's House and was operated for the first time in July 1913; a corrugated iron hut was also erected next to house number 5 to act as the Post Office, only the step and foundations remain to this day. Although the transmitter broke down in October it was serviceable during the winter but its life was short. It was dismantled in the spring due to lack of financial support.

Strangely the First World War was to make a tremendous difference to life on St. Kilda. In January 1915 the Government set up a Signal Station on Hirta near the store-house, giving the people regular contact with the naval ratings who manned it and proved to be extremely kind. After the shelling by the German submarine in May 1918 many more vessels visited Village Bay. These included Naval ships and trawlers from Fleetwood, Hull and Aberdeen, as well as Norwegian Whalers which assembled their catches before leaving for the whaling station on Harris. At last St. Kilda was abreast of the news in the outside world. Free travel on Naval vessels, trawlers and whalers also opened up new horizons with visits to Harris, Lewis and Glasgow.

At the present time, with regular visits of the Army Tank Landing Craft bringing supplies, letters by Air Drop, together with the use of the Army Telephone and a Helicopter in dire emergency, communications are far better than ever before.

LIFE THROUGH THE YEAR

With the Rev. Neil Mackenzie

The Rev. Neil Mackenzie was the Minister on St. Kilda from 1830-1844, during that time he took a great interest in all aspects of life on the islands, primarily caring for the physical and spiritual needs of the people which he did most effectively, but he also made notes about the arrival of the birds, their breeding cycles and their departures. His monthly diary gives a sensitive account of the patterns of life and the hardships in the 1830's.

January. Our coasts continue to be dead, lonely and deserted. Soon they will receive their inhabitants. A gannet has been seen as soon as the 13th of this month. By the beginning of the next month a good number of them will be on their accustomed rocks. Rooks and the blackhood crow are numerous. The latter are very troublesome, taking the thatch off houses, seeking for grains and insects which rest in the thatch. The want of fuel is very much felt. Every good day the natives are from hill to hill, and from crevice to cliff, in search of anything that burns.

February. The shearwater has come to these islands the latter end of this month. One third of all the gannets that arrive this year should now be about our rocks. The black guillemot having assumed the summer plumage is now seen. Our religious meetings have been regularly attended all the season. The scarcity of food and fuel, which is now felt in their intensity, gives a sombre aspect to every thing around us.

March. All the birds are now come except the puffin. Though the last in coming it is first generally that is now caught. Formerly the black and particularly the foolish guillemot used to be very early caught, but their mode of capture being rather more dangerous and certainly more laborious, they discontinued. All the birds are so regular in the time of leaving and coming, laying and hatching, that a kind of calendar might be constructed from their migrations. How well this illustrates the beautiful expression of Scripture, "Yea, the stork in the heavens knoweth her appointed times, and the turtle, and the crane, and the swallow, observe the time of their coming."

April. All classes of sea-fowl are during this month about the island – I mean all such as are accustomed to this coast. About the end of it the puffin, gannet, shearwater, and the black guillemot, begin to lay. No fuel has been got yet; though it should be dry for a few days, there is not a sufficient length of dry weather to dry turf. By the coming of the boat from Harris, and the arrival of the birds, the people's food is greatly improved. Every family got from forty to fifty gannets, besides small fowl. Thanks be to Almighty God for his kindness to us.

May. This is by far the most important season in the year to the fowler. All the birds lay in this month except the stormy-petrel, which lays next month. The reason so many sea-fowl congregate upon our rocky island is to propagate their kind.

June. If deprived of the first laid eggs, that keeps them back two or three weeks, for they take sixteen days to lay a second. And a few – none of the fulmars lay a second egg – will not lay again at all. The people are ill off for fuel yet, they have got little, and still worst off for food.

July. All the birds are rearing their young, except the stormy-petrel, during this month; but that little bird is only beginning to lay about the commencement of it. The people are suffering very much for want of food. During spring, ere the birds came, they literally cleared the shore not only of shell-fish, but even of a species of seaweed that grows abundantly on the rocks within the sea-mark. For a time they were better off particularly as long as fresh eggs could be got. Now the weather is coarse, birds cannot be found, at least in such abundance as their needs require. Sorrel boiled in water is the principal part of the food and even that grass is getting scarce. All that was near is exhausted.

August. In the beginning of this month the guillemots and razorbills left their rocks, having got their young with them; the puffins about the 10th and also the kittiwakes; and towards the end the fulmars, having been robbed of its young.

September. The greater part of the gannets, with the old ones, leave our rocks about the end of this month. All birds leave our rocks as they get their young ones with them. The barley is not half shorn yet, nor the oats. this is decidedly the wettest and windiest season I remember. No fuel is got yet, neither is it likely that any will be this season. How the year is to be gone through I know not. Were it not for the promise that our bread would be given us and our water made sure, we would feel very uneasy.

October. The whole of the gannets are away from our rocks, and even the stormy-petrel. A few gulls, cormorants and black guillemots which turn greyish-white, remain about the shore all year. The fulmar continues coming to land every day the wind is from the west. A species of small duck visit the shores, and now and then an eider-duck. When the weather is stormy, wild geese, and a few straggling swans, may be seen. Our crops are housed. The quantity of straw is large, but the grain very small. Potatoes are very defective, not above half an ordinary crop. No fuel has been got yet. Everything seems to conspire against us this season.

November. This is the deadest month of the year. The bulk of the fowls having deserted our coast leaves the rocks so black and dead. There is a pleasure in seeing any thing move in this more than solitary place. Our minds seem to be revived by seeing a few wild fowls such as swans, geese, woodcocks and snipes, though the most of them pay us but a short visit on their way to more hospitable climes.

December. What has passed of this winter has been rather stormy. All kinds of fowls that come hither to breed are gone, long ago, to their winter quarters. Snipes, wrens, crows, ravens and hawks, remain all the year round. Thrushes, lapwings, curlews, herons and ducks etc., visit us, and some of them remain with us for a long while in the winter. The people have never been worse off for fuel. Last year was not good, but this one turns out a third less.

"Lord, have mercy on us."

*Schoolmaster George Murray, St. Kilda 1886–87.
Photo taken in 1909.*

With George Murray, 1886–87

George Murray was School Master on St. Kilda from June 1886 to June 1887 and he kept a fascinating diary of his experiences and the way of life of the people. Here are a few extracts illustrating the activities in the different months of the year.

July 30   Fishing round Dun in the evening.

    31   Snaring Puffins and catching sheep on Soay.

Aug. 5   "Hebridean" visits with passengers.

    7   Men mending the boat.

  10   Men on Boreray.

  11   I went with the men to Boreray, I shouldered 20 Fulmars and 2 Solan Geese.

  12   Men fowling on the mainland. I fished on the rocks in the evening.

  13   In the evening went to Conachair to see the men fowling.

  14   Set off with a boat round the island to pick up the birds (Fulmars) the men were pitching over the rocks above.

  15   Sabbath. Heard two short English sermons.

  16   Went in the afternoon to the Cambir and killed a good few fulmars. Had the rope on me on the cliffs.

17 Most of the men on the Dun. Went in the evening back to Conachair . . . Went down the steep and brought up burdens.

20 Helped the men in towing in a whale from the Dun, length 28ft.

21 "Dunara" arrived in the afternoon having on board a great number of passengers . . . including 2 doctors . . . one left a box of medicines.

25 Men very busy taking the blubber off the whale.

26 Men at Soay for fulmar. An occasional puffin still seen. Fulmars leaving the island.

27 Held school for 1½ hours and then set out with the men for Soay. On reaching we could not get landed.

28 Very stormy morning . . . Wrote letters to Australia for four parties.

Sept. 2 "Hebridean" arrived . . . the visitors had a proper day of it. They bought a deal of cloth and stockings from the natives.

3 Had no school as I had no less than 23 letters to read for myself besides some through the village.

4 A third sunny day . . . did immense good to the crops. Went with the men to Boreray to catch sheep.

9 Last night was very boisterous . . . the Elements seemed at war with each other. Great damage to the crops. People sick with the 'cuatan' (cold).

11 People cutting barley.

13 Men at Boreray for young Gannets.

14 Went with the men to Boreray, where I saw and took part in the slaughtering of the young Gannets.

16 People busy at harvesting. Yesterday I helped a little at the scythe and today at stacking the barley.

Oct. 1 From the 14th till today we had no rain except a slight shower. On Thurs. 23rd the people started cutting the crops and by Saturday night 25th there was not a sheaf out on St. Kilda. On the 24th. the "Robert Hadden" put into the bay.

4 People cutting hay.

12 People finished cutting the grass and now the cattle are let inside the dyke. Fulmars now begin to return to the island.

13 In the evening I cut down and salted a sheep I bought. I feel desperately sleepy these nights . . . I regret I do not get more reading done.

14 Men, boys and some of the women had a great day at catching the sheep. This lively and exciting work they call "Ruagadh" . . . I found that in every house they were busy slaughtering.

16 Men spending the day at "Ruagadh" the lambs and I set out with them.

18 Listened with more than usual attention to Mr. McKay's afternoon sermon.

19 Men putting lambs onto the Dun and lifting potatoes. The potato crop is very poor, scarcely worth the trouble of lifting.

20 Men at Boreray for the sheep . . . killed a ewe 16 years old.

22 After school I made a bow and arrow for one of the boys and in a few hours every boy in the village had one.

25 Men were engaged in dividing the grass among the rocks.

28 Had no school the latter part of the day as the scholars wanted to leave to go for grass.

30 I went round Osevall for grass.

Nov. 1 Went up the village. The oil in my lamp ran short and I had to borrow a candle to take me home.

3 What a terrible night with wind last night. I really thought the window would be blown in.

15 People were after the poor sheep – these that they do not expect to live, they take home and kill. I went as far as the Cambir. Men went to Boreray and saw one young gannet and two young puffins.

16 Wind and snow. Tops of hills white for the first time this season.

19 Am troubled about a family who are not sending peats to the school as they ought.

24 Last four days wet and misty . . . I improved greatly in my Gaelic since I came to the island.

29 Yesterday there was a baptism in Church, John MacDonald, about sixteen months old.

Dec. 2 Today white with snow. Hard frost last night.

9 The storm continued till about 1.30 this morning, at which time I went to bed. Several stone dykes fell and one house was almost roofed.

14 This morning at 0.30 a.m. was born . . . McKinnon. Parents Neil and Mrs. M.

McKinnon. Child large and very promising. Mother doing well.

18 Great snow storm. Hard frost . . . Today also much drifting.

20 St. Kilda looks well when covered with snow. The people in single file carrying home peats over the white hills presents a a curious spectacle.

22 Mostly all the snow has disappeared. The child that was born a week ago took ill, the jaws fell last night, and it is not expected to live long.

25 Christmas Day. Forenoon snowing heavily. I continued my journey to the "Carn Mor" where I fell in with four men who had gone out for peats and with whom I returned. I cannot help reflecting upon the way and place I used to spend my Xmas holidays . . .

27 Mr. McKay preached yesterday again twice upon the Prodigal Son . . . the sixth sermon on the same subject. Last night at 10.30 the child, after six days intense suffering departed this life . . .

1887

Jan. 1 Another year has run its course. How good the Lord has been to me. 'New Year's Day' in St. Kilda is not held in the new reckoning, so that this day is no different from any other. The men had the lines set last night for ling and this morning they went to lift them . . . They got about twenty ling and as many yesterday.

4 Snow, heavy snow yesterday and very cold. On Sabbath last we had the 7th and 8th sermons on the Prodigal Son. Went today to the top of Conagher. Knee deep in snow there.

Soay Ram.

5	Xmas Day here. Distributed the prizes among the scholars and gave them play for 10 days.
10	Saturday we set out for Soay for sheep for the New Year Feast . . . just 1½ hours on land and in that time caught 20 . . . I am reading Sir W. Hamilton's Lectures on Metaphysics.
17	The bay is one mass of foaming water-waves rolling high and the salt spray driven, I'm sure , half a mile inland.
Feb. 28	A nice girl of ten years is siezed with that terrible disease the 'Lock-jaw' which works such havoc amongst the St. Kildians.
Mar. 5	Beautiful weather since March came in. Oystercatchers came last week. There is much sickness amongst the people at present.
10	Annie Ferguson, after much suffering since this day fortnight, departed this life about 3 p.m. today.
12	Today at 4 p.m., amidst a heavy snow fall Annie Ferguson ages 10½ was buried.
16	Have no School this week owing to the death of the girl.
21	Men still weaving. Ten Guillemots caught on Saturday. They came about the 8th inst.

*View from Boreray on to Stac Lee;
in the distance Soay, right, and the Cambir, left.*

and the Shearwater about the 3rd inst.

28 Up till yesterday the weather was wet and cold. Today mild and calm. Men about finished with weaving.

Apr. 2 Weaving finished a few days ago. Women pulling the cloth. Weather good.

6 Yesterday the minister commenced catechising the people taking five families at a time to the Church.

9 On Thurday 7th I went with the men to Boreray to kill Gannets through the night.

12 Mrs. Ewen Gillies of a son Sabbath 10th. Beautiful weather. Men went to Boreray again last night.

18 Died yesterday at mid-day the child that was born a week ago, of lock-jaw . . .

25 Showers of snow yesterday. Very stormy last night. Hills quite white today. Still (morning) snowing. A bad day for lambs.

May 2 Beautiful weather since middle of last week. People commenced planting the potatoes on Thursday. According to custom they all commenced at the same time. Today they commence the oats.

5 No oats sowed till yesterday the 4th. On the afternoon of the 2nd we went to Boreray, Stack Lee, Stack An Armin for Gannets eggs. It was too early in the Season. Got only about 15 dozen, being 20 eggs per man. No school today as they are busy sowing. Saw the first Fulmar egg of the season. How I long to see the "Robert's" sails in sight!

9 Oat sowing finished today. First Puffin's egg got on Saturday by D. McQueen. Did very little studying of late. Commenced astronomy today.

14 Yesterday I had a great day getting Puffin's eggs in the Dun with the boys. The men were removing the sheep (which had wintered on Dun).

21 Very stormy these last 3 days. Gale still continues. Peat cutting suspended.

28 Lively times at present. On Wednesday 25th we went to Soay for Fulmars . . . Got about 500, and a few eggs (Guillemots and Falca). The Fulmars were all snared on the nest and all the eggs were left in the nests. On Thursday the ewes and lambs were brought to the glen and folded there, where they are milked daily. Today the sheep are to be clipped. I clipped 7 yesterday and learned them the way to use the shears.

June 6 This is terrible. No vessel yet. On Thursday 2nd the men went to Boreray to clip the sheep. The women commenced storing away the peats on Friday, putting them into clacts (stone huts) on the hill.

11 This is almost beyond endurance. Last night the cry was got up that a vessel was come. The place was all astir, but no vessel came. Today the boat is to go to Boreray for the men. They signalled last night that they were finished. This they do by cutting up a large square plot of ground so as to be seen black.

The deserted Village Street, numbers 12-16 of the 1860 Cottages.

LIFE TOWARDS THE END

The Last Inhabitants

The stone shells of the 16 Cottages, built in the 1860's still stand and form the remains of the Village Street; five of these have been re-roofed by the National Trust for Scotland. Walking down the street you cannot help asking, "Who lived here?". Lachlan MacDonald was 24 years old at the evacuation, having grown up in the Village and with people; in 1980 he could still remember vividly the names of the last inhabitants of St. Kilda and the Cottages in which they lived. With the help of notes from the late John Gladstone's diaries we have been able to work out the complicated family bonds. Cottage No.:–

1. *MacKinnons*, Norman and his wife Annie (daughter of Finlay Gillies of No. 7) together with the largest family on St. Kilda – their 8 children – Norman, Donald Ewen, Finlay, Rachel, John, Christine, Mary and Neil. Mr. MacKinnon was considered to be the most skilful tailor on the island, he was also the Precentor at the Church Services. The family had been very short of food in the hard

St. Kilda Parliament of 1927. Photo by Cockburn.
Left to right: Ewan Gillies, Norman MacKinnon (Senior), John Gillies, Ewan MacDonald (above the head of Ewan Gillies),
Donald Gillies (standing), Norman MacQueen (standing), Neil Ferguson (Junior), Neil MacKinnon, Neil Gillies (standing),
Lachlan MacDonald, Donald MacDonald, Norman MacKinnon (Junior), Finlay Gillies, Neil Ferguson (Senior),
Donald Ewan MacKinnon, Malcolm (blind Callum) MacDonald.

131

Finlay MacQueen with a Gannet he had stuffed.
Photo A. A. MacGregor, 1930.

and prolonged winter of 1929-30 and were eager to leave before another one.

2. *MacQueen.* Finlay MacQueen lived alone here, his wife Mary, nee MacKinnon (Mary, Gemima, Otter) had died before the evacuation, his daughter Mary Annie was married to Neil Ferguson, junior; his daughter Annie married Donald Gillies who lived at No. 13. Finlay lived with his son Donald for some time before he left the islands, as did his son Norman and daughters Bessie and Christine. Finlay was a distinguished looking man, tall with a long black beard: he was proud of the puffins and gannets which he himself had stuffed; he was one of Britain's greatest cragsmen and fowlers and was the one who accompanied Heathcote on his visit to the islands and stacs in 1898; understandably he was one of the few who were reluctant to leave Hirta, the scenes of his fabled skills and daring.

3. *Empty.* This had been the house of a remarkable family of MacDonalds who had lived on St. Kilda since 1753. William MacDonald was the first person to evacuate his whole family, which he did in 1924. William had married Mary Ann MacQueen in 1895 and had 11 children, John, Finlay, Annabella, Mary, Mary Betsey, Finlay John, Callum, Kirsty, Rachel, Marion and Mae. His son 'John R' left with him but was to return to live in No.

9. William's father, Neil, had married Isabella Ross Munro, the servant of the Rev. John MacKay, and his grandfather Callum in 1834 had married Betsy Scott from Lochinver, the servant of the Rev. Neil Mackenzie. William himself was a taxidermist and sold specimens to Manchester Museum, he was also the Precentor until he left.

4. *Empty.* This had been the home of Donald Ferguson, whose son Alexander had become a successful cloth merchant in Glasgow, his son Neil became the Postmaster on St. Kilda and his daughter Annie married John Gillies, senior, and another son became a Missionary.

5. *Ferguson.* The home of Neil Ferguson, senior and his wife Annie, the half sister of Finlay MacQueen; also living with them were his son Neil and his wife Mary Annie (MacQueen), the last couple to be married on St. Kilda. Neil, senior, was not only the Postmaster, but also the School Manager, the only Elder of the Kirk, the Flockmaster, Store-owner and Ground-officer of the estate. At the evacuation he took up a job with the Forestry Commission on the Tulliallan Estate.

6. *Empty.* Angus Gillies and his wife Annie had both died well before the evacuation.

7. *Gillies.* Finlay (his wife Catherine and his son Neil had both died previously) lived with Neil's widow

Neil Ferguson, junior, carrying the wool.
Photo by Cockburn in 1927.

Katie and her two boys Ewen and Donald. Finlay had accompanied the Kearton brothers on their visit in 1896 – he was a good man, liked by all, and the oldest inhabitant, being in his 74th. year at the time of the evacuation.

8. *Empty.* Callum MacDonald, often known as "Old blind Callum", had died earlier. He had been married twice, firstly to a cousin, a MacDonald of No. 16 and later to Annie Gillies, a daughter of Norman Gillies and sister of Finlay. His son Donald and daughter Annie both left before the evacuation. He had been a quiet retiring person who took great pleasure in the Sunday Services, in the absence of the Missionary and the Elder he would preach at the Services.

9. *MacDonald.* J. R. MacDonald, the son of William of No. 3, left with the rest of the family, he obtained a job on one of the Drifters but later returned to live here. Also living here were Annie Gillies (Mrs. 'Scalpay' Gillies) whose husband Ewen had died previously in a fall from the rocks beyond Mullach Mor, and her daughter Mary Anne.

10. *Empty.* Donald MacQueen had moved to Glasgow before the evacuation.

11. *MacQueen.* Mrs. Christine MacQueen lived here alone, her husband Norman had been drowned with Lachlan MacDonald's father in a boating accident off Dun. She was Aunt of Norman MacKinnon, senior, and had no children.

12. *Empty.* Ewen Gillies, son of Norman, had lived here until he fell from the rocks, his widow Annie and daughter Mary Anne moved to No. 9.

13. *Gillies.* Donald Gillies, son of John senior, lived with his wife Christine and their two daughters Kathie and Rachel.

14. *Gillies.* Mrs. Annie Gillies, whose husband Donald died of appendicitis on Boreray, lived with her two daughters Rachel and Flora. Their sister Mary died of T.B. in June 1930.

15. *Gillies.* John Gillies, junior, (his wife Mary, nee MacQueen had died earlier) lived with his mother Annie, Queen of St. Kilda (Grannie Gillies), sister of Neil Ferguson, senior; her husband who had died earlier was John Gillies, senior. John Gillies, junior's son Norman John, also lived with them.

16. *MacDonald.* Rachel MacDonald, nee Mac-Kinnon, whose husband Donald died in a boating accident off Dun, lived with her sons Ewen and Lachlan. She was extremely kind and generous. Her son Ewen was chosen by Mathieson to be his companion in his surveying work in 1927, at the evacuation he was leaving the island for the very first time. Of her other children, Rachel had died on St. Kilda, Donald and Angus left, Donald became a

St. Kilda Club Meeting 1977.
Left to right: Làchlan MacDonald, Neil Gillies, Rachel Johnson
(nee Gillies) and Flora Craig (nee Gillies). All born on St. Kilda.

Lay Preacher, Angus died in 1980. Lachlan who was 24 at the evacuation has very vivid memories of life on St. Kilda and returned to visit the island until 1980.

Summary at the time of the Evacuation

Number in the Family	Family	House Number	Members of the Family
10	MacKinnon	1	Norman and Annie, also Norman, Donald Ewen, Finlay, Rachel, John, Christine, Mary Neil.
2	MacQueen	2	Finlay.
		11	Christine.
4	Ferguson	5	Neil, senior and Annie, Neil, junior and Mary Annie.
16	Gillies	7	Finlay, Widow Catherine and boys Ewen and Donald.
		9	Widow Annie and daughter Mary Anne.
		13	Donald and Christine with daughters Kathie and Rachel.
		14	Widow Annie and Rachel and Flora.
		15	John, and mother Annie, and John's own son Norman John.
4	MacDonalds	9	John R.
		16	Rachel and sons Lachlan and Ewen.

Population Decline

Throughout the history of St. Kilda the population has fluctuated considerably from time to time, partly due to disease like cholera and the dreadful outbreak of

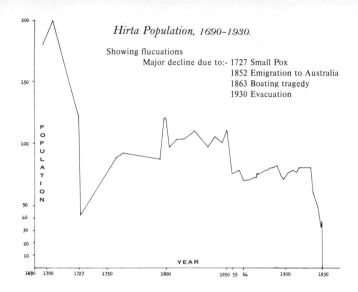

Hirta Population, 1690–1930.

Showing flucuations
Major decline due to:- 1727 Small Pox
1852 Emigration to Australia
1863 Boating tragedy
1930 Evacuation

small-pox in 1727. Boating tragedies reduced the community of the vital man-power on several occasions and during the last 100 years of its occupation emigration to Australia and the Scottish mainland played an important part in the depopulation. In the period between 1856 and 1879 of the 62 babies born, no fewer than 41 died of tetanus. Clegg (1977) points out that in the last 100 years "replacement levels were never sufficient to maintain a constant population size. In the early part of this period the main factor responsible was heavy neonatal mortality, almost all

from tetanus ('eight day sickness'), but latterly the fertility of those who survived was low, even though the mortality rates had declined. In part at least, this decline in fertility could be ascribed to a lower frequency of marriage – a phenomenon seen elsewhere in the Outer Hebrides during the latter part of the 19th. century."

The Evacuation

In an interview with the B.B.C. at the time of the 50th. Anniversary of the evacuation, the Rev. Donald John Gillies, who was born on the island, made the point that, "most of the young people, the moment war was finished left, a dozen in one bunch, and then there was one leaving here and one leaving there. I believe and I'm thoroughly convinced that the evacuation that finally took place in 1930 began in 1915-16." Contact with the armed services and greater communications and links with other visiting vessels widened the horizon of the St. Kildans, many of whom realised that a better life could be obtained on the mainland.

The crunch finally came after the severe and prolonged winter of 1929-30. Neil Ferguson recalled that no mail reached the islands between August and March. "The last winter was the worst ever. For months there had been no contact with the mainland and food was running out." Finally, the islanders persuaded the missionary to write to the Prime

Minister, Ramsay MacDonald, "We are now twelve weeks without news or relief supplies. For weeks all of us have been without sugar or potatoes. Paraffin Oil is running short when we most require it for light to work our looms in the making of Highland Tweed." Towards the end of January Mary Gillies was ill with acute appendicitis, but it was February 15th before a vessel, the Norna, reached the island to take her off. It was too late, she died two days after reaching hospital in Glasgow and the news demoralised the community back on Hirta. The tiny population had struggled to survive under impossible conditions but at last they reached the point of surrender, and on the 10th. of May 1930 wrote to the Rt. Hon. W. Adamson, Assistant Secretary of State for Scotland, "We the undersigned, the natives of St. Kilda, hereby respectfully pray and petition H.M. Government to assist us to leave the island this year, and to find homes and occupations for us on the mainland." The letter continued, describing the islanders' plight in their own words, "Several men out of this number have definitely made up our minds to go away this year to seek employment on the mainland, this will really cause a crisis as the present number are hardly sufficient to carry on the necessary work of the place. These men are the mainstay of the island at present, as they tend the sheep, do the weaving and look after the general welfare of the widows.

The Evacuation. Left: 'Dunara Castle'. Right: 'Harebell'

Should they leave, the conditions of the rest of the community would be such that it would be impossible for us to remain on the island another winter." The letter was signed or marked by 12 of the men.

The population by this time in 1930 had dropped to 36 souls which included 16 Gillies, 10 MacKinnons, 4 MacDonalds, 4 Fergusons and 2 MacQueens. There were also living on Hirta the nurse, Williamina Barclay and the Missionary, Dugald Munro and his wife and two children. The evacuation was to take place later in that year. Most of the sheep and cattle left the island in two shipments, the S.S. Hebrides sailed in July for Tiree and the S.S. Dunara Castle in early August for the markets in Oban. On Wednesday August 27th. at 5 p.m. the Dunara Castle entered Village Bay to collect the remaining sheep with the aid of shepherds brought in from Lewis. They were packed into the rowing boats and towed out by the ships cutter; they also took away 10 cows and 4 calves, the cows having to swim to the awaiting vessel. She also took the bulky luggage, the kists and the furniture, and the last, and possibly the largest bunch of letters to leave the island. On Thursday at 7 a.m. H.M.S. Harebell (the Senior Fishery Protection Vessel) steamed into the Bay to collect the inhabitants and at about 12 noon on the same day the Dunara Castle left for Oban. A final service was held in the Church.

The evacuation of the people took place on the next day, Friday 29th. August 1930. In the early morning Family Prayers were said for the last time in each of the cottages. Bibles were left open on the tables, and at about 7 a.m. the doors were locked for the first and last time in their history. The people made their way down to the jetty where the "Harebell" was awaiting them. Neil Ferguson, senior, was the last to get on board, "I was the last to leave the island . . . I went for a last walk round the Village – it was weird passing the empty houses – it was just like looking into an open grave." By 8.30 a.m. they were on their way, the two Ferguson families and the Missionary were to go on to Oban, while the other families were to disembark at Lochaline where the vessel docked at 6.30 p.m. Some were found accommodation in the Village, others went to Larachbeg, Achabeg, Savaroy and Ardness. All were about to begin a new and very different way of life. One elderly gentleman, as the ship left Village Bay, looked back longingly to the islands and was heard to whisper in Gaelic, "God will help us."

ST. KILDA — FOR THE NATURALIST

ANIMAL LIFE

The isolated position of St. Kilda, separated by 80 km (50 miles) of rough Atlantic from any sizeable land mass, has severely limited the number of species of both animals and plants which have been able to reach the islands, let alone establish a foothold. Amongst the Vertebrates, there is no natural obstacle for Fish, and their huge numbers form the vital food supply for the sea-bird population. With no 'land bridge' in its recent geological history, Amphibians and Reptiles have been unable to colonise St. Kilda – no frogs, toads, newts or snakes and lizards have been recorded on the islands. Of the Birds, only 28 species breed regularly. However, what is lost by the lack of variety is more than compensated by the tremendous density of the population – the vast numbers of individuals, estimated to reach about 1,000,000 visiting St. Kilda in the breeding season. Mammals have only four representatives, one a sea mammal, the Grey Atlantic Seal; two imported for economic reasons, the Blackface and Soay sheep; one which arrived by accident, possibly in a load of hay, the St. Kilda Field Mouse, (the House Mouse now being extinct). Only two wild land vertebrates are to be found, the Soay Sheep and the Field Mouse. The following comparison of species on the Scottish Mainland, the Inner Hebridean Island of Rhum and the Atlantic islands of St. Kilda illustrate the problems faced by the prospective colonisers.

	Mainland	Rhum	St. Kilda
Land Vertebrates	38	9	2
Birds	152	54	28
Plants	850	400	131

In the past the St. Kildans also had horses, cattle, cats and dogs. The fish, the sea-birds and the sheep were all vital for the survival of the human population.

MAMMALS

ST. KILDA FIELD MOUSE (Wood Mouse) – *Apodemus sylvaticus hirtensis*

Field mice are very constant in size, colour and characteristics over the greater part of their range from China westwards, but in the British Isles, the species is represented by distinct forms on St. Kilda, on eleven of the Hebrides and on three of the Shetland group. (Berry, 1979). It was thought that it might have survived the last Ice Age on this remote outpost, but a more reasonable hypothesis postulated by Berry is that "in population language the Scottish island mice are 'Viking Mice'." The consistent similarity between mice

St. Kilda Field Mouse
outside the Factor's House, 1980.

on the Hebridean Islands and Iceland with those Norwegian mainland animals "strongly points to the Vikings as the culprits in introducing the field mice." (Berry, 1977).

In the St. Kilda Field Mouse the lengths of the head, body, tail, hind foot and ears are all longer than in the other British and Icelandic Field Mice. Their weight is 20gm heavier than their Hebridean and British cousins, Males being 32-40gm, heaviest 54gm; Females between 29-38gm, heaviest 48gm (Boyd, 1960), which makes them more like the Norwegian in shape and size. From nose to tail they measure 17-20cm. A few years ago there was no small scare on Hirta caused by a rumour that rats had been seen on the island and if allowed to spread they would be likely to decimate the nesting birds. Fortunately, it turned out to be a case of mistaken identity, the 'rats' were particularly large specimens of the St. Kilda Field Mouse colony near the Army Camp. The coat colour is a peppery-reddish-brown with a dark dorsal line which is well developed, the ventral region is white with brown along the median line. The skull structure shows a number of variants from which it can be distinguished from other Field Mice.

The main concentrations are around the Village, but they are found anywhere on Hirta below 150m as long as they are within the vicinity of dry stone walls, cleitean or houses. They are also found on hill-sides, cliff-faces, and a few have been reported from the top of Conachair, with another discrete community on the boulder beach of Village Bay. They have been found on Dun, but not on Soay or Boreray, although one was taken over to the last island by mistake when a party of St. Kildans landed to collect the birds. There is evidence that the communities above 150m (500ft) may move to lower ground during the winter and return in the spring. They are rarely seen during the day but become active around dusk and during the night, most remaining within 30-90m of their base. In experiments carried out by Boyd and others, mice transported distances up to 500m (1,600ft) were capable of returning in less than 3 hours. Beyond that distance recovery decreased sharply and varied from 3-9 hours.

Food consists mainly of grasses and seeds, but spiders and insects are also taken, some have been reported feeding off the carcases of birds and sheep. They take a delight in supplementing their diet with human left-overs, as well as invading the stores of apples, biscuits and cheese of the residents.

They make poorly developed burrows in the walls of the old thatched houses, cleitean and among the fallen rocks of the pro-talus ridge. The females are pregnant from April to June. Gestation is about 26 days, and the young are weaned at 15 days. Litter size – six or seven.

They have few predators on the islands, just a few breeding Hooded Crows and Gulls. The remains have recently been found in the pellets of visiting birds – Short eared Owl in 1977 and Long eared Owl in 1980. Post mortems have shown that they suffer greatly from endo-parasites which affect the liver and intestines. Altitude, with its increased exposure to the weather has a marked adverse effect on the distribution. Since the islands were designated a National Nature Reserve in 1957 the Army has taken steps to protect the St. Kilda Field Mouse. "Included in the Standing Orders of the Army Unit is a ban on killing mice and on the introduction of pet cats and dogs." (Boyd, 1963).

ST. KILDA HOUSE MOUSE – *Mus musculus muralis*

The St. Kilda House Mouse certainly deserves a mention here, although it is now sadly extinct. It was a sub-species of the Common House Mouse, a smaller cousin of the Field Mouse. The coat colour varied from smoky grey to creamy yellow. The skull had similar characteristics to the House Mouse of the Shetlands and the Faeroes in contrast with those of the rest of Britain. Litter sizes were usually between 6-9. After enjoying life to the full in company with the St. Kildans, when it swarmed all over the houses and cleitean within the cultivated area, it hit hard times when the island was evacuated. Within one year it was reduced to about twelve individuals. Harrisson and Moy-Thomas placed traps in every house and cleitean within the Village in July 1931 but only caught 8 adults, six were females and none were pregnant. These were found in Cottage 8 and 16 where a small amount of flour, fish and sugar had been left. The lack of warmth within the houses, the presence of cats which had been marooned on the island to fend for themselves and a shortage of food greatly reduced their numbers. However, House Mice have survived in the absence of human inhabitants on a number of islands, but not in competition with Field Mice which are quick to disrupt their normal life and take over their habitat. This causes the House Mice to move into other areas and upsets their breeding success so that births become insufficient to replace adults dying from old age. Berry (1977) makes the interesting comparison between the Field and House Mice in a breeding season of similar length, "Field Mice increase their population size by about four-fold, whilst the House Mice increase ten to twenty-fold." Even this rapid breeding rate was unable to save the species in competition with the Field Mice. Within 18 months of the evacuation the House Mouse was extinct.

A naturalist, concerned about the future of the House Mouse at the time of the evacuation, wrote this verse for a newspaper and was quoted by MacGregor (1969), and foretold its untimely fate.

"O what will become of the Post-office Mouse,
   When the Post-office posts no more,
 It will mope, it will mope in the Post-office house,
   And die on the Post-office floor."

Soay Rams in the Village Meadow.

SOAY SHEEP – Ovis aries
Origins.

Soay sheep are one of the most primitive breeds of domesticated sheep in existence, bearing a striking resemblance to the Mouflon (Ovis musimon) of Sardinia and the primitive sheep in Cyprus and Central Asia. How they reached the islands is unknown, but the Vikings probably found them there and gave the name Soay (Sheep Island) to the north west rock. They "may well be direct descendants of the first sheep introduced to the islands in prehistoric times." (Jewell, Milner, Boyd, 1974). Their forebears were probably brought to Britain by Neolithic Farmers. About 200 now live on Soay where they have survived in a remarkable way, unattended by man, at the mercy of the climate and subject to the dangers of inbreeding on this exposed rock, believed to be the least visited island in Britain. The sheep have few predators, just Ravens, Hooded Crows and Greater Black-backed Gulls which attack the weaker lambs.

Hirta Population

The population on Hirta was introduced from Soay by the Marquis of Bute in 1932 when he transferred a balanced flock of 107 Soays which included 20 tups, 44 ewes, and 43 lambs (22 rams and 21 ewes). Since then the numbers have increased but they have varied from being as low as 610 in 1960 to as high as 1783 in 1971. Great losses occur at irregular intervals, due mainly to a hard winter followed by a hard spring, resulting in poor pasture growth and starvation. Adults normally lose 50% of their body weight at this time. Rams are often the worst affected as they do not feed during the rut and enter the winter under-nourished and ill prepared. The 'crash' of 1960 was caused by starvation and enterotoxaemia. In the severe winter of 1978-79 in the Village area alone 50 out of 150 lambs died on their first day due to the lack of milk; many of the ewes carrying twins also died. The lambs are usually born between March and June with most in April and the figures for this month often reflect the pattern of the winter and spring:–

Village Area	Total Number of lambs born in April	Alive at the end of April	Died by the end of April
1978	129	108	21
1979	141	93	48
1980	175	170	5

Soay lambs - figures for April in the Village

Normally, recovery from the 'crashes' is quite quick if the weather is conducive to a good pasture growth as a high percentage of twins are born. 1980 was a good recovery year as the mild winter resulted in a good 'early bite' of grass in January and February enabling

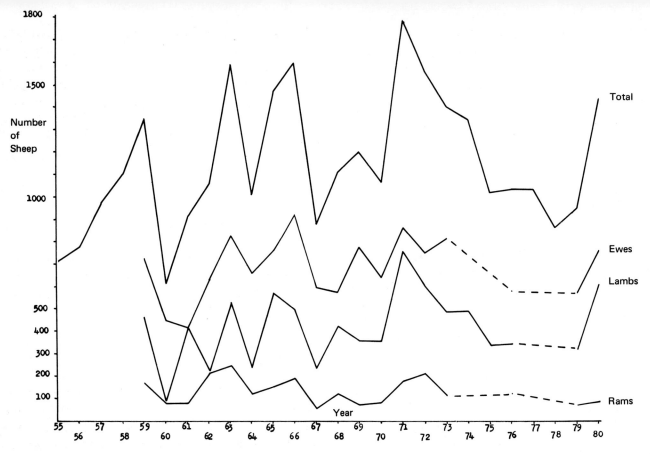

Soay Sheep
Fluctuations in the Hirta Population, 1955-80.

the ewes to be in top condition, in fact only one died in the Village and all the yearlings with their lambs survived – in 1979 all were lost. In 1980 no lambs were lost to Ravens or Hooded Crows as they were so much bigger and healthier.

Occasionally triplets are born, Wally Wright, the Nature Conservancy Warden could only remember one set during the last few years. Macaulay, writing in 1764 recorded how one ewe increased the flock by 9 in 13 months; the ewe had triplets, and the next year she had triplets again and each of her yearlings had one lamb each: The lambs in Glen Bay are often born two weeks earlier than those in the Village, in 1980 they began in mid-March. This is thought to be due to the better pasturage and the smaller number of sheep per hectare.

The Flocks

The Soay sheep on Hirta have formed themselves into separate flocks which keep themselves apart, the Village flock does not mix with those on Ruaival, the slopes of the Lover's Stone nor those on the Cambir or in Gleann Mor. The separate flocks have within them two social units, the adult males go about in 'ram groups' of 6–10 composed of three years olds and above. The other unit is the 'ewe group' which consists of ewes, their lambs and some young adult males.

Between 1964-67, 10 'ewe groups' were identified in the Village area varying in number between 2 and 69 individuals, with a mean between 27-37. Within the 'ewe group' there are family units made up of a ewe with her own lambs which normally stay together for 2-3 years. At this stage they will separate but remain within the larger 'ewe group'.

The separate flocks or 'sub-population' are divided into their distinct units by areas of poor grazing, sometimes by rocky spurs or precipitous cliffs. The sheep are concentrated on the island's grasslands; in spring the rams show a marked preference for the steep grassy cliff slopes around the coasts, whereas the ewes with their lambs are well scattered but have their own concentrations in the Village Glen, which holds the largest flock, with others on Ruaival, the Lover's Stone slopes, the Cambir and Oiseval.

Breeding Cycle

Since the previous rutting season, the 3 year old rams and the older ones have been together in their social groups of about 6-10. The beginning of the Autumn initiates a period of intense activity as the group gradually breaks up into smaller units and then into individuals. They begin fighting and displaying to each other in the form of nudging, also blocking, rubbing and head butting, often followed by the victor's chase of the vanquished. A ewe will only be receptive for a period of 1-2 days, normally, with a possible range of 4 days. At this time a ram will somtimes accompany her for a whole day, keeping away other contenders, in one case mating occured 8 times in 8½ hours and on the next day the same ram tended 6 ewes and attempted to mate on 13 occasions. At this time the family units are temporarily split up but they are soon reunited. The rut takes place in October and November, and the gestation period lasts 148-155 days (mean 151.15 days) and 50% of the lambs will be born within a 7 day period. At the time of birth the ewe will separate from her family unit either into an open place or near to a wall or cleit. During the first few days the lambs will only move a few hundred metres or so, then the ewes begin to lead them to higher ground; those born in the Village meadows will move up through the Village and the Head Dyke into the Old Village. The ewe with her lambs will stay together for 2-3 years as a family unit.

Daily Movements

During the summer the sheep spend the night in the shelter of a cleit or a wall in an up-slope area; at daybreak they collect into their social group and move downhill to the low lying meadows where grazing begins before they disperse. After this they rest and ruminate. In the afternoon they gather together to

Soay Lamb in the Village Meadow.

work their way up the slope, grazing as they go, tending to follow the same routes each day, grazing different plant communities at different times of the day. Rams were observed to be later in coming down in the mornings and first to ascend in the evening! (Grubb P and Jewell, Chapt 7. Jewell, Milner, Morton Boyd, 1974). In the depths of the winter movement is greatly restricted, the sheep only emerging from the shelter of their cleitean to graze in the neighbouring area.

Food

(a) Selectivity. Studies on the Cambir have shown

that from February to May the total amounts of each species of grass for grazing is low and there is no evidence for selection or rejection of individual species. Later in the year, however, from June to August when there is abundant growth and availability of all the species, the sheep show a clear preference for Smooth Meadow Grass (Poa pratensis) and particularly Red Fescue (Festuca rubra), these are selected, whereas they strongly reject the Bents (Agrostis sp.), and Yorkshire Fog (Holcus lanatus) in the Village. From August to January, Red Fescue and Yorkshire Fog reach a peak intake on the Cambir. In the Village Glen, Heather (Calluna) is grazed during this period. Mat Grass (Nardus stricta), sedges and rushes are grazed during their growing period from April to June, and provide winter feed at the time of greatest scarcity from December to March. Other grasses, lichens and mosses are taken at this time to supplement the meagre diet.

The total figures for the whole year reveal that the sheep select the Meadow Grass and Red Fescue which are "fine leaved, glabrous and, on Hirta, rather succulent species. Yorkshire Fog (Holcus lanatus) is hairy and rather coarse, and growing mainly between tussocks of other species suffers damage from trampling and manuring. Fine Bent (Agrostis tenuis) is normally regarded as a desirable species on hill land, but in the particular circumstances of Hirta assumes a form which in the Village area at least is almost completely rejected by the Soay sheep." (Milner and Gwynne Chapt 11. Jewel Milner and Boyd, 1974).

(b) Winter. Milner and Gwynne have calculated that in the months of December, January and February and March the availability of grazing material is insufficient to maintain the sheep and to allow a small increase in body weight, except for those living on the Lover's Stone slopes. Those in the Village with their high density are certainly short of food, and go through the winter in a poor state and in consequence suffer many more deaths than anywhere else on the island. There is low availability during the winter and early spring just when their demands are greatest in terms of survival and embryonic growth in the ewes. The vegetation in the Village Glen recovers much more slowly than on the Cambir, a sudden increase occurs on the Cambir around April 19th (in 1966) which is not matched until June 9th in the Village. This is probably due to the high density grazing, causing severe defoliation and poor storage in the roots and therefore slow growth in the following spring.

Horn Growth

The growth of horn in the rams is most marked in the first year, but the rate decreases during the summer and ceases during the winter giving rise to clear growth rings which can be used to age the rams; the older the ram the smaller the size of the most recent rings. With the ewes the situation is quite different as only about half of them have horns, and the rings of these animals often cannot be distinguished from the normal corrugations within a single years growth and therefore is quite unreliable in attempting to age them.

Coat Colour and Life Span

The colour of the coat varies from light to dark brown and black, with three times as many dark animals as light coated ones. The casting of the fleece begins at the end of April, the process lasting quite a long time and continues during May and into June in many of the individuals.

The greatest periods of mortality are at birth and during the first winter. The rams which survive may live until they are over five and the ewes until they are over ten.

Ownership

It was estimated that on Soay in 1861 there were about 300 sheep, it had been grazed by the families who had emigrated to Australia in 1856; and "when they left St. Kilda, the stock was purchased by the proprietor, and was held in "steel-bow" by the other tenants – that is, they had to return their equivalent in quantity and quality at the end of the lease." (Seton, 1878).

SCOTTISH BLACKFACE AND OTHER SHEEP

Soay sheep were the earliest breed, not only on Soay but also on Hirta; a later import was the old Four Horned Hebridean Sheep, which became known as the 'St. Kilda Sheep'. During the 18th. and early 19th. centuries the Dunface or Old Scottish Shortwool appears to have been the main breed, but in 1872 the Scottish Blackface (originally from the Pyrenees) and the Cheviot stock were introduced and the St. Kildans managed about 1,300 of which 500-600 were on Hirta and the rest on Dun and Boreray. Being larger than the Soay and having a longer fleece they were able to resist the elements with less heat loss and proved to be extremely hardy. The St. Kildans used the milk for cheese when mixed with cow's milk, and the wool for clothing which the men wove during the long winter. In the summer the men made brief visits to Boreray to attend the Blackface sheep which are still there to-day. Mathieson made the comment that, "Sheep shearing consists of pulling the wool off the sheep if it is loose, if not, it is cut with a knife. A St. Kilda sheep after being sheared in this way is the ugliest animal I have ever seen." In 1930 almost all the improved stock was taken from Hirta to be sold in Oban and Tiree. Only a few missed being captured and some of their descendants can be seen today.

GREY ATLANTIC SEAL – *Halichoerus grypus*

This magnificent seal, superbly adapted to ride out the roughest sea, is one of the rarest of the family of seals. With the evacuation of the islands by man the Grey Atlantic Seal moved in as a breeding species, as it did on Rona and the Monachs. The resident population is estimated at 300-400 with the main concentrations in Glen Bay, Soay Sound and on both sides of the neck leading to the Cambir. Here they rest lazily on warm summer days, hauled out on the rocks, their mournful cries echoing in the sea-caves below. Others peer out of the breaking waves at Geo nan Ron, while a few enjoy the racing tide in the tunnel below Gob na h-Airde.

Calves with thick, creamy, fluffy fur and weighing 15kg are born between October and November, mainly on Dun (30 in 1957, 100 in 1958, fewer now due to the disturbance of man), at Mol Ghiasgar and at Mol Shoay. Between the Evacuation and the erection of the Army Camp some calves were born on the beach below the Manse. They are weaned at 2-3 weeks, having been suckled about every two hours on the richest milk and increased in weight by 1½kg each day until they are about 30-40kg. During the third week they shed their coat, the females replacing it with a blue coat and the males with a dark grey or black coat. At this stage they are abandoned by the cows, and make their own way down to the sea in about a week, where they will feed and fend for themselves. After the weaning is over, the adults mate, the bulls having selected a harem of up to 20 cows. Young cows reach breeding maturity at 5 years and the bulls at 6 years. In

Grey Atlantic Seals – Cow and Bull.

Grey Atlantic Seals
hauled out on the rocks to the west of the Cambir.

Martin's day and subsequently a few were taken and were considered to have very good meat, and the skins were used to help to pay the rent.

A visitor to the islands in 1799 described the risky method employed by the St. Kildans in killing the seals in a sea cave on Soay. "There is a remarkable creek resorted to by a vast number of seals. The method of destroying them is as follows. The natives approach the mouth of it which is very narrow, in one of their boats with as little noise as possible and leaving the boat at the mouth, they rush in with large clubs with which they knock down the seals. They, however, sometimes perish themselves in the attempt, for as they never make the attempt except when the wind is easterly, so if the wind happens to change before they retire, the sea rolls into the creek with such violence that the boat and all in her inevitably perish. They used formerly to pay a considerable part of their rent in the skins of these animals, which however, are not found in such numbers now."

Rae (1960) found a varied collection of food taken by the seals – cod, saithe, ling, conger, 'toad-fish', lump suckers, crustaceans, mackerel, skate, ray, dogfish, salmon, sea-trout, halibut, herring, cuttlefish, squid, octopus, lythe, flat fishes, mussels, bib, haddock, whiting, pilchard, brill, wrasse, bass, grey mullet and seaweed.

BIRDS

SEA-BIRDS AND THE ST. KILDANS

St. Kilda has been renowned for centuries for its vast sea-bird colonies from which the inhabitants obtained most of their food. When Martin visited the islands in 1697 he reckoned that his party alone, comprising 70 souls, consumed 16,000 eggs in 3 weeks and that the St. Kildans, man for man, ate many more. He saw 29 baskets of eggs brought down from the rocks in one morning, each held between 400 and 800 eggs. For the birds to survive such human predation indicates that the takings represented only a small fraction of the total population.

Today St. Kilda is one of the most important sea-bird sanctuaries in the North Atlantic with approximately one million individual birds, which includes 18 species of sea-birds and at least 260,000 occupied nests. Harris (1978) elaborates on this, "By far the most important is the gannet, as about 37% and 25% of the British and North Atlantic populations are on Boreray and the Stacs (Cramp et al, 1974). The 300,000 pairs of puffins constitute about half the British total . . . Even following the dramatic spread of the fulmar, St. Kilda is still the single largest colony, with some 13% of the British birds. No estimates are available for the numbers of nocturnal petrels, but the islands must have one of the largest concentrations of storm petrels in Britain and one of the very few colonies of Leach's petrel in the eastern Atlantic which can rank with those in North America."

Nelson (1978) sums up the importance of the seabird colonies to the St. Kildans in the following way. "St. Kilda is the name above all others in the annals of seabird exploitation. There, the entire community built their physical and cultural life around this resource, much as the Bedouins have built theirs around the camel or the Eskimos the animals of the Arctic." On 24th. June 1869 an Act of Parliament was passed for the Preservation of Sea-Birds, naming 32 species, which included the puffin, guillemot, shearwater, fulmar and gannet, stating that from 1st April to 1st August these birds were not to be slaughtered – the penalty of £1 would be extracted from any contravener. Fortunately, for the St. Kildans an extra clause was added declaring that the operation of the Act "shall not extend to the islands of St. Kilda", the reason being, "the necessities of the inhabitants." (Seton, 1878).

ST. KILDA WREN AND OTHER BIRDS

ST. KILDA WREN – *Troglodytes troglodytes hirtensis*

The St. Kilda Wren was described as a distinct sub-species in 1884 by Seebhohm; it shows a tendency with

St. Kilda Wren on Dun.   Photo – C. P. Quine.

many Hebridean birds to be darker than its mainland relatives. The Hebridean Wren (T. t. hebridensis) was separately named by Meinertzhagen in 1924 because it showed characteristics intermediate between the Shetland Wren (T. t. zetlandicus) and the Scottish mainland form, but the St. Kilda Wren is a greyer and more barred form, similar to the Fair Isle (T. t. fridariensis) off the Shetlands. Berry (1979) concludes "While it could be maintained that the convergence between the St. Kilda and Fair Isle races is adaptation towards life on a small exposed island . . . it seems more plausible to argue that the distinguishing characteristics of the four sub-species arose from genes fortuitously carried by the original founders."

At around 4 a.m. from May to mid-June the male St. Kilda Wren will be singing his heart out perched on top of an old chimney stack or on the end wall of a cleit. The song is faster, sweeter, more vibrant and higher pitched than the mainland species. It is remarkable to find this tiny, weak flying woodland species surviving and flourishing on such treeless and wind-swept islands. But such is this sub-species. It is slightly larger and greyer and more barred than its close relatives, with a longer beak. Its habitat varies from the comparative protection of the Village where there are usually 6-12 pairs, to the cliffs of Conachair, Dun and the exposed island of Boreray. Three pairs regularly nest among the broken rocks on Stac an Armin. The main concentrations are to be found on Carn Mor, the Mullach Bi coastline and the grassy gullies of Oiseval.

There is no shortage of nest sites in the ruined houses, cleitean and in the crevices in the walls. However, 80% of the nests are hidden among the boulders of the cliff faces. James Fisher (1951) recorded, "The wrens nest among the steepest cliffs, at the bottoms and the tops of the precipices and slopes. In this steep ground they are not easy to find." The adults use about 200 pieces of grass and moss in the construction of their nest in which 4-6 eggs are laid. Incubation is carried out by the female only. She does this in short spells of 6-25 minutes at a time, then she leaves to feed and returns within 3-7 minutes (Waters, 1964). After 20 days the eggs hatch, normally within 24 hours of each other, usually between mid-July and early August. The shells are soon removed some distance away from the nest. The eyes of the young open at about 5 days. At this time there is a lull in the singing as all the energy of both birds is required to obtain enough food for the brood. Two days after hatching the adults will return to the nest about 10 times each hour: by the time the nestlings are 10 days old the visits will be stepped up to between 20 and 30 per hour. The young are fledged at 16-17 days. Their food consists mainly of small beetles, flies, centipedes, earwigs, larvae, spiders and occasionally small seeds.

By 1894 it was thought that there were only 15 pairs left, many eggs had been taken and sold to visitors and adults were being killed to add to people's collections. In 1904 a special Act of Parliament was introduced by Sir Herbert Maxwell and passed for the protection of the Wren and also the Leach's Petrel. By 1931 the numbers had increased to 68 pairs, 45 on Hirta (12 in the Village); 11 on Dun, 9 on Soay and 3 on Boreray. Further counts in 1938, 48, 49 recorded 12 pairs in the Village also. The species now seems secure with a total population of 100-125 pairs in a good year on the whole island group.

OTHER BIRDS

Also to be found within the Village area are Snipe (Capella gallinago), often peering down from the chimney stacks and cleitean, and nesting in the bracken in the meadows; it is thought that they have colonised Hirta from the Faeroes. Small groups of Starlings (Sturnus vulgaris) are constantly on the move with 100-200 pairs breeding, a few Collared Doves (Streptopelia decaocto) are often seen, and Oystercatchers (Haematopus ostralegus), some 50 breeding pairs on Hirta, are always emitting their noisy alarm calls.

Further away from the Village, Wheatears (Oenanthe oenanthe) use the walls of the cleitean and sheep fanks for their nests, pairs vary from 6-50 in different years, a few pairs of Meadow Pipits (Anthus pratensis) breed in most years, less than 20 pairs, whereas often 100 pairs of Rock Pipits (Anthus spinoletta) nest on Hirta. A few Swifts (Apus apus) carry out their aerial manoeuvres over the cliffs and an occasional Swallow (Hirundo rustica) pays a visit. A pair of Whimbrel (Numenius phaeopus) often breed and several Curlews (Numenius arquata) are present in most months, as well as a few Golden Plover (Charadrius apricarius) which occasionally breed on the moorland and Turnstones (Arenaria interpres) are seen on the rocks at sea level all the year round. About

Great Skua in Gleann Mor.

12,000 pairs of Kittiwake (Rissa tridactyla) have their precarious cliff colonies on Hirta (5,500 nests), Dun, Soay, Boreray and the Stacs.

Predators are surprisingly scarce, especially when one realises that the Bonxie or Great Skua (Stercorarius skua) did not breed until 1963, since then numbers have steadily increased to 20 pairs in 1978, 28 in 1979, and 36 in 1980 on Hirta, as well as nests on Soay. Ravens (Corvus corax) are frequently seen over Conachair with 3-6 pairs normally breeding on Hirta with another pair on Dun and almost certainly pairs on Soay and Boreray; some 4-10 pairs of Hooded Crows (Corvus cornix) breed. There are between 50-80 pairs of nesting Greater Black-backed Gulls (Larus marinus), a bird detested by every St. Kildan and exterminated on sight, on the island group; about 150 pairs of Lesser Black-backed Gulls (Larus fuscus) nest mainly in Gleann Mor with very few Herring Gulls (Larus argentatus), 40 pairs on Hirta, 24 on Dun and about 10 pairs on Boreray and only 3-4 on Soay. There is a resident population of less than 100 Herring Gulls present in the winter, 850 Greater Black-backs have been counted at this time but no Lesser Black-backs. In 1980 a single pair of Common Gulls (Larus canus) reared one young on the lower slopes of Oiseval, near the Village, the first for many years.

There are no resident Eagles (although Sea Eagles

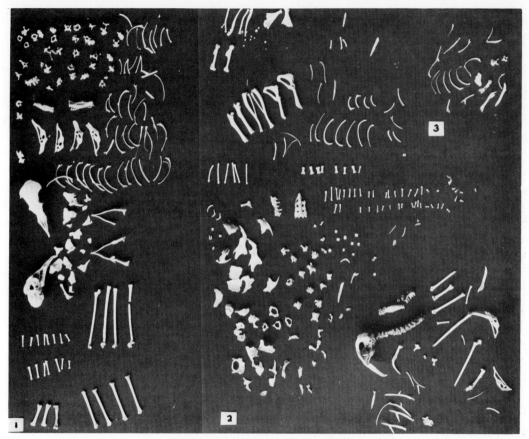

Contents of 3 Pellets of a Long-eared Owl
found on Conachair in 1980. Includes 3 Storm Petrel skulls and bones of the St. Kilda Field Mouse.

used to breed), Buzzards, Hawks, Falcons or Owls. There were 3 pairs of Peregrine Falcons (Falco peregrinus) in 1928, 2 pairs in 1934, but none since 1939 except for an occasional winter visitor, although a pair were prospecting the northern cliffs in 1980. Merlin (Falco columbaris) visit in the spring, one stayed during April and May 1979 feeding on Redwings until they left for their northern breeding grounds. A Rough Legged Buzzard (Buteo lagopus) is sometimes seen. There are several records of Short Eared Owls (Asio flammeus) on Hirta mostly in May; three fresh pellets of a Long Eared Owl (Asio otus) found in July 1980 contained skulls and other bones of 3 Storm Petrels and 1 St. Kilda Field Mouse. An occasional Snowy Owl (Nyctea scandiaca) visits the islands, one staying for 2 weeks in April 1979.

Shags (Phalacrocorax aristotelis) are seen all the year round and breed in large numbers. Cormorants (Phalocrocorax carbo) are only rarely seen. About 50 pairs of Eider Ducks (Somataria mollissima) nest but comparatively few young survive the predatory gulls and skuas.

MIGRANTS

Harris (1978) points out that, "Owing to the isolated position of the islands, the only regular migrants are the relatively few species which nest in Iceland and Greenland. In spring, Wheatear, Meadow Pipit, White Wagtail and Geese are common and there are usually a few Ducks, Swans, Merlin, Dunlin, Redshank and Common Gulls. In autumn the same three passerines and redwings are common, and there are usually a few Ringed Plover, Dunlin, Sanderling and Ruff. Most other species can be regarded as lost individuals, either overshooting mainland Britain during their spring migration (e.g. Hirundines, Warblers, Chats, Spotted Flycatcher), or being drifted westwards towards the open Atlantic by easterly winds with overcast skies in the autumn (e.g. Willow Warbler, Pied Flycatcher, the less common Warblers)." In the best year only 113 species have been recorded.

The following birds were recorded in April 1980:–

Laughing Gull	Chiff-Chaff
Upland Gull	Brambling
American Green Winged Teal	Robin
Eider	Snow Bunting
Pintail	Whimbrel
Mallard	Curlew
Pinkfooted Goose	Dunlin
Greylag Goose	Golden Plover
Barnacle Geese	Wheatear
Peregrine Falcon (Pair)	House Martin
Merlin	Swallow
Ring Ouzel	Redwing

GANNET – *Sula bassana*

The St. Kildans called the Gannet, 'Suleire', the sharp-eyed. John Ross the school-master in 1889 observed, "He is an elegant diver and must be sharp sighted as he sometimes makes a perpendicular dart down upon his prey from a height of fully 30 feet. It is easy to tell from what direction the wind blows when this bird is seen fishing as he always rises off the water with his head into the wind." The most recent count for Boreray and the two Stacs is 59,000 pairs nesting, none breed on Hirta or the other islands. These magnificent white birds with contrasting black wing tips, and nearly 2m wing span travel large distances in small parties to their fishing grounds. They are frequently found in the Sound of Harris and off the shores of the Long Isle and far beyond to Dunvegan Loch on Skye (144km, 90 miles) where they dive for mackerel, and also take coalfish, haddock, pollack, whiting and sprats. They are beautifully adapted for fishing by their 'plunge diving' method from a height of up to 50m. Their whole body is streamlined, the skull is specially strengthened, nostrils hidden and they have well developed air sacs in the neck to cushion the impact of hitting the water at great speed. Buchanan (1793) recorded a most unusual incident when the tacksman was sailing to St. Kilda and passed over a shoal of fish where the gannets were fishing. One gannet had selected a fish and had begun its dive when the fish passed under the boat and "rushing so violently through the air, instead of the fish, darted his strong bill quite through the barge, and was actually carried back to Harris dead, with his bill through the plank, as a testimony to the fact."

Breeding

A few adults return to their breeding sites in early January, by the end of February about a third of the total population will be in the vicinity, and the numbers continue to build up throughout March. It was in March that the St. Kildans made their sorties to the Stacs to collect the adults by night. Later in the season the sloping upper parts of the Stacs and every available ledge and corner are white with the Solan Geese (Gannets), sitting on their nests. Copulation takes place at the nest site or in 'clubs'. "On a quiet Spring day the colony is full of the sound of pattering feet, departure-groans and the strident calls of birds coming in with nest material." (Nelson, 1978). The adults have an impressive greeting ceremony at the nest site as they shake necks and bills, tucking them under each wing, one after the other, and then rattling their bills together in a friendly sword fight. Neighbouring gannets are often very argumentative and aggressive towards each other, Tom Weir made the observation "If the gannets are not quarrelling, they are about to!" When disturbed

157

Gannets displaying on Boreray.

during the breeding season the air is literally filled with a blizzard of gannets.

Egg laying begins in early May and incubation of the single egg lasts about 6 weeks and is shared by both adults, keeping the egg warm under their feet as they have no brood patch. At this time the St. Kildans would collect thousands of eggs from Boreray and Stac an Armin, but not normally from Stac Lee as they wanted all the young to be ready at the same time for the Harvest. On hatching the young are fed on partly digested fish which they take out of the gullet of the adult. At 11 weeks they are deserted by the parents, the time when the St. Kildans would strike again; normally the large speckled fledglings wait for another 10 days or so before launching themselves from the cliff ledge and glide their way down to the sea. Being too heavy to take off they will remain on the water until they have fasted and lost sufficient weight to enable them to become airborne when they will begin to fish for themselves.

The young migrate furthest in their first year to winter off the coast of West Africa, older birds simply disperse through home waters during the winter. They acquire their full adult plumage in their 4th year but do not breed until they are 5 or 6 years old.

Gannet Harvest

Weather permitting the St. Kildans would collect

Gannets nesting near the summit of Boreray.

Photo – R. Castro.

the adults in March or April, the eggs in May and the young between August and October. Donald Og, a good cragsman in his day but later crippled by an accident, gave this account of taking the adults in March to Sands in 1876. "About the middle of March the St. Kildians launch their boat and go to Boreray and Stack Armin to catch the old birds in the dark. Two men fastened at either end of a rope ascend the rocks, and on all fours crawl along the ledge where the geese are resting. The latter have always a sentinel posted, who, if he thinks all is well, cries "Gorrok! Gorrok!" on hearing which the fowlers advance; but if the sentinel cries "Beero!" the men remain motionless, with their bonnets drawn over their brows and their faces on the rock. If the sentinel fancies it was a false alarm, and cries again "Gorrock!" the first fowler progresses until he is near enough to grasp the sentinel, and twist his powerful neck. The sentinel gone the whole flock fall into a state of panic and bewilderment. But it sometimes happens that the whole troop takes flight with a "Beero! hurro! boo!" when the men have to crawl back without any game for that night." (Sands, 1878).

This was a time of great excitement, the winter was nearly over, there would be the opportunity of fresh food; it was time to make the necessary preparations.

"Away bent spade, away straight spade.

Away each goat and lamb;

Up my rope, up my snare, –
I have heard the gannet upon the sea."

(MacCrimmon, late 1700's)

Sometimes the Missionary would join the expedition, occasionally this brought added hazards as recorded by Lachlan MacDonald. "You have to be awful quiet when you get out of the boat; no noise at all as you climb. You see the watchman Gannet, and that's the one you make for. The Missionary got it right enough, but he hadn't the knack of killing it by twisting the neck. The Gannet started 'Ka-Ka-Ka' and all the birds were flying, and the stones came rattling down and the folks were in danger. He got a good telling off!"

Connell (1887) recalled an expedition in 1886, conditions on this particular night were poor and the 3 men took 160 adults, "On a favourable night three expert fowlers have no difficulty in killing thrice that number. In all more than 500 birds were killed that night, and there was naturally, great rejoicing at the success of the expedition when the party returned in the morning to St. Kilda." (see also sections on Bird Fowling, Boreray and the Stacs).

Martin claimed that in his day, in 1697, the St. Kildans would keep 20,000 young and adult birds in their cleitean for the winter, they were plucked and gutted but not salted. In later years the natives bought salt from the Factor; the eggs were simply preserved in the ashes of peat for several months. They not only ate the young and adult birds but boiled up the fat into a gruel, "which they called 'brochan' and drank for removing the cough." The number of birds taken decreased after Martin's time – the late James Fisher considered his figures were exaggerated. By the 1830's Mackenzie recorded that never more than 5,000 young were taken, and often the number was 2,000 or less. By 1900 the raids were beginning to stop as the St. Kildans concentrated on the more accessible Fulmars, only 300 were taken in that year; in 1910 about 600 adults were taken but no young were caught, and after 1910 gannet taking seems to have petered out altogether.

Salted 'gugas', the young Gannets, "are clearly an acquired taste, for while one islander extols them to me as 'not unlike good kippers', Dr. Morton Boyd finds them 'more akin to a rather tough goose that has been pickled in cod liver oil for at least a year!" (Murray, 1973).

No part of the Gannet was ever wasted, some bones were used for spoons, its wings tied together for brooms to sweep out their houses, the neck and head skins were used for shoes, feathers sold for bedding, oil for lamps, flesh for food, inedible parts for manure and their beaks for pegging down their thatched roofs.

Fulmar on nest at the Gap.

FULMAR – *Fulmar glacialis*

The Fulmar was known to the St. Kildans by the name, 'Grey Fowl'. Fulmar from Norse Fyl-mar = vomiting man! (from its protective method of spitting oil).

Population

At present about 20,000 pairs of Fulmars nest on Hirta, of which 6,000 are on the cliff ledges of Conachair, and an estimated 44,000 pairs on the St. Kilda group of islands. St. Kilda had been the only breeding station south of Iceland and the only one in Europe until in 1878 it colonised the cliffs of Foula in the Shetlands. During the last 100 years its spread has been dramatic with nesting sites scattered right round the British Isles and across to Norway. The Fulmar is rarely away from the islands, just leaving at the end of August after the breeding season and returning in late October or early November. On land they shuffle around awkwardly, but, "They are masters of the air, planing effortlessly over the wave crests or hanging motionless, steering themselves with their webbed feet, in upcurrents along the cliff faces." (Cramp et al, 1974).

Breeding

The Fulmar does not normally breed until its 7th. year, adults will be inspecting possible sites from November and December, the numbers increasing as the winter goes on; their main display consists of prolonged bouts of cackling to each other which they engage in at the site and also on the sea. Copulation has occurred at or near the nest site on the few occasions it has been observed. Some of the nest sites are easily accessible, some on ledges with vegetation, some preferring an overhang above, others nest among boulders and some take over a cleit, but the vast majority choose a cliff ledge or crevice where the single white egg is laid. Most of the eggs are laid between May 12-14th., when robbed they are not replaced, for this reason, although they are very palatable, only a few were taken. After laying the egg the female incubates it for a few hours before handing over to the male who begins a marathon stretch of 7-11 days. After this period, the incubation is shared by both adults in spells of about 4 days at a time until the egg hatches at about 7 weeks. The young take a further 7 weeks before being fledged. Ringing has shown that the young disperse as far as Newfoundland, the Barent's Sea and the Bay of Biscay, while the older birds are found mainly in Western European Waters.

Fulmar Harvest

Hatching usually occurs around June 26th. or soon after, and the St. Kildans kept a close watch on their development in order to select the right day for the start of the young Fulmar Harvest. It usually began on August 12th. or a few days later and lasted about 8-10 days. Lachlan MacLean, writing in his book of 1838, gives this account, "The young Fulmar is valued by the natives more than all the other tribe of birds taken together; it may be said to be their staff of life; they therefore never meddle with the egg. The twelfth of August, if a notable day on the moors is more so on the rocks of St. Kilda. A day or two before every rope is tested, every oil dish cleaned, and every barrel emptied. Some of the ropes are older than their owners, and are chiefly made of thongs of cow-hide, salted and twisted into a cable. The twelfth arrives, the rope is made fast round the waists of the heavier party, whilst the other and lighter party is let down the perpendicular rock several hundred feet. Here the work of destruction goes on night and day for a given space; the St. Kildan man has nothing to do but to take the young Fulmar, wring his neck, and then suspend him by a girth he wears round his loins. This is the harvest of the people of St.

Fulmar Harvest in 1884.   *Photo by G. W. Whyte.*

Left to right:– Angus Gillies, Malcolm MacDonald, Donald MacDonald, Finlay Gillies, Donald MacQueen, Malcolm MacDonald, Mrs. Donald MacQueen, Neil MacDonald, John Gillies, Neil MacKinnon, Donald Ferguson, Norman Gillies, Finlay MacQueen, John MacKinnon (on Stone), Mrs. Donald MacDonald (extreme right).

Kilda. They are aware it is to last only eight days, and therefore sleep is banished for this space. The number killed in this one week may be from eighteen to twenty thousand. They are from two to three pounds in weight, about 200 will go to fill a herring barrel; yet each family, after serving the poor, shall have from four to five barrels salted for winter use." (MacLean, 1838).

Everyone in the Village was involved, going to the rocks where the men were not only lowered to the ledges to kill the young but also at the same time to extract ½ pint, 300ml of oil from each bird. "When

Exporting Fulmar Oil.

Photograph by Heathcote, 1898.

genuine it is a clear dark, slightly reddish sherry colour, and has a powerful and peculiar odour . . . it is certainly a fish oil, and it possesses nearly all the properties of cod liver oil." (Stanfield E.C.C. in Gray, 1871). Seton (1878) explains how the oil is obtained, "The oil is extracted from the stomachs of both the old and young birds, and enclosed in long distended bags, formed from the stomachs of old solan geese. The receptacle is held open by one man while another, squeezing the body of the fulmar, forces the oil through its gaping bill." In 1875 the community exported no less than 560 gallons of Fulmar Oil towards the payment of their rent, and kept a large volume for their own use. They were paid £45.

The women and children would take the dead young Fulmars and pile them in a heap, where they were divided into equal numbers, and lots were cast, before they were taken home. Work went on well into the night as the birds had to be plucked, the feathers stored, the internal fat disposed of and the carcases salted for winter food. Next morning the whole process was repeated and continued for 10 days. Mackenzie recorded that "their clothes were literally soaked in oil, and everywhere inside and outside their houses was nothing but feathers, often looking as if it had been snowing." Inedible parts were used for manure. About 200 carcases were salted in each barrel, and each family kept four or five barrels in their cleitean. They tasted like salted pork!

A Visitor on the Cliffs

An article appeared in the Manchester Guardian for March 21st 1907 in which a lady visitor, Zillah Goudie described her experiences as she joined the St. Kildans at their Fulmar Harvest in the previous August. "A long and arduous climb over the damp and slippery Mullach Mor and round the Glen brought us at length to the top of the Cambargh, at whose base, some 800ft below, thundered the long Atlantic rollers. Here we found the men armed with long ropes, making ready for the descent. This yearly raid on the fulmar is made at the beginning of August, just before the young birds can fly, and they are caught in the hands or, if the bird is out of reach, by throwing a running noose over its neck. Like all the petrel tribe, the fulmar is in the habit of squirting a vile-smelling oil at any enemy who comes to close quarters. As this oil is valuable in several ways, part of the art of fulmar-catching lies in siezing the bird by the neck before it has time to eject the oil. During the hunting the women and children remain on the top of the cliffs and draw up the birds in bundles as the men catch them. The men work in pairs, tied together by a long rope. Bare feet are the order of the day, for it would be impossible to get the toe of a boot into some of the cracks along which these expert cragsmen make their way.

"When we arrived at the top of Cambargh the descent was about to begin. Men, women and children, we all climbed down to a small grassy plateau some twenty feet below the summit. The scene was magnificent and awe-inspiring in its grandeur. As I stood contemplating the frowning majesty of the cliffs one of the older men came behind me and, laughing, slipped a rope round my waist and knotted it, inviting me by signs to join in the hunt. The women expostulated shrilly in Gaelic, fearing, I suppose, that "Mees" might take an involuntary "header" into the waves below. But the opportunity was not to be lost, for no "Sassenach" had ever before hunted fulmar in St. Kilda; so with my heart in my mouth and an uneasy feeling at the pit of my stomach, I gaily followed my guide along a twelve inch ledge with a distinct list to sea-ward. After about five minutes of this we came to the first corner. The ledge narrowed to four or five inches, and it became necessary to face the cliff, hugging it with both arms, with the cheerful assurance that one's heels were over about eight hundred feet of nothingness. But once round the game began.

"I was the last of the three on the rope, and we were divided by about thirty feet of slack. Bird after bird was seized, killed, and slung on to a rope round the

Mrs. MacKinnon and her son carrying Fulmars from Conachair.

Photo by Cockburn, 1927.

shoulders of the men. Every now and again we stopped on a ledge a little wider than the rest, and one man let down the other to work the ledges behind us. Any easy catch fell to me. The young fulmar is an exquisitely pretty creature, a great ball of snow-white fluff, with two beady black eyes and a yellow bill. It was some time before I could make up my mind to wring the neck of one. I caught them and passed them to the men to be killed, and was laughed at for my pains. Up and down we went, now along a wide ledge, now working our way with toes and fingers along a mere crack. There was no time to feel dizzy. All one's energies were taken up in seeking toe and finger holds and scanning the cliffs for birds. Now and again on some good wide ledge we stopped, and tied all our birds together by the neck, and one of the men gave a wailing call which brought the women to the edge above. They let down a rope and hauled up the birds . . . We caught that day 1,241."

The Vital Importance of the Fulmar

From 1829-1929 an average of 10,000 young fulmars were taken each year, about 125 for each inhabitant for the winter. In March the St. Kildans were ready for a change in diet from the regular salted young, and they enjoyed going to the cliffs to noose the adults on their ledges. Oil and feathers were used to pay the rent. In

1815 the £40 rent was paid in feathers, and in 1847 each family paid rent by 84kg of feathers of the fulmar, gannet and puffin (80 fulmars made 11kg of feathers). But by the end of the 19th century the bottom had dropped out of the feather trade.

The taste of the fulmar was so delicious that it appeared in one of the St. Kilda 'Love Lilts', this is part of the one composed by the mother and father of Euphemia MacCrimmon before they were married.

> "Thou art my handsome joy, thou art my
> sweetheart,
> Thou gavest me first the honied fulmar . . .
> Thou art my hero, thou art my basking sunfish,
> Thou gavest me the puffin and the
> black-headed Guillemot."

Fulmars cackle and chatter incessantly to each other on their cliff ledges, 'sark-ag-ag-ag-ag-ag', the volume rising with excitement. So strange and rare were the sounds of spoken English that the St. Kildans described it as being "like the cackling of the fulmar." (Sands, 1878).

School-master Ross in 1889 wrote in his diary, "The fulmar is the principal bird, being to the St. Kildan almost what the Reindeer is to the Laplander." As a main item of diet it was replacing the gannet, not only because of its delicate taste but because it was more accessible. As the human population diminished the number of skilled cliff climbers was reduced and so the fulmar became the primary target. It is almost impossible to exaggerate the importance of the fulmar to St. Kildan life. "Can the world exhibit a more valuable commodity? The fulmar furnishes oil for the lamp, down for the bed, the most salubrious food, the most efficacious ointment for healing the wounds. Deprive us of the fulmar and St. Kilda is no more." (Macaulay, 1764 quoting a St. Kildan). Visitors to the island often made a different assessment – the oil gives off such a strong "odour of which the whole island and all its inhabitants smell!" (Gray, 1871).

MANX SHEARWATER – *Puffinus puffinus*

The Manx Shearwater, which pats the water with its feet on take off, leaving a shallow trough in its wake, was called 'sgrabaire' by the St. Kildans from the Gaelic root meaning to scratch or make a furrow. It was also called 'cromag', crescent shaped, from the appearance of its curved narrow wings as it glides and skims over the surface of the waves before rising above the crests at great speed. Occasionally it gives a few quick wing beats to gain greater height before tilting its whole frame to show at one moment the totally black upper surface and at the next the white under parts and wings. It has a thin black bill, hooked at the tip and tubular nostrils. The webbed feet are positioned well back,

Manx Shearwater with young in burrow.

good for diving but making them clumsy on land.

Large numbers breed on the main island and on all the subsidiary ones, being most abundant on Soay. The breeding adults collect in rafts on the water towards the end of February and prospect for suitable burrows among the boulders and grassy slopes of Carn Mor and Oiseval in March, before laying the single egg. Studies have shown that they often return to the same nest year after year. Occasionally, the St. Kildans took eggs or young and found them tasty, but they were more difficult to reach than the puffins. The adults are most vulnerable when they crash land on the ground near their burrows at night, and so the natives would sit in the colonies after dark and send their dogs to catch them before they reached the safety of their burrow.

From the nest site the adults communicate in the dark by a staccato cackle and a crooning caw, followed by a brief, harsh indrawing of air – "Cack-cack-cack-carr-hoo!"

The St. Kildans would take adult Shearwater for food, catching them both at night and by day. Lachlan MacLean recalled, "He trains a dog, places him sentinel at the hole all night; when the Scrabaire, or Shirwater first alights, he pauses to look around: the dog now pounces upon him and carries him to his master. A good dog will kill from 60 to 70 in a night. (MacLean, 1838).

Murray in his diary for April 9th. 1887 described hunting adults by day. "Today we went in the morning to kill Shearwaters . . . These birds are to be found in holes far in beneath the ground or below stones. The dogs get the smell of the birds and by scraping make it known in what holes they are. We got about sixty only – very few for the men's work all day."

Both adults take part in incubation, sitting continuously for about 6 days at a stretch, until the single egg hatches after about 51 days. The young are fed on regurgitated food, usually 2 out of 3 nights, until they are nearly twice the weight of their parents; they are fully fledged at about 62 days when they are deserted by the adults. The young remain in the burrow for a further 7-10 days before finding their own way down to the sea at about 10 weeks. They feed on plankton on the surface and also dive for small fish, especially herring fry and sprats.

Away from the breeding grounds they appear to migrate in a clockwise direction round the Atlantic. The young birds do not return to European waters until their second year when they visit their colonies, but most do not breed until they are five years old.

STORM PETREL – *Hydrobates pelagicus*

The St. Kildans had the delightful name 'Aisleag' or little ferryman for the Storm Petrel from its habit of flying back and forward from point to point. Old sailors often called them 'Mother Carey's chickens' derived from 'Mata Cara' – Mother Dear, referring to the Virgin Mary who was considered to protect sailors, and the sight of these tiny birds, like chickens, assured them of her interest, hence 'Mother Carey's chickens'. With a wing span of only 30cm (12 inches) it is the smallest of the seven Atlantic Petrels and the smallest webbed footed bird known. Of 50 caught for ringing behind the Factor's House on one July night in 1980 the average weight was only 26.3gm, varying from 21-31gm. At sea it often follows in the wake of ships feeding on the plankton churned up by the rotating propellers. Through the daylight hours it flits around here, there and everywhere in tireless flight, and when seen at night in the ship's light it closely resembles a House Martin, being the same size and having the bright white rump. Its black feet hang low and often dangle just over the water, appearing to walk on it, like St. Peter, from whom all the Petrels derive their name.

They breed on many islands off the west coast of Scotland and Wales making their first visits under cover of darkness to possible nest sites in April or May. They make a rough nest in a burrow or rock crevice where they lay one white egg about one metre from the entrance in May or June. The adults are completely nocturnal at the breeding site and give away their position and presence by a continual purring, described by Charles Oldham as a "not loud but penetrating sound, consisting of a harsh uneven purring – 'urr-r-r-r-r,' long and sustained, ending with a hiccough, like a fairy being sick!" Incubation by both parents lasts 38 days and a further 61 days elapse before the young are fledged. In 1978 over 2,000 adults were caught in mist nets behind the Factor's House at night for ringing. 1,000 of these were caught on only two nights which gives an indication of the large numbers of this species on the island.

Storm Petrels ringed on St. Kilda have been recovered on Fair Isle, the Summer Isles, Foula, Fetlar, the Shetland Mainland, and one each on the Orkneys, Sule Skerry and the islands off Co. Derry and Donegal.

Outside the breeding season numbers of this species are found on the east side of the Atlantic and in the Mediterranean.

> "She swept the seas, and as she skimmed along
> Her flying feet unbath'd on billows hung."
>
> Anon. 1799 or earlier.

LEACH'S FORK TAILED PETREL –
Oceanodroma leucorrhoa

The very first British specimen of Leach's Petrel was found in a burrow in loose rock near the summit on Dun by Bullock in 1818. It can be distinguished from the Storm Petrel by its larger size and greyer appearance, its larger wing span of 45cm (18 inches), and its deeply forked tail with the white across the rump divided by a black line from the centre of the tail feathers. The call is also distinctive, "an ascending trill, a succession of 8-10 notes in a definite cadence and of varying pitch, rather like a staccato musical laugh." (Darling, 1964). From the burrow they maintain a continuous song with similar snippets echoing the flight call. There are probably at least 1,000 pairs in the St. Kilda Group nesting on Dun, Soay, Boreray, Levenish and Hirta. St. Kilda is one of only 5 known breeding sites in Europe, the others being the Flannan Isles, Sula Sgeir, North Rona and Mykinesholmur on the Faeroes.

*Leach's Petrel
caught for ringing behind the Factor's House, 1980.*

169

Kearton in 1896 found them on Boreray nesting in burrows among the rocks. The nest sites may be among boulders or in the stone walls of the cleitean; the entrance is always tiny and often obscured by mayweed or thrift. Many excavate their own shallow burrow with their hooked beaks and feet, some making 'lay-bys' in the passage for the partner to rest and some line the nest with dead leaves or sheep's wool. They lay their single white egg at the end of the tunnel, in May or June. In the 19th. century many eggs were taken by the St. Kildans and sold to visitors and collectors. Occupied nests have a characteristic musky petrel smell and at night the site is given away by their lovely song. Kearton commented that when they were taken out of their nests they would squirt quantities of a very strong smelling oil which varied in colour from amber to orange. Incubation is shared by both parents and lasts about 7 weeks, and the fledgling period is about another 5 weeks.

Each night the first birds return to their breeding area in silence, among the huge boulders on Carn Mor small parties collect and chase each other round the rocks in bouyant, batlike flight. When a company has gathered the calling begins and increases in excitement and this continues until the coming dawn when the activity gradually dies down again and the off-duty birds go back to the sea. Non breeding birds travel over the oceans and are found as far as South Africa and the North Coast of South America.

Puffins on Dun.

PUFFINS – *Fratercula arctica*

The Puffin was known to the St. Kildans as 'Buigire' – the damp fellow, because he usually arrived on the nesting cliffs in damp or wet weather in early April. If you enter Village Bay in stormy weather or take a casual walk along the cliffs you could get the impression, mistakenly, that there were comparatively few of these friendly, inquisitive little birds. However, drop down to the tumbled boulders of Carn Mor, in the breeding season, and you will see them perched in small groups on the rocks, others will be whirling round in constant succession, as if racing round an invisible 400 metre track over the colony and out over the sea. Some are returning hurriedly with a large beakful of small fish, only to pause for a moment before dashing out of sight to feed a hungry squeaking youngster deep down within the rocks. But Dun is the great place for Puffins where 60,000-80,000 pairs nest on the soily slopes, lush with vegetation. A sight difficult to imagine as thousands circle and wheel overhead like a swarm of lucusts.

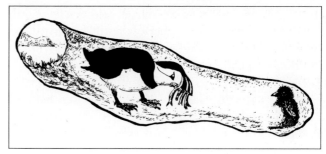

Fish for supper.
Adult Puffin and young in the burrow.

Breeding

Having spent the winter months far out in the ocean, the onset of the breeding season brings about an urge to visit their island nesting haunts again. One day in March hundreds will suddenly appear on the sea, but it will be a few weeks before they will actually venture onto the cliffs and begin to select a nest site. If the weather is damp it is usually between April 18th-22nd, if dry and after a mild winter it will be in the first few days of April. Adults engage in excited bill rubbing as their main form of courtship display, but vicious fights occasionally occur over a mate or a choice nest burrow, which one of them may have dug out with its multi-coloured and multi-purpose bill. Mating takes place on the water. Incubation of the single white egg is undertaken by both adults and lasts for about 42 days. The chick receives his food deposited on the floor of the burrow, usually in the form of Sprats (Sprattus sprattus) Sand-eels (Ammodytes marinus) and Whiting (Merlangius merlangus). He will remain in the burrow until fully fledged at about 49 days. During the last week he will have been deserted by his parents, so he has to leave the burrow by himself, making his first flight to the sea, under cover of darkness to avoid predators. At this stage the fledglings from Dun are often attracted by the lights from the generating room in the Army Camp; in most years over 1,400 find their way on their first flight into the confines of the camp where they are collected up, weighed, ringed and returned to the sea the next morning. Surprisingly, there are quiet days in the large colonies, even on Boreray and Dun, when there is hardly a bird to be seen, the whole nesting area seems deserted, with all the non-incubating birds far out to sea, and perhaps just one or two rocks attracting a few off duty birds.

From 1973-78 Harris (1980) with the help of Murray and others carried out an intensive study of the Puffins nesting on Dun. Two areas were selected, a 'dense' colony of nests below Bioda Mor, with a mean number of 0.5 nests per square metre, and a 'sparse' colony 500m to the west where between 0.2 and 0.001 nests per square metre were to be found. Within these about 190 and 130 nests respectively were observed throughout the breeding season. Harris found four main factors influencing breeding success. *(i) Egg laying date.* Young adults laid later than experienced birds, and birds in the sparse area laid a few days later than those in the dense area, although they were not young birds. This had a disadvantageous effect only if an egg was taken. *(ii) Nest burrow density.* In all the years the pairs nesting in the high density colony did better than in the other. In the years 74-77 the eggs producing fledged young in the dense and sparse areas were 76% and 50.7% respectively. *(iii) Predation.* The difference in the success rate was considered to be due to the predation and disturbance caused by the gulls. About 40 pairs of Greater Black-backed Gulls nest on Dun and from late April until late July feed almost entirely on Puffins, taking as many as 2,600 in some years, 4.2% of the breeding adults in the sparse area each year, but only 0.9% of those in the high density area. *(iv) Characteristics of the year.* Breeding success and chick weights varied from year to year depending mainly on the availability of the right food. 1974 was the worst year, Sprats, with their high calorific content, were not available at the peak growing time and the chicks were fed less frequently and on fish of less value, namely Whiting and Sand-eel larvae. Harris concluded that on Dun there is room for many more Puffins as the density is only half that of many other colonies.

Feeding

The Puffins feed mainly on Sprats and Sand-eels, with smaller quantities of Rockling and Whiting. These they catch by swimming under water, beating their wings and using their feet as rudders. On average they bring in 5-10 Sand-eels in a load for their young, but one adult brought in 61 Sand-eels and one Rockling weighing a total of 5gm. To hold these slippery creatures the inside of the beak has rows of tiny backward pointing spikes. Most of the fish are caught within 2-10km of the nesting sites. By August the colonies are completely deserted, all the birds having left for the open seas.

Population and Exploitation

It has been estimated that on the St. Kilda Group of islands there are no fewer than 300,000 pairs of Puffins, about half the British population. Recent counts record the following pairs:–

Hirta 8-13,500   Soay 150,000
Dun 70,000   Boreray 100,000 (in 3 colonies)

When St. Kilda was inhabited men, women, boys and girls with their dogs would pursue the adult puffins incessantly, and they would eat large numbers during the summer months. Kearton, in 1896, recorded no fewer than 620 taken by Angus Gillies in a single day. They were caught by using a pole, 5 metres long, supported by a curved stick, and carrying a running noose of horse hair on a gannet's quill. The noose was slowly and silently moved towards the inquisitive puffin at head level, the mesmerised bird eventually allowing the noose to be lowered over its head!

Sands in 1876 reported that, "in one year alone close on 90,000 of this species were killed by the natives. They were plucked, split open like kippers, cured and hung out to dry on strings across the cottages; and whenever a native feels hungry he simply pulls one down from the line, flings it in the fire to grill and forthwith has his lunch without the aid of knife, fork, plate or napkin." In the summer, "the smell of roasted puffins – 'a very ancient and fish-like smell' – came from every door. These birds also furnish a feast for all the dogs and hooded crows that haunt the village. I ate a puffin by way of experiment, and found it tasted like a kippered herring, with a flavour of dog–fish. Custom could no doubt make it more palatable . . . Some of the women caught as many as six hundred in a day. I calculate that eighty-nine thousand six hundred puffins must have been killed by both sexes. The fingers of the girls had become so sore from plucking the feathers that they were obliged to use their teeth in drawing the tail and pinions!" (Sands, 1877).

Lachlan MacDonald said that in the 1920's you would usually have a pot on the fire with some birds in it to form a puffin soup. "With the puffin you would also split them and put them next to the fire, roast them there – they were lovely, too – that's if you were wanting a wee snack!"

Nowadays, puffins are still killed in the Faeroes for food, others meet their deaths in oil slicks, some ringed on St. Kilda were picked up completely engulfed in oil which had escaped from the Amoco Cadiz off the Brittany coast in March 1978.

BLACK GUILLEMOT – Uria grylle

The Black Guillemot, often known as the Tystie, is found breeding all round the Arctic Ocean and the

173

North Atlantic but is only found in very small numbers round St. Kilda, normally preferring shallower waters. There are only about 10 pairs, and these are centred on Glen Bay and Dun Passage. They are easily recognised by their sooty appearance and distinctive white patch on the wing, black beak and coral red feet. They feed mainly on molluscs, crabs and sand-eels and other small fish; their high pitched whistle can often be heard above the noise of the waves, even when they cannot be seen.

The nest is usually near the water, hidden away among the boulders or in rock crevices or on a cliff ledge. In the safety of such a site, in contrast with the Common Guillemot and the Razorbill, they lay two white, boldly blotched eggs, which are incubated by both parents for 30 days, the young remain for a further 40 days until they are fully fledged and they are able to look after themselves.

COMMON GUILLEMOT – *Uria aalge*

The Common Guillemot was known to the St. Kildans as 'lamhaidh' – a handful. A total of 20,000 pairs are to be found on the whole group of islands. In the breeding season they are growling and trumpeting on their ledges and can be seen and heard on many sites near the Cambir, on the stacs on Soay Sound, near the Gap and on the cliffs or Ruaival. On Boreray there are about 14,000 pairs. They first visit the cliff ledges for a few days in early February: mating takes place at the nest site, and they lay the one large pyriform egg, blotched and streaked with brown, on a bare ledge, in company with several of their species, in rather slum conditions, in the middle of May. Incubation is undertaken by both adults and lasts 32-34 days, and the young leave the cliffs after only 18-25 days when they flap their tiny wings as they fall almost vertically to the sea. This hazardous journey is taken at dusk to escape predatory gulls and skuas.

A good place to watch Guillemots is on the cliffs of Ruaival below the Mistress Stone, opposite Dun. At about 100m above sea level there is a narrow vertical ledge occupied by about 10-12 off duty birds, the number varies all the time as some leave in search of fish, and return again, others just go for exercise! Behind the ledge on the landward side the rock slopes steeply down for 1m before flattening out to form a rough gully with murky pools and guano; to the rear, the rock-face rises high above the ledge in an overhang. In the gully thus formed three young Guillemot chicks squeak incessantly, attended by only one female who is nestling two of the young on her feet, their fluffy bodies hidden under her white feathers, the third one attempts to climb the steep slope aided by

Guillemots and young on a ledge on Ruaival.

sharp claws and the flapping of tiny wings, pausing to carry out strange head pumping movements, just like the adults. On the ledge above the adults, three of which are 'Bridled' and wear white 'spectacles', bow low to each other and waddle about, trumpeting all the time. Another adult lands clumsily and pushes his way past the others, slides down the slope carrying a fish lengthways in the beak to lessen the chance of losing it to one of his interested companions. He bends low and presents the meal to the hungry youngster.

The St. Kildans would aim to take the adult Guillemots about three weeks after the first birds returned to the cliffs in the spring. The birds were

"suddenly driven away from their favourite ledges late one evening, and long before dawn on the following morning a man is lowered to each. He sits motionless as a statue when the birds stream up from the sea and alight upon him, thinking he is a rock, and are promptly secured and killed. One hundred can be taken by one man in one hour." (Kearton, 1897). MacLean recorded that the dead birds are laid at the feet of the person, as if alive. This lulls the suspicion of those coming, who light at the same spot. (MacLean, 1838). It was a risky operation and a number of natives slipped to their death off the wet ledges in the dark.

Large numbers of eggs were also taken, in the 1830's Mackenzie (Mackenzie, 1911) reported, "I have seen 17 baskets of eggs taken at one time off Stac Biorach and at another time in the same season, 14. These baskets hold each about 400 of these eggs . . . they are very good for eating when fresh. Some have a gamey flavour . . . others are as bad as the most vivid imagination can depict. Many were blown and sold to visitors."

RAZORBILL – *Alca torda*

Only about 1,000 pairs of Razorbills breed on St. Kilda. It can be distinguished from the Guillemot by its sooty black beak and crown, the Guillemot is more chocolate coloured. At close quarters the beak is seen to

Razorbills on Dun.

laid in mid-May and is incubated by both parents for 34-39 days. Food is brought cross-wise in the beak to the fluffy black and white young. When only a third of the adult size, at about the 18th day, the chick will take the plunge from the cliff ledge after dusk. Even at this stage the young can swim and dive without any difficulty. By the middle of August, when fully grown, the youngster will probably be accompanied by one of its parents. Many birds from Scottish sites travel to Scandinavian waters for the winter.

The St. Kildans did not consider the flesh of the adult good to eat, but eggs were taken, blown and sold to the visitors for one old penny each.

GREAT AUK – *Alca impennis*

The Great Auk, now extinct, deserves a mention among the birds of St. Kilda. It was like a huge flightless Razorbill. It stood even more erect than the Razorbill and Guillemot reaching a height of one metre, although twice their size the wings were no larger, the longest primary feather being only 8cm. The Greenland name for it was 'Isarokitsok' – 'Little Wings'. It was a strong swimmer and a powerful diver, submerging quickly when alarmed and in order to capture crabs, marine invertebrates and fish which included the Lumpsucker and the Sea Scorpion. The mandibles were large, with a series of grooves which increased with age, mature

be flattened from the sides and has a white stripe lengthways, looking like the old fashioned cut-throat razor in its sheath. It is found in much smaller numbers than the Guillemot, preferring to have its own individual niches on the cliffs of Ruaival and near the 'fort' on Dun.

Frequent visits are paid to the nest sites in March and April, where mating takes place. The single large blotched egg, more rounded than the Guillemot's, is

Great Auk – now extinct.

Denmark, the Faeroes, St. Kilda, Iceland. Greenland and Newfoundland. Others were reported from the Orkneys, Fair Isle and the Isle of Man. Whalers off Greenland used the gullet and stomach of the birds as air filled bags, inflated bladder-like floats which they attached to their harpoons. The St. Kildans called it the 'Garefowl' or by the Gaelic 'bunnabhuachaille'. 'Garefowl' has Norse origins, 'Geyr-fugl' being its Icelandic name. 'Geyr' is Icelandic for a spear, which could describe the large spear-like beak or its extraordinary speed in the water, like the flight of a spear; it could refer to their use with harpoons. There was a rock bearing its Gaelic name on either Boreray or one of the Stacs where it used to breed but the actual site is no longer known.

Being unable to fly the nest site had to be close to the sea or easily accessible, making it vulnerable to bird and human predators alike, as well as being in danger from gales and high seas. Because of its shyness it usually nested on flat rocky islands or lonely remote skerries, often in colonies. On St. Kilda it would come ashore occasionally to lay one large pyriform egg, like the Guillemot's, variously covered with fine scrawls and blotched with black and brown, sometimes with grey and green. The egg was laid on the bare rock, the adults appearing in May and returning to sea again in June or July. There was a distinct "contrast between the

birds having 8-10 on the upper mandible; the inside of the mouth was orange. The irides were chestnut and the eyelid margins black, a large white patch of feathers reached between the eye and the bill.

In the 16th century it was often seen and caught for food by fishermen off the northern coasts of Norway, adults clumsiness and vulnerability when it was on land and its speed and agility in the water." (Halliday, 1978). It was quite capable of outpacing a rowing boat and could remain submerged for several minutes. An observer made the following comment having watched an adult which had been caught on St. Kilda in 1821, "it dives and swims under water, even with a long cord attached to its feet, with incredible swiftness." (Fleming, 1828). Its flesh was delicious, its oil was used in their lamps and the feathers were sold. One bird, caught on Stac an Armin in 1840 was kept for two days before being killed. The last pair of the species was captured on the island of Eldey, off Iceland on June 4th., 1844, both birds were clubbed to death. Bones of the Great Auk have been found in the kitchen middens in Denmark, Caithness, Oronsay, Colonsay and Newfoundland, and in America as far south as Florida. An ignominious end to a stately bird, once abundant in the North Atlantic, due to the spread of man and his thoughtless greed.

A NIGHT ON CARN MOR – *The Big Rocks*

A visit to St. Kilda would be incomplete without a night spent on the great boulder field of Carn Mor. Only the alarm calls of Snipe and Oyster-catcher disturb the still air as we leave the Village at about 11 p.m. The mist is down to 200m. On the coll of Am Blaid

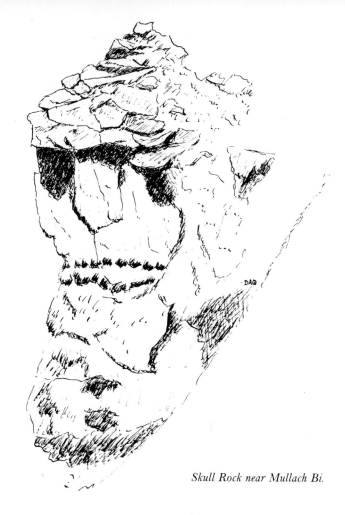

Skull Rock near Mullach Bi.

all is quiet except for a single Snipe and the sound of the waterfall descending from Mullach Mor. We follow the wall above the Great Glen, which looks eerie and beautiful, filled with mist and lit by the moon, and pause by a cleit beyond the Lover's Stone where four nesting petrels are pouring out their night song. We pass the dark outline of 'Skull Rock' peering through the mist, then, below the summit of Mullach Bi, turning left by the two cleitean we drop down the very steep grassy slope into the mist again, through the funnel formed by the huge rocks on either side. Turning right we clamber clumsily in the dim light over a rugged rocky outcrop, with a vertical cliff overhead and enter the extensive boulder field of Carn Mor.

At 1 a.m. sitting among the huge boulders, enveloped in mist in the semi-darkness, the first weird cries are heard from below ground, two or three Manx Shearwaters are calling to their partners flying in from the sea to help them to locate their own burrow among the rocks. During the next two hours there is a rapid build up in the numbers of birds flying passed at very close quarters as they circle round trying to 'home in' on their own nest – a remarkable feat in the dark. Their wings 'whirr' as they bank to avoid the strewn boulders before landing with a distinct 'thud' on a small grassy patch near the site, pausing for a few seconds to check bearings before disappearing out of sight into the nest

Manx Shearwater returning to its burrow on Carn Mor, 1980.

burrow. On entering the nest the greeting, which has been described as the 'dying screams of an asthmatic cockerel' is noisy, prolonged and hysterical.

Another sound from underground is the occasional 'Ah-ha' of the Puffin with a few high pitched squeaks from the young, also the continual purring of the tiny Storm Petrel and the rarer Leach's Petrel which has a delightful laughing call in flight, often echoed by the partner in the burrow below. 'Little Ferrymen' was Martin's apt description of the Storm Petrels as they journey to and from their feeding grounds, even travelling 320km (200 miles) out to the Rockall Bank where they take minute oceanic plankton. Before leaving this magical place in the early hours of the July morning, Wally Wright, the Warden called us over, we watched excitedly as he with-drew his hand from the grassy entrance of a burrow. It was clutching the tiny sooty body of a Storm Petrel. With the aid of a torch he hesitatingly read out the numbers on the ring – 2122413. The bird had been ringed somewhere on St. Kilda seven years previously. With the first signs of dawn the off-duty birds return to the sea, the sounds die away, apart from the shrill 'Kleep' of the Oyster-catcher and the gruff 'Caw' of the Hooded Crow and the continual roar of the restless sea.

FISH CONSUMPTION

The question arises as to the quantity of fish consumed by such huge colonies of breeding sea-birds. Nelson estimated that "a gannet can swallow four large mackerel in succession, ten herrings or codlings. A captive gannet takes up to 1,000gms (36ozs) in a meal and up to seven large herring per day!" With 120,000 adults around St. Kilda something like 480,000 mackerel or 740,000 herring or their equivalent, 120 tonnes are likely to be consumed each day. It has been estimated that there are some 300,000 pairs of nesting puffins – 900,000 individuals including young. It has been calculated that an adult puffin in the wild requires 80-100gms of fish per day, and a young bird on average

84gms from hatching to fledging so that puffins are likely to take around 100 tonnes of sand-eels, sprats and whiting per day. If we include fish brought to young gannets as well, then puffins and gannets alone could consume over 250 tonnes of fish each day in the height of the breeding season! To obtain all this food puffins fish between 2-10km from the colonies, whereas the gannets feed below the nesting cliffs and up to 140km away.

GAELIC NAMES OF ST. KILDAN BIRDS

At the end of John Ross's account of life on St. Kilda during the time he was school-master in 1889 he adds the following list "For the benefit of anyone visiting the island and wishing to buy eggs, I give the St. Kildan names of the birds whose eggs can be had, spelling them phonetically:–

English	St. Kildan
Fulmar	Fulamar
Puffin	Bonur
Guillemot	Lavy
Razorbill	Falca
Gannet	Sular
Gull	Fulag
Starling	Druid
Oyster-catcher	Trislachan
Tree Sparrow	Biggan Caill

Fork-tailed Petrel	Irbul Scoilt or Aslag Mor
Gray Crow	Fennag
St. Kilda Wren	Dreidhan dow
Raven	Fiach du
Eider	Tunag a mhara"

PLANT LIFE

There are many factors which together make the plant life of St. Kilda particularly fascinating. The fact that the Quaternary Ice Sheet did not reach the group means that the islands form a reserve for the pre-glacial species of plants. The dominant vegetation is grass moorland, but this has been modified by several environmental pressures. These include:–

High winds which blow most of the year round. The prevailing wind is from the south west but 20% is from the south east from which Village Bay receives no protection. For 85% of the time a wind speed of force 3 and over will be recorded, whereas force 5 or above occur for more than 30% of the year. These high, persistent winds clip the heather to the same degree as at a height of 800m on the mainland, and cause a great reduction in plant size to avoid water loss.

Selective Grazing by the Soay sheep (see Soay sheep section) affects many species; it has favoured heather and bracken to the detriment of others.

Lack of Burning has enabled Bilberry and the Great Woodrush to grow and spread unhindered. The luxuriant growth of the latter covers large areas on the summit of Mullach Bi, and to the east of the summit of Conachair.

Salt Spray provides an aggressive environment for plants to live and has severe adverse effects on many species, causing damage to roots, leaves and other tissues, thus limiting the number of species which are adapted and able to survive such harsh conditions. Some plants like thrift and the plantains have developed thick cuticles and small or spiked leaves to reduce the surface area on which the salt can fall, and to minimise water loss. Others, like the Oraches have developed a salt pump on the leaves to exude excess salt. On exposed headlands which receive continuous salt spray well developed plantago swards have formed. (see para on Plantago Sward).

Sea-bird Guano is another dominant factor influencing the plants on the cliff ledges where Common Sorrel is one of the few plants which is able to withstand the high nitrogen content of the guano, both in the soil and on its leaves and this accounts for its great abundance in the fulmar and puffin colonies.

Altitude. A considerable part of the land surface on Hirta is between 200 and 425m above sea level, and this reduces the plant growth rate by as much as 5% for every 30m in spring, and 18% in June.

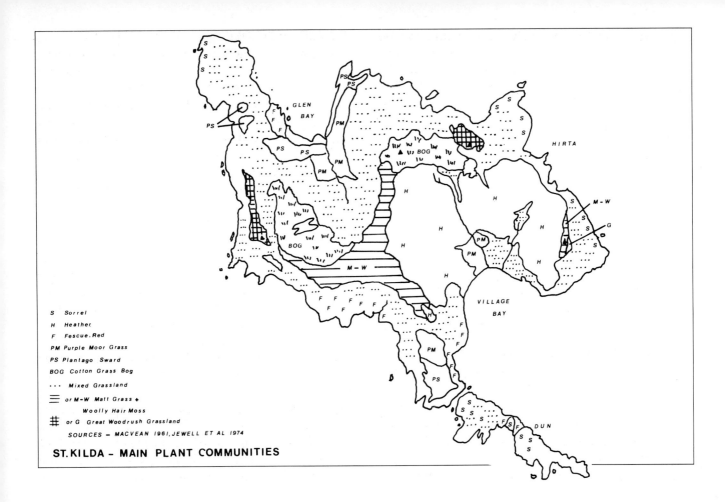

GLEN BAY

HIRTA

BOG

BOG

M-W

M-W

G

VILLAGE BAY

DUN

S   Sorrel
H   Heather
F   Fescue, Red
PM Purple Moor Grass
PS Plantago Sward
BOG Cotton Grass Bog
··· Mixed Grassland
≡ or M-W Matt Grass +
        Woolly Hair Moss
♯ or G Great Woodrush Grassland
   SOURCES — MACVEAN 1961, JEWELL ET AL 1974

ST. KILDA – MAIN PLANT COMMUNITIES

Temperature. St. Kilda has mild winters with very little frost or snow, although 1979 saw both above normal, the mean January temperature is 5.6 °C, but the summers are cool with a July mean of 11.8 °C. This reduces plant growth considerably and had a similar effect on the crops which the St. Kildans attempted to grow.

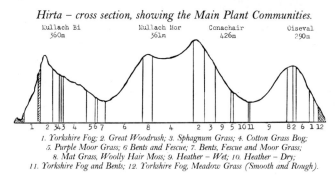

Hirta – cross section, showing the Main Plant Communities.

Mullach Bi 360m   Mullach Mor 361m   Conachair 426m   Oiseval 290m

1 2 343 4 567 6 8 4 2 3 9 5 1011 9 82 6 112

1. Yorkshire Fog; 2. Great Woodrush; 3. Sphagnum Grass; 4. Cotton Grass Bog; 5. Purple Moor Grass; 6 Bents and Fescue; 7. Bents, Fescue and Moor Grass; 8. Mat Grass, Woolly Hair Moss; 9. Heather – Wet; 10. Heather – Dry; 11. Yorkshire Fog and Bents; 12. Yorkshire Fog, Meadow Grass (Smooth and Rough).

THE MAIN PLANT COMMUNITIES

For an intensive study reference should be made to the Chapter in Island Survivors (Jewell, Milner and Morton Boyd, 1974) in which a detailed vegetation map is included showing the different plant communities. The cross section illustrated here is compiled from the map and shows the communites in relation to the topography. The land can be divided into the following regions:–

VALLEY BOTTOMS

Village Glen. In the Village Glen the plants have been greatly influenced by the removal of stones and past farming and the present grazing of Soay sheep. In the meadows Yorkshire Fog (Holcus lanatus) and Fine Bent (Agrostis tenuis) dominate, while Sweet Vernal Grass (Anthoxanthum odoratum) and Rough and Smooth Meadow Grass (Poa species) are abundant, with Meadow Buttercup (Ranunculus acris) common. Lining the banks of the stream from the Tobar Childa, Yellow Flags (Iris Pseudacorus) are prolific with Ragged Robin (Lychnis-flos-cuculi) near its source and patches of Bracken (Pteridium aquilinum) on drier ground nearby. Large clumps of Stinging Nettles (Urtica dioica) are in some of the ruined houses and the neighbouring area. Stonecrop (Sedum species) fills the gaps in many stone walls and Rye Grass (Lolium perenne) grows in the Village street.

Gleann Mor. At the head of Gleann Mor, Purple Moor Grass (Molinia caerulea) is dominant together with Bents (Agrostis species), Red Fescue (Festuca rubra), Mat Grass (Nardus Stricta), Tormentil (Potentilla erecta) and Sea Plantain (Plantago maritima). There are also Cotton Grass communites (Eriophorum bog) with an increase in Heather (Calluna vulgaris) and two insectivorous plants, the Common Butterwort (Pinguicula vulgaris) and the

Greater Sundew (Drosera anglica). Areas round the cleitean, the tarn and natural springs have their own plant communities.

HILL SLOPES

Dry Hill Slopes. On the dry hill slopes to the north and west of Oiseval the dry heath conditions favour Heather (Calluna vulgaris) which is dominant with only a few species managing to push their way through, namely, Bell Heather (Erica cinerea), Purple Moor Grass (Molinea caerulea), Mat Grass (Nardus stricta), Tormentil (Potentilla erecta) and the Heath Spotted Orchid (Dactylorchis maculata). Elegant St. John's Wort (Hypericum pulchrum) is present in greater than normal abundance.

Wet Slopes. On the wetter slopes to the east of the Village where the drainage is poor, Heather is dominant with Purple Moor Grass and Deer Grass (a sedge – Trichophorum caespitosum) equally frequent. In these wetter areas other plants are in association, Mat Grass, Viviparous Fescue (Festuca vivipara), Cotton Grass (Eriophorum angustifolium) and Crowberry (Empetrum nigrum).

Grassland. Sphagnum moss species occur in most of the sloping grasslands due to the wet climate. The grasslands are mixed, predominantly Bents and Fescue (Agrostis – Festuca) but subject to great variations and can be classified into the following:–

Sphagnum
Yorkshire Fog – Bents – Sphagnum
            (Holcus – Agrostis – Sphagnum)
Purple Moor Grass (Molinia)
Bents – Fescue (Agrostis – Festuca)
Great Woodrush (Luzula)
Yorkshire Fog (Holcus)
Yorkshire Fog – Meadow Grass (Holcus-Poa)
Yorkshire Fog – Bents (Holcus – Agrostis)

SUMMIT PLATEAU

The Summits. The summits of Oiseval, Conachair and Mullach Bi have similar distinctive plant communities, namely the grassland in which the Great Woodrush (Luzula sylvatica) appears closely associated with the dominant Fine Bent (Agrostis tenuis) together with an abundance of Mat Grass (Nardus stricta) and Sweet Vernal Grass (Anthoxanthum odoratum).

Between the Summits of Conachair and Mullach Mor there is a poor drainage which has caused the development of the main Cotton Grass Bog (Eriophorum Bog) community with dense cover of very short Heather (Calluna vulgaris) together with Crowberry (Empetrum nigrum), Tormentil (Potentilla erecta), Creeping Willow (Salix repens), Great Woodrush (Luzula sylvatica), Bog Asphodel

(Narthecium ossifragum) and Heath Spotted Orchid (Dactylorchis maculata).

The Summit Ridge between Mullach Mor and Mullach Sgar is characterised by Mat Grass and Woolly Hair Moss, Nardus-Rhacomitrium community with Heather (Calluna vulgaris) and Viviparous Fescue (Festuca vivipara) dominant. Mat Grass and Woolly Hair Moss replace Heather where the soil is thin on the less steep slopes and summit plateau.

CLIFF LEDGES

On the cliff ledges sea spray, grazing sheep and bird droppings all have a pronounced effect on the vegetation, the following plants are dominant:–

Common Sorrel (Rumex acetosa), Scentless Mayweed (Matricaria maritima). Sea Pink or Thrift (Armeria maritima), Sea Campion (Silene maritima) and Sea Plantain (Platago maritima).

Sea spray has a marked effect on the western cliffs, in some places Yorkshire Fog is replaced by White Bent and in some gullies Red Fescue is the only grass able to survive the salty conditions. Red Fescue is the dominant grass on many of these cliffs and also occurs in fulmar and puffin colonies and is closely grazed by sheep. White Clover (Trifolium repens) and Sea Plantain (Plantago maritima) also exist in this hostile environment.

On the east of Oiseval and Conachair, Bents and Fescues are dominant on the upper ledges, while on the lower ledges with a higher bird concentration, the main vegetation is Common Sorrel (Rumex acetosa) and Yorkshire Fog with Meadow Grass (Holcus-Poa). It is modified to 'lair flora' where sheep flatten the vegetation and add dung and urine. Many examples of 'lair flora' where the sheep rest are found all over the island: on the NW slopes of Mullach Mor there is luxuriant growth of Yorkshire Fog, Smooth and Rough Meadow Grass, with occasional specimens of Common Mouse-ear and White Clover.

MINOR COMMUNITIES

Other minor communities which will reward study may be found at:–

i. The edges of the tunnel at Gob n h-Airde . . .
    Sea Spleenwort (Asplenium marinum)
    Babbington's Orache (Atriplex glabriuscula)
    Mountain Sorrel (Oxyria digyna)

ii. The surrounds of the Cleitean in the bottom of Gleann Mor. the luxuriant growth includes:–
    Yorkshire Fog (Holcus lanatus)
    Broad Dock (Rumex obtusifolius)
    Common Sorrel (Rumex acetosa)
    Meadow Buttercup (Ranunculus acris)
    Common Chickweed (Stellaria media)

PLANT LIFE – SUMMARY

Land Categories	Area/Communities	Typical Plants (* = Dominant)
Valley Bottoms	a. Village Glen	*Yorkshire Fog *Fine Bent Sweet Vernal Grass Smooth and Rough Meadow Grass Yellow Flag Bracken Stinging Nettles Stonecrop
	b. Gleann Mor	*Purple Moor Grass Bents Red Fescue Mat Grass Tormentil Sea Plantain Cotton Grass Communities Sundew Butterwort
Hill Slopes	a. Dry Heath	*Heather, tall Bell Heather Purple Moor Grass Mat Grass

Land Categories	Area/Communities	Typical Plants (* = Dominant)
		Tormentil Heath Spotted Orchid Sweet Vernal Grass Wavy Hair Grass Red Fescue
	b. Wet Heath	*Heather Purple Moor Grass Deer Grass (Sedge) Mat Grass Viviparous Fescue Cotton Grass Crowberry Sphagnum Moss
	c. Grasslands	Sphagnum Grasslands Yorkshire Fog, Bents, Sphagnum
		Purple Moor Grass Bents + Fescue Great Woodrush Yorkshire Fog Yorkshire Fog + Meadow Grass Yorkshire Fog + Bents Sorrel

Land Categories	Area/Communities	Typical Plants (* = Dominant)
Summit Plateau	a. Great Woodrush Grassland	*Great Woodrush *Fine Bent Mat Grass Sweet Vernal Grass
	b. Mat Grass and Woolly Hair Moss Heathland	*Mat Grass Woolly Hair Moss Heather Viviparous Fescue
	c. Cotton Grass Community	*Cotton Grass *Heather Crowberry Tormentil Creeping Willow Great Woodrush Bog Asphodel Heath Spotted Orchid Grasses scarce – some:– Wavy Hair Grass Purple Moor Grass

Land Categories	Area/Communities	Typical Plants (* = Dominant)
Cliff Ledges	a. Maritime Red Fescue Grassland	*Red Fescue Yorkshire Fog Thrift Sea Plantain Poa
	b. Bird Cliffs Sorrel Grassland	*Common Sorrel Yorkshire Fog Rough Meadow Grass White Bent Meadow Buttercup Lesser Celandine Common Mouse-ear Common Chickweed Purslane
	c. Sheep Ledges Yorkshire Fog and Meadow Grassland	*Yorkshire Fog *Rough Meadow Grass Red Fescue Meadow Buttercup Common Chickweed Common Sorrel

iii. The spring to the south of the Amazon's House
Marsh Willow Herb (Epilobium palustre)
Blinks (Montia fontana)
Mossy Pearlwort (Sagina procumbens)
Marsh Pennywort (Hydrocotyle vulgaris)
Bog Asphodel (Narthecium ossifragum)
Bog Pondweed (Potamogeton polygoniforius)
iv. Following the course of Amhuinn Mhor
Creeping Willow (Salix repens)
Devil's Bit Scabius (Soccisa pratensis)
Common Primrose (Primula vulgaris)
flowering in July.
Purple Saxifrage (Saxifraga oppositifolia)

PLANTS WITH A DIFFERENCE

ARCTIC-ALPINES

Most of the Arctic-Alpine species are very rare on St. Kilda (Turrill, 1928), however the following are particularly adapted to survive in exposed situations and have been identified on Hirta.

Moss Campion – Silene acaulis   Flowers July-August
Found in the Highlands between 700-1,250m on St. Kilda at about 100m. It has a good root system for obtaining moisture and keeping food stored; above ground it forms a small compact cushion of bright

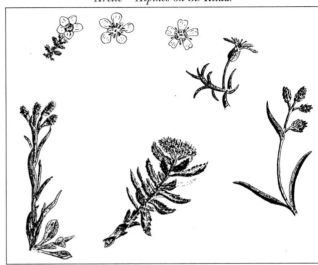

Arctic – Alpines on St. Kilda.

Purple Saxifrage   Moss Campion   Stiff Sedge
Mountain Everlasting   Rose Root

green moss-like leaves, packed closely to avoid water loss. Small numbers of pink star-like flowers form on each clump, made up of 5 petals in a flat disc on a bell shaped calyx. Some cushions have male flowers, others female, but it is rare to find both. Found on Na h-Eagan.

Purple Saxifrage –   Flowers March-May,
Saxifraga oppositifolia   sometimes July to August
Prefers crevices among the moist rocks of the North

and East where the suns heat is less. The long roots penetrate into cracks and the slender branches creep along the rocks with leafy shoots forming a dense cushion. The leaves are paired, very small and shiny: the reddish purple flower is bell shaped with five small petals. At the apex of each leaf is a chalk gland designed to conserve moisture. Found on Na h-Eagan, and Ruaival.

Rose Root – *Sedum rosea*   Flowers May-August

Plentiful in the rock crevices where the thick underground stem acts as a storehouse for food and moisture reserves. The leaves are thick and fleshy to conserve water on exposed sites. The flowers are bright yellow forming an attractive terminal cluster. Found – Amhuinn Mor, Mullach Bi, Gob na h-Airde and Glacan Mor.

Mountain Everlasting or Catsfoot – *Antennaria dioica*   Flowers May-July

It is related to the Edelweiss and found between 100-175m. The tufted stem with hairy oblong leaves gives it a white appearance. The male and female flowers are on different plants. The male florets are inconspicuous, tubular and short, but the inner bracts have broad petal like tips spreading out like a daisy. In the female the spreading bracts are missing, the corollas are very fine and protrude giving the head a snow white effect. (Holden, 1952). Found on the Pro-talus ridge.

Mountain Sorrel – *Oxyria digyna* Flowers July-August

Belongs to the family of Docks and Sorrels having a long leaf stalk with dark green shaped leaves and a slender leafless flowering stem, terminated by many small greenish flowers. It is wind pollinated and found on the north face of Conachair, and the west entrance of Gob na h'Airde.

Dwarf Willow, the only tree on St. Kilda, Height, 2 cm.

Dwarf or Least Willow – *Salix herbacea*   Flowers in June

Sometimes called "the smallest tree in the world." It has a woody underground stem and short shoots covered with thin, finely toothed leaves with many veins and terminated by very small catkins, parachute seeds are formed. The plants form a dense carpet on the north face of Conachair

Stiff Sedge – Carex rigida　　　　Flowers June-July
The three sided stem distinguishes it from the grasses. The plant forms dense low colonies with flat rigid leaves. The glumes are dark brown or black with a green midrib, the male and female flowers are separate, the female having 2 instead of 3 feathery stigmas to aid wind pollination. It is found on Mullach Mor and other summits.

WOODLAND PLANTS

WOODLAND SPECIES

In 1928 Turrill noted and attached great importance to the fact that five woodland species are found on St. Kilda which he thought might "be relics of a woodland flora." Lesser Celandine (Ranunculus ficaria) found everywhere, flowering from March to May, Hedge Vetch (Vicia sepium) is very rare only on the Cambir and Soay and flowers from April to September. Common Honeysuckle (Lonicera periclymenum) flowers luxuriantly from June to September on the east cliff of Oiseval, Conachair and on Mullach Bi while the Common Primrose occurs mainly in sheltered spots by the sea and flowers from March to May. The Great Woodrush (Luzula sylvatica) could only be found within 7m of Conachair's summit (426m) in 1928, now it is much more extensive on several summits and flowers from June to July.

POLLEN ANALYSIS

Pollen Counts from peat samples on Hirta reveal Hazel (Corylus), Birch (Betula), Alder (Alnus), Pine (Pinus), Elm (Ulmus) and Oak (Quercus) It was thought that these trees must have been present on St. Kilda in the form of scrub or woodland, recent research on Lewis clarifies the picture. In the study area at Little Loch Roag which is virtually a treeless landscape, 9% of the modern pollen rain consists of tree pollen, the highest level of tree pollen during the whole of the Flandrian (10,000 years before present, onwards) only reached 18%. These figures clearly do not suggest the former occurence of extensive woodland. Low arboreal pollen values occur on St. Kilda and other sites in the Outer Hebrides and also on Canna, Shetlands, Orkney Mainland and NE Caithness. This "suggests a virtually forestless zone throughout the Flandrian in northernmost Scotland and the Outer Islands" (Birks and Madsen, 1979). However the high count on St. Kilda for Birch and Hazel suggest scrubland with subordinate Alder.

Birks summarises the present views in the Outer Isles, "Pollen diagrams from small Hebridean islands (Canna, Barra and St. Kilda) all indicate that no tree development occurred during the Flandrian, presumably because of intense exposure to westerly gales. The main vegetation was maritime grasslands and dwarf-shrub heaths with Plantago maritima, P.lanceolata, and Armeria maritima."

PLANTAGO SWARD

A luxuriant Plantago Sward is to be found, mainly on Ruaival, but also on the Cambir and on Gob na h'Airde below 200m, and on a few other gentle slopes. The heavy grazing by the sheep may be responsible in part for its successful growth. In each of the three locations there is a cover of very short Red Fescue, the three Plantago species are present together with a non tussocky Sea Pink (Armeria maritima) forming a dense mat. Buck's-Horn Plantain (P. coronopus) is often small and grows out from the centre like a basket with leaves divided into leaflets with a simple vein, it flowers from May to July. Ribwort or Ribgrass (P. lanceolata) flowers from April-August and is the species very common in everyone's lawn and in hedge-rows, having erect leaves with 3-6 veins and flower spikes shorter and more compact than in the other species. Sea Plantain (P. maritima) flowers from June to August and has a rosette of long narrow fleshy leaves with flowers on a tall stout stem arranged in a long spike with greenish stamens and pistils on the same flower. It is wind pollinated. All these specially adapted maritime species seem to have replaced an earlier grassy vegetation which was unable to withstand the inundation of salt spray from the more frequent gales brought on by a change in the climate.

FERNS

The following ferns have been identified on Hirta:–

Scottish Filmy Fern – Spores,
Hymenophyllum wilsonii July-August
Found in wet and shady habitats. The fronds are up to 10cm in length and are divided into narrow sections which turn back on themselves.

Bracken – Pteridium aquilinum Spores, July-August
Prefers acid soil and is common in the meadow within the Head Dyke. It has spread considerably since the Evacuation due to sheep grazing the nearby grass and avoiding the bracken. Spreads by spores and far reaching rhizomes.

Hard Fern – Blenchnum spicant Spores, June-August
Prefers acid soil and shade and is found in many gullies and on the rocky banks of Amhuinn Mhor. Fertile stems stand erect, narrow and long, like a

fish's back-bone, they die back in winter whereas the sterile ones remain green.

Black Spleenwort –   Spores,
Asplenium adiantum-nigrum   June-October

Found in rock crevices and walls. Fronds are triangular at the ends, the stalks are dark and brittle, leaves leathery. The sori are long and narrow and at the centre of the leaf.

Sea Spleenwort –   Spores,
Asplenium marinum   June-October

Found in rock crevices by the sea, several on the sloping track leading down to the tunnel at Gob na h'Airde. The leaflets are tough, thick and broad, and are able to withstand the sea spray.

Lady Fern –   Spores,
Athyricium filix-femina   July-August

Forms in dense clumps, preferring damp areas. Variable in shape, but usually has doubly pinnate fronds with a long scaly stem. "Its delicate texture and graceful feathery appearance has earned it the name Lady Fern." (Phillips, 1980). Spores form in sori on the underside and look like a 'comma'.

Bladder Fern –   Spores,
Cystopteris fragilis   July-August

Grows in rock crevices and walls. The stem is very brittle and is about half the length of the frond. Spores develop in sori in two rows on each part of the frond. In the early stages they are covered by a thin layer which swells into the shape of a bladder.

Broad or Common Buckler Fern –   Spores,
Dryopteris austriaca   July-September

Prefers shady rock ledges. The tip of the fronds narrow quickly and the stem scales have diagnostic dark brown streaks on them.

Common Polypody –   Spores,
Polypodium vulgare   July-August

Found on the tops of walls and rock ledges. The fronds are long and flat, with lobes of more or less equal length.

Moonwort –   Spores,
Botrychium lunaria   June-August

Prefers dry grassland and rock ledges. "Lobed sterile fronds are 5-20cm with branched spore structures arising near the base. Alchemists believed it could turn mercury to silver." (Phillips, 1980).

Adder's Tongue –   Spores,
Ophioglossum vulgatum   May-August

Found in damp grassland growing from 5-20cm. Its shape is similar to a snakes tongue.

FUNGI

162 species of Agarics were recorded for Hirta and 2 for Dun in September 1967 by Watling and Richardson (1971). By far the most common were

Omphalina ericetorum and Nolanea staurospora. The following were also widespread:– Dung Roundhead (Stropharia semiglobata) and Liberty Caps (Psilocybe semilanceata) where sheep congregate round the cleitean; also Hygrophorus laetus and marchii were found between acid and richer soils; and Galerina vittaeformis was found widespread in many different habitats.

LICHENS

Lichens are fascinating dual organisms, made up of a combination of fungi (forming most of the bulk) and a microscopic green algae, which provides the chlorophyll for photosynthesis. They are very slow growing, some only increasing by one millimetre a year, others by one centimetre, but all flourish best in moist climates and normally grow on trees. Dr. O. Gilbert in 1978 found and identified 188 of the 194 species which have been found on St. Kilda. Far fewer species have been found on other Scottish islands, Fair Isle 108, Foula 72, North Rona 87 and the Flannans 63 species. It is surprising to find so many on such a treeless habitat, clearly they appreciate the pollution free atmosphere, the 90% humidity and the greater height of the island over others enabling some lichens to exist which are unable to withstand the salt spray at a lower level. There is a particularly rich lichen flora in the grasslands and on the cliffs, and other communities benefit from the rich nutrients from the sea-bird guano. Some lichens are eaten by sheep which leaves a grazing line on the walls and boulders after feeding during the hard winter season.

For a full account of the lichens of St. Kilda Dr. Gilbert's Study (1979) should be read. Some of the species he records are particularly interesting. He points out that Verrucaria laetebrosa has only previously been recorded in Lentrim in Ireland, but it is to be found on vertical rock faces with other extreme Atlantic Species. Lecanora straminea is a rare polar maritime species but is found in company with others on the guano rich boulders of Dun and Carn Mor where as many as 25 species may be found on one rock. Lobaria pulmonaria, a large species normally growing on trees, flourishes on the rocks high up on Mullach Bi, Carn Mor and Glacan Mor. It is thought that several other species are likely to be identified around the high tide mark in the future.

USEFUL PLANTS

Food

The staple food crops were barley, oats and potatoes but the yield in each case was poor, usually only about three times the quantity planted. The visitors in 1799 reported that the "only vegetables eaten are potatoes, the scurvy-grass, and the roots of the silver wood (silver weed) and the common dock."

Scurvy-grass (Cochlearia officinalis) was famous as a major source of Vitamin C on long sea voyages. It is unpleasant and bitter. It grows to about 20cms in height with small white flowers and dark green heart shaped leaves, abundant on the cliffs and banks near the sea.

Laver (Porphyra umbilicalis). Large quantities of this important seaweed grow on rocks and stones on the shore – the fronds are thin, purplish and irregularly shaped like membranous lettuce leaves. After simmering it looks like well cooked spinach. It is probably this plant, which in time of famine "they literally cleared the shore, not only of shell-fish but even of a species of seaweed that grows abundantly on the rocks within the sea-mark." (Mackenzie, in the 1830's). Macaulay and the visitors of 1799 both recorded their fondness for laver and the former noted the inhabitants' concern for the conservation of supplies (see People, Compensation and Fines).

Silver-weed (Potentilla anserina) has silvery grey undersides to the leaves but it was the roots which were eaten. Mabey (1972) has some interesting comments. "The roots were cultivated as a crop from late prehistoric times. In the upland areas of Great Britain they were used right up until the introduction of the potato – and later, in times of famine. The roots were boiled or baked or even eaten raw, and the botanist John Ray likened their taste to parsnip. They were also dried and ground into flour for bread and gruel."

Common Dock or the Broad-leaved Dock (Rumex obtusifolius). The leaves of this plant would be gathered young for food but they had a very bitter taste. With the sea fowls they would boil or eat raw a quantity of 'sourocks', a large leaved sorrel, "a sad and watery substitute for the mealy potatoes of more genial climes." (Seton, 1878).

Large quantities of *Carragheen (Chondrus crispus)* were to be found at the Landing Place and although eaten on many Hebridean Islands the use seemed unknown at the time of MacGillivray's visit in 1840. They used to make a fairly lethal brew of ale in olden days, "making use of the roots of the nettle steeped in a vessel of water mixed with a small quantity of oatmeal instead of barm." However, the practice had died out by the time the visitors made this comment in 1799.

Dyeing

Both Martin in 1697 and Macaulay in 1758 found the St. Kildans unacquainted with the art of dyeing, but in later generations the people collected some of the many different species of grey lichens which they called 'crotal'. These they scraped from the rocks with an old spoon or hoe, boiled them up outside their cottages in a large cauldron to produce an acid which dyed the wool the reddish-brown colour of Harris Tweed. They also collected lichens for sale (Atkinson, 1949). Sometimes they would use soot as they did in Harris which dyed the wool, not black but brown. To make the dye fast they added a mordant, the chopped up roots of the docken, probably the Common Sorrel.

Tanning

Macaulay refers to the successful tanning of leather with the root of Tormentil (Potentilla erecta) which was done to "great perfection". They would "lay the leather when sufficiently prepared . . . in the warm infusion of this bark for two nights, and afterwards keep it in the hollow of a rock, which is under water at every full sea, with some of this root pounded into it, until it is sufficiently tanned." (Macaulay, 1764).

Thatching

After the barley was gathered in the heads were cut off and threshed, and the lower parts of the stalks were used for thatching the old houses; iris leaves collected from the edge of the Tobar Childa were also used.

MARINE LIFE

SKIN DIVING

In 1979 Gordon Ridley chartered the converted trawler, the Kylebhan, for his team of experienced skin-divers. They erected their tents in the enclosure just below the Factor's House. Having dived for several weeks off Dun, in Soay Sound and round Am Plastair to the north of Soay, the team planned to spend 8 hours off Stac an Armin and Boreray on the next day and offered to take a few members of the National Trust party. Five of us were keen to go and joined their expedition; after lunch for two hours we were able to

Skin Divers off Stac an Armin,
Conachair in the distance.

197

explore Boreray. The landing off the inflatable craft was tricky and we needed to be roped for the first awkward section of the rock-face but after that, although steep the going was safe. The day was glorious, blue sky, sun and cloud, cliffs, sheep, puffins and gannets, panoramic views – a day not to be forgotten.

Gordon Ridley talked about his experiences and recalled the attractions St. Kilda has for the skin-diver. "What is special about St. Kilda is the visibility, the water is clearer than in any part of Britain, this includes the West coast of Scotland as far as the Butt of Lewis, which is nearly as good. It is as rugged and grand below the surface as it is above, and with very little sediment to stir up, the visibility remains incredibly good. The waters are also very rich in marine life with brilliant colours, predominantly reds, oranges, yellows, purples and blues. Some encrusting species cover huge areas of rock walls. Another peculiar feature is the tremendous wealth of rock structures under water. Off Stac Lee and Stac an Armin vertical rock walls, in places over-hanging, reach down to depths of over 50m (about 170ft). There are huge under-water caves and tunnels, some opening at a depth of 30m. Below Conachair, a valley has eroded into the sea and the water is not so deep. One surprising thing is the absence of territorial fish, like Wrasse. There are plenty of shoals of fish; seals are to be seen everywhere in narrow clefts, tunnels and in the huge sea caves, which might well account for the small number of fish. It is not a place for wreck-hunters. There is no trace of the legendary ship from the Armada which was said to have gone down at Mina Stac, or of the trawler which sank in the 1920's in a storm in Glen Bay. Off the Cambir the cannon found in 1977, trapped under a two tonne boulder has now sadly disappeared. The island is so exciting and romantic above the surface – it is equally so below!"

MARINE BIOLOGY

One of Gordon Ridley's team, Dr. Christine Howson, kindly shared with me the observations made in the two seasons diving around the islands and stacs. I am greatly indebted to her for the information in this section.

Village Bay is typical of many exposed shores of Western Scotland. It has a sandy bottom and is edged to the south by fallen boulders which have broken from the vertical underwater cliffs of Dun, which reach down to a depth of 20m. The vertical surfaces have characteristic features of this type of shore:–

ZONES
i A greatly extended upper zone of black lichen (Verrucaria sp.) together with a dark green

seaweed (Prasiola stipita) which is influenced by seabird guano.

ii A wide band of Dulse (Poryphyra umbilicalis), in some places limpets have cleared some rocks completely of weed, and the few sheltered shores provide anchors for the fucoid seaweeds, including one uncommon species (Fucus distichus).

iii A deep zone of Barnacles (Balanus balanoides with some Chthalamus stellatus).

iv An Alaria zone forms the top layer of the sub Littoral area where the main species are the Oar-weed (Alaria esculenta), and the Coralline algae (Corallina officinalis) with some 'hand-like' Laminaria (Laminaria digitata).

v The Kelp zone. This forms an extensive forest from a depth of 6-30m. One surprising feature is that some of the kelp is found even below 30m. This is due to the clarity of the water allowing the light to penetrate such depths and to reach the plants, however, the plants themselves are extremely small. The major species is the large 'hand-shaped' seaweed (Laminaria hyperborea). Amongst the kelp are large areas of pinkish-purple encrustations (Lithothamnion sp.), also sponges and sea squirts, including the 'light bulb' tunicate (Clavelina lepadiformis) and extensive colonies of Sea Mats or Bryozoans.

JELLYFISH AND SEA ANEMONES – *Coelenterates*

Anemones abound, they include the small white species (Sagartia elegans) and the Plumose anemone (Metridium senile) which is particularly common on overhanging rocks. There are also Dahlia anemones (Tealia felina), and the Pink and Green Beadlets (Actinia equina) which are very common on the shore and the shallow sub-littoral region. Large colonies of the beautiful Jewel anemone (Corynactis viridis) cover rock walls between 10 and 20m and lower, in huge patches of purple, blue, green, yellow and pink.

Cup Coral (Caryophyllia smithi) is common in the deeper waters on cliff faces and over-hangs and in the sea caves, especially at Dun and Levenish. There are isolated patches of Dead Men's Fingers (Alcyonium digitatus) on rock faces and the Sea-Firs or Hydroids, Tubularia species predominating in the tunnels and deep caves where the sea surges through.

In the surface waters, during the summer, there is a profusion of Comb Jellies or Ctenophores and large shoals of 'By-the-Wind Sailor' (Velella velella), which are often stranded on the beach. Larger species of Jellyfish include the Common Jellyfish (Aurelia aurita) and the Blue Umbrella (Cyanea lamarki).

WORMS – *Annelids*

Fanworms are represented by the colourful Peacock

Worm (Sabella pavonina) which is found in small numbers at the back of deep sea caves, like the one 20m below the surface under the highest point of Dun, on the Village side, here the worms find sheltered backwaters. Serpulid Tubeworms, protected by their own encrusted tubes are found on many rock surfaces and on the kelps.

CRABS AND LOBSTERS – *Crustaceans*

The only Hermit Crabs (Eurapurus bernhardus) seen were on the sandy floor of Village Bay. There are plenty of Norway Lobsters (Nephrops norvegicus) in the deep water between Hirta and Boreray, and huge Crayfish (Palinurus vulgaris) inhabit the rocks below Am Plastair to the north of Soay. Large numbers of Squat Lobsters (Galathea strigosa and G. squamifera) hide in rock crevices. There are a few well camouflaged small Spider Crabs (Inachus dorsettensis), and a good number of Edible Crabs (Cancer pagurus) and some large Lobsters (Homarus vulgaris). Barnacles (Balanus balanoides) abound in the inter-tidal region.

SHELL-FISH – *Molluscs*

The Topshells are very common, particularly the Grey Topshell (Gibbula cineraria) and the Purple or Flat Topshell (Gibbula umbilicalis). The Painted Topshell (Calliostoma zizyphinum) is common near the surface and in deep water. The Common Limpet (Patella vulgata) browses the seaweed off many rocks, while the Blue-rayed Limpet (Patina pellucida) is abundant in the kelp forest. The Cowrie (Trivia monacha) feeds on the sponges and sea-squirts, and the Sea Hare (Aplysia punctata) is found in the arches at the end of Dun feeding on the Coralline algae. There are several species of nudibranch Sea Slugs, and an occasional Lesser Octopus (Eledone cirrhosa) is encountered.

SEA-URCHINS AND STARFISH – *Echinoderms*

The Common Sea-urchin (Echinus esculentus) is abundant and varying in size from tiny specimens to monsters, all occuring on Dun. The Common Star (Asterias rubens) and Brittle-stars (Ophiura sp.) are found everywhere, the Purple Starfish (Henricia sanguinoleta) is also quite common. There are many Spiny Starfish (Marthasterias glacialis) and huge numbers of Feather-stars (Antedon bifida) occuring locally on rock-faces, with the Cushion-star (Porania pulvillus) found at depths of 20m and below.

FISH

There are surprisingly few fish to be seen close to the rocks, possibly due to the large number of seals, just an occasional large Ballan Wrasse (Labrus bergylta) and

Pollack (Pollachius pollachius), Lumpsuckers (Lumpus cyclopterus) and Conger Eels (Conger conger) which reach a length of 2m. Shoals of 300–400 smaller Pollack were often encountered on the Village Bay side of Dun Passage. On the sandy bottom of Village Bay between the jetty and Dun Passage the only creatures seen were a few Flat-fish and some Hermit Crabs. In late July and August large shoals of Mackerel (Scomber scombrus) enter Village Bay and attract feeding Gannets and Porpoise.

The under-water scene is not unique but is one of great profusion and massed colours. A typical example is found on passing through the tunnel at the end of Dun and turning north west into a deep cove with its own free standing stac, the floor being lined with huge fallen boulders. Here, Grey Atlantic Seals inspect visitors in their own curious way. Ahead, a single slab of rock, 3 x 4m forms a vertical wall which is completely covered with three colour groups of Jewel Anemones, giving one large patch of deep purple and blue, a wide band of pink and an extensive area of yellow and green.

ST. KILDA —
FOR TODAY'S VISITORS

PRESENT

THE NATIONAL TRUST FOR SCOTLAND

St. Kilda, having been bequeathed to the National Trust for Scotland in 1956 was to come under much discussion before it was eventually accepted by the Trust in 1957. It was at this time that the islands were leased to the Nature Conservancy Council to manage them as a Nature Reserve and the St. Kilda Club was formed in 1958. The Trust arranges working parties to

National Trust Working Party, 1979.

stay on the island and these have re-roofed five of the 1860's Cottages, and have prevented the decay of many cleitean and the grave-yard wall, as well as repairing and refurnishing the Church. Safari holidays are arranged in small parties to stay in the cottages on Hirta under the leadership of someone who has experience of the islands. A small area of the main island, Hirta, is sub-leased to the Ministry of Defence.

THE NATURE CONSERVANCY COUNCIL

Since 1958 the Nature Conservancy Council has been managing the islands as a Nature Reserve of international importance. During this period much valuable research has been carried out on the flora and fauna, particularly the free ranging flocks of Soay sheep on Hirta. The results have world-wide application to management techniques. Constant watch is kept on the populations of seabirds, wrens and field-mice, insect and plant lists have been compiled and the vegetation mapped out.

THE MINISTRY OF DEFENCE

In the past many voices have been raised in protest against an Army presence on St. Kilda, expressing fears about possible damage to the archaeological sites and the flora, also the disturbance to the varied fauna and the spoiling of the natural scenery by modern man-

Photo by R. A. Hebrides.

possible to the wild life on the islands. Today the Army has its job to do in a difficult, hostile, environment and in doing so provides a wonderful back-up for today's visitors.

After the evacuation in 1930 St. Kilda remained uninhabited until 1957 when an Air Ministry Construction Unit began work on establishing a rocket tracking station. Since 1958 it has been garrisoned by men of the R.A. Guided Weapons Range on the Hebrides. "The Officer Commanding and his Sergeant Major do a tour of 9 months on St. Kilda; they are not volunteers and although they get a short leave during their tour the posting is a lonely one, particularly in winter. The Army sends bachelors to these two appointments! Certain other key men, such as the Royal Engineer Warrant Officer who runs the Power Station, and the Sergeant in the Army Catering Corps and the Medical Sergeant, do between 3 and 6 months at a time while the remainder rotate between Benbecula and St. Kilda for a period of approximately 6 weeks.

"The function of the Royal Artillery Range is to provide technical and administrative fascilities for units of all three services and representatives of the Science Research Council and the Meteorological Office for the firing of various guided weapons and rockets into a range area about 100 miles long and 60 miles wide. The

made buildings. These fears were not unfounded in many cases. The original plan was to demolish the houses along the Village Street to form hard-core for the new road. Fortunately, this was just stopped in time and the road was re-routed. The camp buildings are an eye-sore and offend many, but care has been taken to lessen the visual impact of the radar installations. Every precaution is taken to cause as little disturbance as safety arrangements for this range are based on radar coverage to ensure that ships and aircraft are never placed at risk. The western end of the range is beyond the "radar horizon" for radars sited on the Uists and hence there is a need for two radars on St. Kilda; the sole purpose of the detachment is to operate and maintain these two radars. Although the unit is called the Royal Artillery Range its members are drawn from several branches of the Army and the St. Kilda detachment also includes Gunners, Sappers, Pioneers, Royal Corps of Transport seamen, electronic and mechanical engineers of the REME and members of the Royal Signals. The detachment is supplied in the summer by a Landing Craft Tank of the Royal Corps of Transport which makes periodic visits and in winter by a helicopter." (St. Kilda Mail, Jan. 1978).

While on the island some of the personnel become concerned about the conservation of the Soay sheep lambs, many of which die in the spring if the weather is bad and the ewes are in poor health. One group collected a few and herded them into a cleit where they fed them at regular intervals on milk from the kitchen. On his way to visit the cleit on one dark night, after an extended period in the Puffin Inn the 'shepherd', crawled in on all fours holding the bottle of milk in one hand. Suddenly he staggered backwards as he was completely bowled over. He had entered the wrong cleit and had disturbed half a dozen sheltering rams which had bolted at the sight of the intruder.

Living at close quarters for weeks on end inevitably leads to strained relationships from time to time. To take one man down a peg or two, a group decided to form a 'Cleit Club'. A suitable Cleit was chosen, spring cleaned and furnished with a table and chairs, drinks and subdued lighting. A £3 membership fee was taken off the offending person as he entered and a very pleasant time was had by all. Next night, feeling a bit low, he paid his second visit to the Cleit Club, but alas when he got there he was not a little surprised and annoyed to find that the Cleit was bare – apart from the foul smelling carcases of some recent Soay sheep casualties.

Fitness can be a problem – the gym is available for those who enjoy such activities. One O/C was anxious about the general lack of fitness of some of his men so he decided to organise a compulsory run. The route took them on the road through the village meadows, over Amhuinn Mhor and up the steep inclines towards Am Blaid. It was a strange sight on St. Kilda to see a long straggling line of bodies, of all shapes and sizes, jogging their way like a white snake along the road. The O/C was at the head reaching the turning point while the tail was still ambling over the flat part of the meadows.

The O/C's have to be adaptable and on the alert for strange contingencies. What do you do with two canoeists who suddenly appear in the Village Bay having paddled across 80km of the Atlantic? How do you rescue the occupants of an inflatable craft belonging to a Dutch trawler, – after the men had visited the Puffin Inn they were swept past their own boat in a gale until they were 60km out to sea by the morning. For some it is all in a day's work.

Cooperation with Visitors

The occupants of the Camp are always most helpful in taking visiting parties over to Dun to see the Puffins, provided there is very little swell. In July 1980 it was touch and go as to whether the crossing was possible. With the rising swell one woman had difficulty in setting foot on the rocks and in the process Wally Wright, the Warden was knocked off balance and into the water. He returned quickly to the Factor's House for a complete change. Meanwhile the wind rose and the sea roughened, the O/C graciously joined the rescue party, together with Wally Wright. Unfortunately, at the call to 'Jump' the said lady hesitated, rather froze to the rocks, and the O/C, who

The O/C the Army detachment takes the plunge in a rescue bid, Dun 1980.

had one foot on the side of the boat and the other on the rocks did a fine cart-wheel into the sea and was eventually hauled back into the boat. He was to take another ducking before he and his helpers successfully got the complete party back on board. He took it very well indeed. All had a good soaking by the breaking waves before reaching the jetty, cold and wet but relieved to be able to have a steaming shower and a hot meal – thanks to the Army.

In such an isolated spot, apart from Television and the regular films, billiards, darts and table tennis, people have to make their own entertainments. Often other visitors from trawlers and yachts, as well as those on National Trust working parties, are encouraged to join in. A fancy dress competition gave wide scope for all – the O/C appeared as an attractive Girl Guide Captain, a witch was attired in a cloak made from black plastic bin liners with a cauldron borrowed from House Number 2. Two fellows had spent many hours making papier-maché masks of the heads of a Puffin and Fulmar; both were extremely realistic. However, the first prize was won by the Sergeant Major, dressed up to the hilt as President Amin.

The presence of the detachment on the island makes life for the visitor both possible and pleasant with the launch service and the Gemini crew, unlimited electricity, constant hot water, the use of freezers, a first aid service, a weekly postal service, an opportunity to use the telephone at certain times, a shop and the Puffin Inn.

FUTURE

What of the future? There have been many differing ideas. Heathcote back in 1900 commented that some had "suggested that St. Kilda would be admirably suited for a convict station in the event of the present inhabitants being removed. I am not much afraid of this; and I trust that the 50 miles of Atlantic swell will always have sufficient terrors to prevent its being made use of as a health resort. It might be useful as a meteorological station . . . !"

The face of St. Kilda could be drastically changed overnight by a single unwanted visitor, like the 'Maersk Angus', the 101,000 tonne oil tanker which nearly went aground when she suffered a total engine failure on December 9th., 1981. She was on her way from Milford Haven to Dundee and in theory was empty, but in fact, was carrying 4,000 tonnes of fuel oil for her own use and thousands of tonnes of oily ballast water. We all remember with horror the foul treacly black oil which spilled out of the Amoco Cadiz when, off course, she broke her back on a submerged reef, ruining large stretches of the Brittany Coast. Not only was the shore-line spoilt beyond recognition, but

The Danish Oil Tanker, the Maersk Angus, drifting helplessly off Hirta, December 1981.
Photo – Cpl. Jim Gallagher, RAOC, RA Hebrides.

thousands of seabirds died and a whole fishing industry was wrecked. The damage that could be done to St. Kilda by one of these huge man-made monsters going aground in the seabird breeding season is unbearable to contemplate. And yet this incident, when the tanker drifted out of control within 2,000m of Boreray, is a clear reminder of the awful possibility.

Fraser Darling (1964) has made the point that, "St. Kilda, Monach Isles, Haskeir, Gasker, Flannan Isles, Sula Sgeir and North Rona are but small spots on the map, but their size is out of all proportion to their importance in the natural history of the British Isles. Within their small compass there is a welter of life and unsurpassed interest to the naturalist." Those who have had the opportunity to visit this spectacular group of islands, considered by many to be the finest reserve in Western Europe, would surely agree that the fauna and flora must continue to be protected and studied in depth, and that as much as possible should be done to preserve the remaining traces of habitation as a memorial to a wonderful people and a unique way of life. Many will echo the words of Lachlan MacLean (1838) as he steamed out of Village Bay after his visit in 1838.

> "We are off – farewell St. Kilda!
> Wherever my lot may be cast,
> my mind will ever revert to thee;

> unique in thy structure
> as in the manner of thy sons,
> thou sittest queen of the Atlantic."

POSTSCRIPT — A Way of Escape

If you should be unavoidably detained on St. Kilda you could use the old method of communication whereby you enclosed your letter in a home made wooden boat with a float attached and launch it on the ebb tide. It usually takes about a couple of weeks to reach the shore of the Long Isle, but in winter it may take several months before it is spotted. One letter was recently found in Norway 15 months after the launch, and another reached the remote island of Soroya in the Arctic Ocean only 60 miles from the North Cape. Sands was on his second visit to St. Kilda in 1876 when he found himself marooned because the relief boat failed to appear. The winter days dragged on until he was joined by some Austrians who had left their sinking ship, the Peti Dabrovacki, and were washed ashore on January 17th. 1877. Sands relates his interview with the Captain:–

He – "Vat island is dis?"

I – "St. Kilda"

He – "Is dere telegraph?"

I – "Telegraph! God bless You! No"

He – "Is dere a post?"

I – "No! No post."

He – "Is dere a steamer?"

I – "A steamer sometimes calls by chance, once in two or three years, perhaps. A small smack called here last June, and ought to have called again in August, but she did not come."

He – "Who does dis wretched island belong to?"

I – "To Great Britain, I believe," and I blushed for my country.

He – "How long have you been here?"

I – "I have been a prisoner here for nearly seven months."

He – "A prisoner!" (and here he glances sharply from my brogues to my bonnet, fancying, as he afterwards told me, that he had got into a penal settlement). "Oh dear! dear! vot am I to do. I have one wife and an old mother; they will think I am dead and put on black cloth."

I – "I am sorry for you, but there is no help."

He – "But I have no tobacco, and I have smoked for forty years."

I – "Chew your waistcoat pocket, as we have been doing, and wait patiently until Spring, when it will be possible for a boat to reach Harris."

Understandably, patience was soon exhausted. On January 30th. Sands and the Captain launched a life buoy from the wrecked ship. To it a small sail was erected and a bottle enclosing a message to the Austrian Consul. It was picked up over 200 miles away to the north east on the island of Birsay in Orkney on February 8th. On the 22nd. of February, only 3 weeks after sending the letter, at about 7 a.m. by "most of the clocks" Sands heard the whistle of a steamer, H.M.S. 'Jackal' had arrived to rescue the distressed Austrians. Sands was quick to take his opportunity and to jump on board!

St. Kilda Mail Boats.

Left – carried a letter from Neil Ferguson to Richard Kearton, 1897.   *Right – sent by Sands in 1877, reached Birsay in the Orkneys.*

APPENDIX

ST. KILDA CHRONOLOGY

B.C.

1850 Boat Shaped Settings built on)
An Lag)

500 Earth-house built in the)
Village) Approximate

A.D.) Dates

600 Calum Mor's House built)

600-1400 Gleann Mor Occupied)

900-? Vikings on St. Kilda)

1202 Icelandic ship shelters off Hirta, recorded in Icelandic Saga.

1373 Charter ratified for John, Lord of the Isles, a MacDonald, to give St. Kilda and other Hebridean Islands to his son, Reginald.

1549 Dean Monro's visit and first written description of St. Kilda. Publish. 1774.

1615 Visit by the outlaw Coll Ciotach (Ketoch alias Macgillespick) who killed horses, cows and sheep and took them away.

1678 Visit by Sir Robert Moray.

1680 Visit by George Mackenzie of Tarbut.

1686 Party of French and Spanish sailors sheltered by the islanders.

1686 Earthquake for some minutes, several gannet rocks fell into the sea.

1697 Martin Martin's visit, full description and first map published in 1698. He was literary Tutor to the MacLeods of Skye.

1705 Alexander Buchan began work on St. Kilda as the first permanent missionary under the S.S.P.C.K., 1709 appointed School Teacher. 1710 Ordained.. Wife Katherine had 13 children. He died in Feb 1730.

1712 Boat lost on Boreray.

1727 Small-pox outbreak between Aug 15, 1727 and May 1728, causing 94 deaths, leaving 4 adults and 26 children from 21 families. Among survivors were 3 men and 8 boys marooned on Stac an Armin in Aug 1727 while collecting Solan Geese.

1728 June. Visit by the Rev. Daniel Macaulay to inspect Buchan's work. He reported back to S.S.P.C.K. and gave details of the small-pox outbreak.

1730 Roderick MacLennan, Missionary from King's College, Aberdeen. Ordained 1730.

1733 Alexander MacLeod, Advocate was pleased to mortify £333-6s-8d for endowment of a Missionary on St. Kilda, leaving the nominations with his family.

1734-42 Lady Grange in exile on St. Kilda.

1735 Violent storm, boat smashed, replaced at a cost of £7-16s-1d sterling.

1738 Lady Grange launched letters wrapped round cork to try to contact friends in Edinburgh.

1743 Alexander MacLeod, Missionary, a native of Skye, educated at King's College Aberdeen, died about 1755. Son, Col. Donald MacLeod, bought St. Kilda in June 1804.

1746 June 19. Five boatloads of soldiers searched St. Kilda for Bonnie Prince Charlie.

1752 Calendar corrected by adding 11 days. When adjusted this brings Martin's egg laying dates into line with present studies.

1758 Visit of the Rev. K. Macaulay from Ardnamurchan, author. Stayed from June-July 58.

1759 At the beginning of October, 10 men landed on Boreray, the boat smashed on the rocks in Village Bay with the total loss of boat and crew. Men on Boreray not relieved until June 1760 when the Steward called.

1774 Donald MacLeod, Missionary, a native of Skye, catechist in 1774. Known as Mac Ian Oig.

1777 Violent storm – boat smashed.

1780 Angus MacLeod, Missionary, known as MacDhonil Oig, died in 1788.

1782-91 Occasional visits by the Rev. John L. Buchanan, Missionary Minister to the Isles from the Church of Scotland.

1788 Lachlan MacLeod, son of Angus above (1780), Missionary, born on St. Kilda in 1762, educated on Skye, left in 1821, demitted in 1830.

1799 St. Kilda with Harris sold to Captain Alexander MacLeod for £15,000.

1799 Visit by Henry Brougham and his party on the way to Iceland. A full anonymous account written by one of the party, possibly Robert Campbell, otherwise John Joseph Henry or Charles Stuart.

1804 St. Kilda bought by Col. Donald MacLeod, died 1813, later in 1871 sold by his son, Sir John MacPherson MacLeod.

1815 Visit by John MacCulloch, Geologist and writer.

1822 Alex. Mackenzie – the Gaelic School Society sent him to open a school on Hirta, he stayed until 1829.

1822, 24, 27, 30 Visits by Dr. John MacDonald, the Apostle of the North. Preached on St. Kilda and while on the mainland collected money for the new Christ's Church in its present position. Meetings held in the barn.

1830-44   Rev. Neil Mackenzie, the first resident Minister for over 100 years. He was appointed in 1829 and was introduced to the St. Kildans on July 4th 1830 by Dr. John MacDonald, and was the master mind behind the New Village of the 1830's. In 1844 he was translated to Duror where he remained within the ranks of the Church of Scotland.

1830 before July   Christ's Church erected at a cost of £600 on its present site, and the Manse was built.

1831   Visit by G. C. Atkinson, Naturalist.

1834   Visit by Sir Thomas Dyke Acland in his yacht. He left 20 guineas with the Minister for the first person to demolish and rebuild his own house.

1834-38   The building of the improved 'Thatched Houses – 1834 Houses' on their present site, also the erection of the Head Dyke.

1835   Prussian vessel foundered off St. Kilda. Crew off 11 safely ashore.

1838   The 'Vulcan' called at St. Kilda, the first tourist vessel to do so, with brass band, and Lachlan MacLean, writer, together with two ecclesiastical men, Drs. Dickson and MacLeod. For some time Village Bay was called 'Dickson's Bay' and Glen Bay 'MacLeods'.

1839   'Charlotte' of Hull wrecked on Rockall. 18 of crew land on Hirta, stay 11 days.

1840   Visit by John MacGillivray, naturalist.

1841   Visit by James Wilson, F.R.S.E., M.W.S. Author and traveller.

1846   St. Kildans declare their adherence to the Free Church in the presence of a Deputy visiting the island.

1847   Visit of Sir W. M. E. Milner, zoologist, landed on Boreray.

1851   Teacher sent out by the Free Church Ladies Association, stayed for 2 years.

1852   The 'Priscilla' leaves for Melbourne, Australia with 36 St. Kildans on board, 20 died of fever on the way.

1853   Visit by Dr. John MacKenzie on board S/V Jessie.

1853   Catechist of the Free Church, stays for 2 years.

1856-63   Duncan Kennedy, Catechist and Registrar, sent by the Free Church.

1858   Visit of T. S. Muir, writer concerning ecclesiological matters.

1858   Visit by H. Sharban on July 8, 9, mapped out the Village and contents of cleitean.

1860   Visits by John E. Morgan, interested in the 'boat cold', Capt. Thomas R.N., folk-lore specialist, and the Duke of Athole on H.M.S. 'Porcupine'. He stayed for 2 days and had a St. Kilda meal with Norman MacDonald at No. 9.

1860   October 3rd. Terrific storm, several roofs carried off. 'Porcupine' with Capt. Otter nearly lost.

1860   Map of the Village made by Sharban, showing field strip, owners and contents of the cleitean within the Village.

1861   Visit of Alex. Grigor, Examiner of Registers, came on 'Porcupine' the Admiralty Survey Ship.

1861-62   The 16 New Cottages built.

1862   Visit by Miss Anne Kennedy, niece of the present Missionary.

1863   April. Boating tragedy. Seven men and one woman, Betty Scott, lost in the 'Dargavel' en route to Harris. Nothing further heard of her, a few clothes washed up on Mealista, an island to the west of Lewis.

1863-65   Mr. A. Cameron, Catechist of the Free Church.

1864   April 7th. 'Janet Cowan' went aground on the rocks in dense fog. She was on the way from Calcutta to Dundee with a cargo of jute. Captain and crew saved. The bell was used by the Church.

1865   October. Rev. John MacKay, Minister of the Free Church, on St. Kilda for 24 years, until 1889. He had previously been School-master at Garve and Minister on Uist and Eigg.

1868   Visit by H. J. Elwes, naturalist.

1869   May 31st. Death of Euphemia MacCrimmon, last of the 'senachie', the verbal historians, aged 88.

1871   St. Kilda sold back to Norman, 22nd Chief of MacLeod. Remains in the family until 1934.

1871   Factor visited 3 times in the 80 ton sailing schooner, the 'Robert Hadden'.

1871   Visit by Alex. Grigor, Examiner of Registers on H.M.S. 'Jackall', gun-boat.

1873   Visit by Dr. R. Angus Smith on the Nyanza.

1874   Visit by Sir William and Lady Baillie of Polkemmet.

1875   Visits by Sir Patrick Keith Murray in his yacht 'Crusader', also Dr. Murchison of Harris.

1875 and 76   Visits by John Sands, writer, marooned on his 2nd Visit.

1877   Jan 17. Captain and 8 of crew of 'Peti Dabrovacki' land after ship wrecked off St.

Kilda. Stay for 5 weeks.

1877 Jan 30th. First 'Mail Boat' launched by Sands. Reaches Austrian Embassy.

1877 May. 'Flirt' arrives with stores on Saturday, unloaded on Monday.

1877 Visit by Lord and Lady MacDonald in the yacht 'Lady of the Isles' with Miss MacLeod of MacLeod, daughter of the Proprietor, who stayed in the Factor's house.

1877 July 2nd. 'Dunara Castle' reached St. Kilda on first Western Isles Cruise and was to visit regularly until the outbreak of 2nd World War in 1939. In the party of about 40 was George Seton, Advocate and author – they landed for 4 hours.

1878 Visit by 'S.S. Mastiff' on her way to Iceland with Anthony Trollope on board.

1882 Crops failed. In April men went to Skye in a small fishing boat to obtain food.

1883 June. Commission of Inquiry held on Hirta, interviewed Rev. J. MacKay and some natives.

1883 Visit by R. M. Barrington, a botanist who explored every corner and climbed Stac Biorach.

1884 Visit by G. W. Whyte, photographer from Inverness, Alex Ross, architect, Mr. MacWhirtir R.A. and Mr. Evans the boat owner. Also visit by Charles Dixon who collected mice from which H. Seebohm named the new sub-species of field mouse.

1884 Mr. Campbell, the first School-master sponsored by the Ladies Society of the Free Church. A room in the Factor's House was made available as a school-room for him.

1884-86 Ann McKinlay came as resident Nurse.

1885 Storm ruined crops. Alex G. Ferguson launched 'mail boat' which resulted in supplies being sent.

1885 Visit by Malcolm Ferguson.

1885 and 86 Two visits by Robert Connell, journalist and author, Glasgow Herald.

1885-86 Hugh MacCullum, School-master.

1886-87 George Murray, School-master, school held in the church.

1887 Visit by Alfred Newton with E. and J. Wolley and Henry Evans.

1888-89 Mr. McRee, School-master.

1888 Visit by Henry Evans, who made 9 previous visits from Jura.

1889 Mr. John Ross, School-master.

1889 Visit by D. W. Logie.

1889-1903 Rev. Angus Fiddes, last of the ordained Free Church Ministers.

1890-92   Nurse Chishall in residence.

1892   Alex G. Ferguson emigrated to Glasgow.

1894   Visit by Ellis Malcolm who was collecting for H. A. MacPherson, also J. S. Elliot. Steele Elliot first person to recognise two species of mice on St. Kilda, thought Wren reduced to 15 pairs.

1895   Visit by Sir Archibald Geikie, also J. Wolly, H. Evans, and in 1896.

1896   Visit by Richard and Cherry Kearton, Photographers and Naturalists.

1897   Visit by H. A. MacPherson.

1898   Masons and carpenters from Dunvegan begin to build the new school room.

1898   First visit of 'S.S. Hebrides' – she was to call several times each summer.

1898   Visit by Norman Heathcote and his sister, Naturalist and author, both climbed Stac Lee and were present at the laying of the School Foundation Stone. They paid a second visit in 1899.

1899   Visit by Henry Evans of Jura, and on 11 previous occasions.

1900   The Church now supported by the United Free Church.

1900-01   James MacKenzie, School-master.

1900   In July the St. Kilda Post Office was fully operational for the first time with the Rev. Angus Fiddes as sub-postmaster, situated in lower floor of the Factor's House.

1902   July-August. Mary Mackenzie, School-teacher from the Royal Academy, Inverness.

1902   Visit by Dr. Wiglesworth, Ornithologist and writer, climbed Boreray and Stacs.

1903   Lachlan MacLean, Missionary.

1903   July-August. Edith Findlay, Teacher from Central School, Inverness.

1903-06   John Fraser, Missionary.

1903-04   Mr. MacDonald, School-master.

1903   Visit by J. A. Harvie-Brown, naturalist.

1904   July-August. Kathleen Kennedy, Teacher from High School, Inverness.

1904   Sir Herbert Maxwell's Bill and Act of Parliament for protection of Wren and L. Petrel.

1904-05   Mr. R. MacDonald, School-master.

1905   Visit by J. Waterston, naturalist.

1905   July-August. Miss W. Gollan, Teacher from Glenfintaig Primary School.

1906   Visit by Miss Zillah Goudie.

1906-09   Peter MacLachlan, Missionary, with his wife Ann who was the teacher. Neil Ferguson senior became sub-postmaster until the Evacuation.

1907 Visit by Bentley Beetham, bird photographer, and collector Harry Brazenor.

1908 Visit by Oliver Pike, early naturalist cine photographer, and Bentley Beetham.

1909-12 Miss Annie MacLean, Teacher from Glasgow.

1910 Visits by Oliver Pike, the Duchess of Bedford, W. Eagle Clarke.

1910-11 Eagle Clarke prep 60 skins of Field and 40 of House Mouse.

1911 Visit by J. H. Gurney, Author of the "Gannet".

1912 'H.M.S. Achilles' called with supplies after a trawler had found people near starvation.

1912-14 Mr. MacArthur, Missionary.

1913 Post Office now situated in the corrugated iron hut between Cottages No. 4 and 5.

1913 July 29th. Wireless Station installed in the Factor's House. Messages sent to the King and the Daily Mirror which led the campaign for the transmitter. Closed down in 1914 due to lack of funds.

1914-19 Alexander MacKinnon, Missionary with his wife who was the teacher.

1914 Visit by E. W. Wade, and the Duchess of Bedford.

1915 Jan 12th. Signal Station set up near the Store-house, manned by Naval Ratings based on Aultbea, later from Stornoway.

1918 May 15th. Hirta shelled by German Submarine.

1919 Naval Garrison evacuated and the wireless station closed down.

1919-26 Donald Cameron, Missionary with his wife Mary and 2 daughters, Mary and Christina.

1924 William MacDonald of Cottage No. 3 was the first to leave with his whole family.

1925 Donald John Gillies left for Glasgow and Toronto, became Presbyterian Minister.

1926 May – four St. Kildans died from influenza.

1926 Nurse Littlejohn working on the island.

1926-29 John MacLeod, Missionary and Teacher with his wife and two boys, Ewen and Alexander.

1927 Nurse Flett in residence on Hirta.

1927 Visit by Seton Gordon.

1927 The islands Surveyed by John Mathieson, assisted by A. M. Cockburn.

1928 Mr. A. M. Cockburn continued and completed his Geological Survey of St. Kilda.

1928 Nurse Williamina Barclay arrived on the island and stayed until the Evacuation.

1929-30 Mr. Dugald Munro, Missionary and

Teacher with his wife Ann.

1929 Visit by F. A. Lowe, Bird photographer.

1930 Feb 15th. Fishery Cruiser 'Norna' called to take off Mary Gillies with appendicitis.

1930 Friday August 29th. The Evacuation of the people.
Visit of Alasdair Alpin MacGregor, Correspondent for the Times.
Film of the Evacuation taken by John Ritchie.

1934 The islands, previously owned by the MacLeods of Skye, now purchased by the Earl of Dumfries, the 5th Marquis of Bute.

1956 St. Kilda bequeathed to the National Trust for Scotland by the Marquis of Bute.

1957 St. Kilda accepted by the National Trust for Scotland.
Ordnance Survey Team work on the Official Map of St. Kilda.
Air Ministry send R.A.F. Task Force, 'Hard Rock' consisting of 300 officers and men to begin work on the road, camp and tracking station.

1958 The Nature Conservancy Council took over the management of St. Kilda as a National Nature Reserve.
The first of the St. Kilda Working Parties arranged by the National Trust for Scotland.

The Formation of the St. Kilda Club.

1971 Visit by the Royal Family in the Royal Yacht, filmed by John Wilkie.

1979 Plaque placed in the Kirk to commemorate the crews of the aircraft which crashed on St. Kilda during the 2nd World War.

1980 Wednesday August 27th. Service of Rededication of the Kirk on the 50th Anniversary of the Evacuation.

PLANT CHECK LIST

Angelica, Wild – Angelica sylvestris
Asphodel, Bog – Narthecium ossifragum
Bedstraw, Heath – Galium saxatile
Bilberry – Vaccinum myrtillus
Bittercress, Wavy – Cardamine flexusoa
Bugle – Ajuga reptans
Buttercup, Meadow – Ranunculus acris
Butterwort, Common – Pinguicula vulgaris
Celandine, Lesser – Ranunculus ficaria
Chickweed, Common – Stellaria media
Clover, White – Trifolium repens
Clubmoss, Fir – Lycopodium selago
            Lesser – Selaginella selaginoides
Cotton Grass (sedge) – Eriophorum angustifolium
Cowberry – Vaccinium vitis-idaea

Crowberry – Empetrum nigrum
Daisy – Bellis perennis
Dandelion – Taraxacum sp.
Dock, Broad – Runex obtusifolius
    Clustered – Rumex conglomeratus
    Curled – Rumex crispus
Eyebright – Euphrasia sp.
False Oat – Arrhenatherum elatius
Ferns, Adder's Tongue – Ophioglossum vulgatum
    Bladder – Cystopteris fragilis
    Black Spleenwort – Asplenium adiantum
                  nigrum
    Bracken – Pteridium aquilinum
    Common Buckler – Dryopteris austiaca
    Common Polypody – Polypodium vulgare
    Hard – Blenchnum spicant
    Lady – Athyricium filix-femina
    Moonwort – Botrychium lunaria
    Scottish Filmy – Hymenophyllum wilsonii
    Sea Spleenwort – Asplenium marinum
Flag, Yellow – Iris pseudacorus
Foxtail, Marsh – Alopecurus geniculatus
Gentian, Field – Gentianella campestris
Grass, Broad Bent – Agrostis canina
    Fine Bent – Agrostis tenuis
    Good Friday (Woodrush) – Luzula
                  campestris

Heath – Sieglingia decumbens
Mat – Nardus stricta
Meadow, Annual – Poa annua
    Rough – Poa trivialis
    Smooth – Poa pratensis
Purple Moor – Molinia caerulea
Red Fescue – Festuca rubra
Rye – Lolium perenne
Scurvy – Cochlearia officinalis
Sheep's Fescue – Festuca ovina
Small Hair – Aira praecox
Sweet Vernal – Anthoxanthum odoratum
Viviparous Fescue – Festuca vivipara
Wavy Hair – Deschampsia flexuosa
White Bent – Agrostis stolonifera
Yorkshire Fog – Holcus lanatus
Hawksbits, Autumn – Leontodon autumnalis
Heather (Ling) – Calluna vulgaris
Heather, Bell – Erica cinerea
    Cross leaved – Erica tetralix
Honeysuckle, Common – Lonicera periclymenum
Horsetail, Common – Equisetum arvense
Lousewort – Pedicularis sylvatica
Lovage – Ligusticum scoticum
Milkwort, Common – Polygala vulgaris
Moss Campion – Silene acaulis
Moss, Sphagnum – Sphagnum sp.

Woolly Hair – Rhacomitrium sp.
Mountain Everlasting – Antennaria dioica
Mouse-ear, Common – Cerastium holosteoides
      Dark Green – C. Tetrandum
Nettle, Stinging – Urtica dioica
Orache, Babbington's – Atriplex glabriuscula
Orchid, Bog – Malaxis paludosa
      Heath Spotted – Dactylorchis maculata
Pearlwort, Heath – Sagina subulata
      Mossy – S. procumbens
Pennywort, Marsh – Hydrocotyle vulgaris
Pimpernel. Bog – Anagallis tenella
Plantain, Buck's-horn – Plantago coronopus
      Great or Rats Tail – Plantago major
      Ribwort – Plantago lanceolata
      Sea – Plantago maritima
Pondweed – Potamogeton polygoniforius
Primrose, Common – Primula vulgaris
Purslane – Montia lamprosperma
Purslane Blinks – Montia fontana
Ragged Robin – Lychnis flos-cuculi
Ragwort, Common – Senecio jacobaea
Roseroot – Sedum rosea
Rush, Bulbous – Juncus bulbosus
      Common (Soft) – J. effusus
      Heath – J. squarrosus
      Jointed – J. articulatus

      Toad – J. bufonius
Saxifrage, Purple – Saxifraga oppositifolia
Sea Campion – Silene maritima
Scabius, Devil's Bit – Succisa pratensis
Scentless Mayweed – Matricaria maritima
Sedge, Carnation – Carex panicea
      Common – C. nigra
      Cotton Grass – Eriophorum angustifolium
      Flea – C. pulicaris
      Glaucous – C. flacca
      Large, Yellow – C. flava
      Moor – C. binervis
      Pill – C. pilulifera
      Star – C. echinata
      Stiff – C. rigida
      Tawny – C. hostiana
      Yellow, Common – C. demissa
Self Heal – Prunella vulgaris
Silverweed – Potentilla anserina
Sneezewort – Achillea ptarmica
Sorrel, Common – Rumex acetosa
      Mountain – Oxyria digyna
      Sheep's – Rumex acetosella
Spearwort, Lesser – Ranunculus flammula
Speedwell, Common – Veronica officinalis
Spike-rush, Few flowered – Eleocharis quinqueflora
      Slender – E. uniglumis

St. John's Wort, Elegant – Hypericum pulchrum
Starwort, Water – Callitriche stagnalis
Stonecrop – Sedum sp.
Sundew, Common – Drosera rotundifolia
      Great – D. anglica
Thistle, Creeping – Cirsium arvense
      Spear – C. vulgare
      Prickly Sow – Sonchus asper
Thrift (Sea Pink) – Armeria maritima
Thyme, Wild – Thymus drucei
Tormentil – Potentilla erecta

Vetch, Bush – Vicia sepium
Violet, Common Dog – Viola riviniana
      Marsh – V. palustris
Willow, Creeping – Salix repens
      Dwarf – S. herbacea
Willow Herb, Marsh – Epilobium palustre
Woodrush, Great – Luzula sylvatica
      Good Friday Grass – L. campestris
      Heath – L. multiflora
Yarrow – Achillea millefolium
Yellow Rattle – Rhinanthus drummond-hayi

BIBLIOGRAPHY

BOOKS

Anonymous. Unpubl. "An account of the island of St. Kilda and neighbouring islands, visited in August 1799." Written by one of Brougham's party, probably Robert Campbell.

Alvin K.L. 1977. Lichens. The Observer's Book. Frederick Warne.

Atkinson R. 1949. Island Going. Collins.

Bannerman D.A., Lodge G.E. 1953–63. Birds of the British Isles. 12 Vols. Oliver & Boyd.

Berry R.J. 1977. Inheritance and Natural History. New Naturalist. Collins.

Berry R.J., Johnston J.L. 1980. Natural History of Shetland. New Naturalist. Collins.

Birks H.J.B. 1977. The Flandrian Forest History of Scotland. In Brit. Quaternary Studies, Recent Advances. Edited by Shotton F.W. Clarendon Press.

Brougham H. 1871. Life and Times of Henry Lord Brougham (3 Vols.) Vol. 1 Blackwood. Edin.

Buchan Rev. A.A. 1752. A Description of St. Kilda. Repr. Aberdeen Univ. Pr. 1974.

Buchanan Rev. J.L. 1793. Travels in the Western Hebrides from 1782–90. London.

Cameron J. 1979. Yesterday's Witness. B.B.C. London.

Carruthers R. 1843. The Highland Note-book; or sketches and anecdotes.

Connell R. 1887. St. Kilda and the St. Kildians. Hamilton Adams and Co. London.

Cramp S., Bourne W.R.P., Saunders D. 1974. Sea Birds of Britain and Ireland. Collins.

Darling F., Boyd J.M. 1964. Natural History in the Highlands and Islands. Collins.

Ewing W. 1914. Annals of the Free Church of Scotland. 2 Vols. T. & T. Clark. Edin.

Ferguson C. 1885–86. The Gaelic Names of Birds. Trans of Gaelic Soc of Inverness Vol. 12.

Fisher J. 1948. The New Naturalist. Collins.

Fisher J. 1952. The Fulmar. New Naturalist.

Fisher J., Lockley R.M. 1954. Sea Birds. New Naturalist. Collins.

Fleming J. 1828. History of British Animals. Edinburgh.

Gladstone, John. Unpubl. St. Kilda Diaries, concerning his visit in 1927.

Gray R. 1871. Birds of the West of Scotland. T. Murray and Son.

Halliday T. 1978. Vanishing Birds. Holt, Rinehart and Winston.

Harris M.P., Murray S. 1978. Birds of St. Kilda. Instit of Terr. Ecol. Cambridge.

Heathcote N. 1900. St. Kilda. Longman's Green and Co.

Hewer H.R. 1974. British Seals. New Naturalist. Collins.

Holden A.E. 1952. Plant Life in the Scottish Highlands. Oliver and Boyd.

Holliday F. 1979. Wildlife in Scotland. Macmillan. London.

Jewell P.A., Milner C., Boyd M.J. 1974. Island Survivors. Athlone Press.

Kearton R. and C. 1897. With Nature and a Camera. Cassell and Co.

Kennedy J., 1866. The Apostle of the North. London.

Mabey R. 1972. Food for Free. Collins. Fontana 1975.

Macaulay Rev. K. 1764. History of St. Kilda. Repr. James Thin 1974.

MacCulloch J. 1819. A Description of the Western Islands of Scotland. (3 Vols) Vol 2. Constable. Edin.

MacDonald J. 1811. General View of Agriculture of the Hebrides. Edinburgh.

MacDonald J. 1823. Journal and Report of a visit to the island of St. Kilda. Edin. SSPCK.

MacFarlane. 1908. Geographical Collections Vol. 3. Mar.

MacGregor A.A. 1931. A Last Voyage to St. Kilda. Cassell and Co.

MacGregor A.A. 1969. The Furthest Hebrides. Michael Joseph.

Mackenzie Rev. J.B. 1904. Antiquities and old customs in St. Kilda, compiled from notes made by the Rev. Neil Mackenzie, Minister of St. Kilda, 1829-43. Proc. Soc. Antiq. Scot. 38 p 397-402.

1905 Notes on the birds of St. Kilda compiled from memoranda of the Rev. Neil Mackenzie. Ann Scot. Nat. Hist. 75-80 p141-53.

1911 Episode in the life of Rev. Neil Mackenzie at St. Kilda from 1829-43. Privately printed.

MacLean C. 1972. Island on the Edge of the World. Canongate.

MacLean, Lachlan. 1838. Sketches of St. Kilda.

Martin M. 1698. A Late Voyage to St. Kilda. Repr. Mackay 1934.

Martin M. 1716. Description of the Western Isles of Scotland. Repr. Thin. 1976.

Monro D. 1774. A Description of the Western Isles of Scotland. Auld. Edin.

Muir T.S. 1885. Ecclesiological Notes on some of the islands of Scotland. Douglas.

Murray W.H. 1973. The Islands of Western Scotland. Eyre Methuen.

Nelson J.B. 1978. The Gannet. T. and A.D. Poyser.

Nelson J.B. 1980. Seabirds, their biology and ecology. Hamlyn.

Nethersole Thompson D. 1971. Highland Birds. Highlands and Islands Dev. Board.

Phillips R. 1980. Grasses, Ferns, Mosses and Lichens. Pan.

Pococke R. 1887. Tours in Scotland 1747, 1759, 1760. Ed. Kemp D.W. Edin Scot. Hist. Soc. Vol 1.

Read H.H., Watson J. 1966. Beginning Geology. MacMillan and Co.

Sands J. 1878. Out of this World or Life on St. Kilda. Maclachlan and Stewart.

Scott H. 1928. Fasti Ecclesiae Scoticanae. New Ed. Vol VII. Oliver & Boyd. Edin.

Scott H. 1950. Fasti Ecclesiae Scoticanae Vol VIII. Oliver & Boyd. Edin.

Seton G. 1878. St. Kilda Past and Present. William Blackwood and Sons.

Shaw M.F. 1977. Folksongs and Folklore of South Uist. Oxf. Univ. Pr.

Small A. 1979. A St. Kilda Handbook National Trust for Scotland.

Smith R.A. 1879. A Visit to St. Kilda in the Nyanza. Glasgow Univ. Pr.

Steel T. 1965. Life and Death of St. Kilda. R. and R. Clark. Fontana 1975.

Stokes T. 1968. Birds of the Atlantic Ocean. Country Life.

Svensson R. 1955. Lonely Isles. Batsford, London.

Thompson F. 1970. St. Kilda and other Hebridean Outliers. David and Charles.

Walker J. 1808. An Economical History of the Hebrides. 2 Vols. Edin.

Whittow J.B. 1977. Geology and Scenery of Scotland. Pelican Books.

Williamson K. and Boyd J.M. 1960. St. Kilda Summer. Oliver and Boyd.

Williamson K. and Boyd J.M. 1963. Mosaic of Islands. Oliver and Boyd.

Wilson J. 1842. A Voyage round the coasts of Scotland and the Isles Vol 2. Adam and Charles Black. Edin.

OTHER REFERENCES

Adam T. Unpubl. An account concerning Mrs. Ann McKinlay, Nurse on St. Kilda 1884-86.

Arrowsmith A. 1807. Memoir relative to the Construction of the Map of Scotland. Aaron Arrowsmith, London.

Bailey R.S., Hislop J.R.G., Manson J. 1979. "The fish and shellfish resources in the seas adjacent to the Outer Hebrides." Proc. Roy. Soc. Edin. 77B, 479-94.

Barrett-Hamilton G.E.H. 1899. On the species of the genus Mus inhabiting St. Kilda. Proc. Zool. Soc. London, pp 77-88, London Feb 7th.

Berry R.J. 1969a. History in the evolution of Apodemus sylvaticus (Mammalia) at one edge of its range. J.Zool., London 159: 311-28 (pp 202 ff).

Berry R.J., Tricker B.J.K. 1969b. Competition and extinction: mice of Foula, with notes on those on Fair Isle and St. Kilda. J.Zool., London 158, 247-65.

Berry R.J. 1979. "Outer Hebrides; where genes and geography meet." Proc. Roy. Soc. Edin. 77B 21-43.

Birks H.J.B., Madsen B.J. 1979. Flandrian Vegetational History of Little Loch Roag, Isle of Lewis. Jour. Ecol. Vol 67, 825-842.

Black R. 1973. Colla Ciotach Trans. Gaelic Soc. of Inverness, XLVIII, 201-43.

Bourne W.R.P., Harris M.P. 1979. Birds of the Hebrides – seabirds. Proc. Roy. Soc. Edin. 77B, 445-75.

Boyd J. Morton. 1960. Observations on the St. Kilda Field-mouse. Proc. Zool. Soc. London Vol 133, 47-65.

Boyd J. Morton. 1960. The distribution of numbers of Kittiwakes and Guillemots at St. Kilda. British Birds 53, 252-64.

Boyd J. Morton. 1961. The Gannetry on St. Kilda. Jour. Animal Ecol. 30, 117-36.

Boyd J. Morton. 1963. Home range and homing experiments with the St. Kilda Field-mouse. Proc. Zool. Soc. London 140, 1-14.

Boyd J. Morton. 1964. St. Kilda, National Nature Reserve, Management Plan. Nature Conservancy HC 5.

Boyd J. Morton. 1979. Natural Environment of the Outer Hebrides. Proc. Roy. Soc. Edin. 77B.

British Regional Geology, Scot. 1952. Tertiary Volcanic Distric. H.M.S.O.

British Regional Geology, Northern Highlands. 1960. H.M.S.O.

Clegg E.J. 1977. Population changes in St. Kilda during the Nineteenth and Twentieth Centuries. Journ. Bisoc. Sc. IX, 3.

Cockburn A.M. 1935. Geology of St. Kilda, Trans. Roy. Soc. Edin. 58(21) p511-48.

Cottam M.B. 1973-74. St. Kilda, Archaeological Survey I and II. Private for the National Trust for Scotland.

Cottam M.B. 1979. Archaeology of St. Kilda. St. Kilda Handbook. Nat. Trust Scot.

Dixon T.J. 1971. Estimates in the number of Gannets breeding on St. Kilda 1969-73. Seabird Report.

Ellett D.J. 1979. Some oceanographic features of Hebridean waters. Proc. Roy. Soc. Edin. 77B 61-74.

Gaelic School Soc. 1822 (yearly thereafter). The 11th Annual Report of the Soc. for the Support of Gaelic Schools. The Society. Edin.

Gilbert O.L., Watling R., Coppins B.J. 1979. Lichen Ecology of St. Kilda. Lichenologist 11(2), 191-202.

Goudie Z.H. 1907. Fulmar Hunting in St. Kilda. Manchester Guardian. March 21st.

Harding R.R. 1966. Mullach Sgar Complex, St. Kilda. Scot. Jour. Geol. Vol 2. Part 2.

Harding R.R. 1965-66. The Major Ultrabasic and Basic Intrusions of St. Kilda. Roy. Soc. Edin. Vol LXVI No. 17.

Harman M. 1976-77. An Incised Cross on Hirt, Harris. Proc. Soc. Antiquaries Scot. Vol 108.

Harris M.P., Murray S. 1977. Puffins on St. Kilda. Brit. Birds Vol 70 No. 2. Feb.

Harris M.P., Hislop J.R.G. 1978. The Food of Young Puffins. Jour. Zool. Soc. London 185.

Harris M.P. 1980. Breeding performance of Puffins, Fratercula arctica in relation to nest density, laying date and year. Ibis Vol 122, p.193-209.

Heron R. 1794. General View of the Hebudae or Hebrides. Patterson Edin.

Laing D. 1874. Mrs. Erskine, Lady Grange, in the island of St. Kilda. Proc. Soc. Antiq. Scot. p.722-30. June 8th.

Macdiarmid J. 1878. On St. Kilda and its inhabitants. Trans. Highland and Agric. Soc.

MacDonald C. Unpubl. Callum MacDonald (1908-79) Autobiography.

MacDonald J. 1825. Appendix to "A sermon preached before the Society in Scotland, June 2, 1825." (Concerning his 2nd visit in 1824). Edin. SSPCK.

MacGillivray J. 1841. Account of the islands of St. Kilda. Cuverian Nat. Hist. Soc.

Macgregor D.R, 1960. The Island of St. Kilda – a survey of its character and occupance. Scot. Studies 4.

Mackenzie J.B. 1905. Antiquities and old customs in St. Kilda, compiled from notes by the Rev. Neil Mackenzie, Minister on St. Kilda 1829-43. Proc. Soc. Antiq. Scot. pp.397-402. Vol 39.

Mackay J.A. Island Postal Series No. 1. Harris and St. Kilda. Publ. by author, 11 Newall Ter. Dumfries DG1 1LN.

MacVean D.N. 1961. Flora and Vegetation of the Islands of St. Kilda and North Rona in 1958. Jour. Ecol. 49.

Mathieson J. 1927-28. Antiquities of the St. Kilda Group of Islands. Proc. Soc. Antiq. Scot. (6) 2 p.123-32.

Mathieson J. 1928. St. Kilda. Scot. Geog. Mag 44.

Milner W.M.E. 1848. Some account of the People of St. Kilda and the Birds of the Outer Hebrides. Zoologist.

Mitchell A. 1901. List of accounts of visits to St. Kilda 1549-1900. Proc. Soc. Antiq. Scot.

Murray G. Unpubl. St. Kilda Diary from June 11th 1886-87.

Muir T.S. 1861. Notice of a Beehive House on the Island of St. Kilda. Proc. Soc. Antiq. Scot. III 225-32. Session 1858-59.

Rae B.B. 1960. Seals and Scottish Fisheries. Mar. Res. Scot. Edin. H.M.S.O. (2).

Report of the Commissioners of Inquiry into the Condition of Crofters and Cottars in the Highlands and Island of Scotland. Parliamentary Papers 1884 XXXII. Appendix p.38. PP Evidence Vol II 1884 XXXIV. pp864-65.

Report on the State of Education in the Hebrides (by A. Nicholson) 1886. Education Commission (Scotland) PP 1867 XXV.

Ross A. 1883-88. A Visit to the Island of St. Kilda. Trans of Inverness Scientif. Soc. and Field Club. Vol III.

Ross J. Unpubl. Diary of the Schoolmaster on St. Kilda 1889. Bute Collection, Nat. Trust for Scot.

Rutherford H.R. Unpubl. St. Kilda 1970, Conservation of the Built Environment. Report of Nat. Trust for Scot. 1970.

Sand J. 1877. Life on St. Kilda. 3 articles in Chambers Journal, Edin. May 5, 19, 26.

Sands J. 1877. Notes on the Antiquities of the island of St. Kilda. Proc. Soc. Antiq. Scot. pp.186-92. Apr. 9th.

Smith J.A. 1879. Notice of the remains of the Great Auk or Gare-fowl (Alca impennis) found in Caithness with notes of its occurence in Scotland and of its early history. Proc. Soc. Antiq. Scot. Jan. 13th.

S.P.C.K. 1710. Minutes of the Committee.

Stevenson D. 1980. Alasdair MacColla and the Highland Problem in the Seventeenth Century. Edinburgh, John Donald.

Stewart M. 1937. St. Kilda Papers 1931 for Private Circulation. Oxf. Univ. Pr.

Taylor A.B. 1967. Norsemen on St. Kilda. Saga – Book of the Viking Soc. XVII.

Taylor A.B. 1969. The Name St. Kilda. Scot. Studies 13.

Thomas Capt. F.W.L. 1857-60. 'Notice of a Beehive House in the island of St. Kilda' by T.S. Muir with additional notes by Capt. F.W.L. Thomas. Proc. Scot. Antiq. Soc. Vol 3, pp.225-32.

Thomas Capt. F.W.L. 1867. On the primitive dwellings and hypogea of the Outer Hebrides. Proc. Soc. Antiq. Scot.

Thomas Capt. F.W.L. 1874. Letter from St. Kilda by Miss A. Kennedy, Communicated with notes by Capt. F.W.L. Thomas. Proc. Soc. Antiq. Scot. Vol 10, pp.702-11.

Turril W.B. 1927. Flora of St. Kilda. Report B.E.C.

Waters W.E. 1964. Observations on the St. Kilda Wren. Brit. Birds. 57 pp.49-64.

Watling R., Irvine L.M., Norton T.A. 1970. Marine algae on St. Kilda. Trans. Bot. Soc. Edinb. 41.

Watling R., Richardson M.J., 1971. The Agarics of St. Kilda. Trans. Bot. Soc. Edin. 41.

Weir T., 1969. Two men on the Stacs. Scots Magazine. Dec.

INDEX
OF PEOPLE QUOTED